HOLOCAUST

TESTIMONIES

Lawrence L. Langer

HOLOCAUST

TESTIMONIES

THE RUINS

OF MEMORY

Yale University Press

New Haven and London

Published with assistance from the foundation established in memory of Philip Hamilton McMillan of the Class of 1894, Yale College.

The sources for the epigraphs on page vi are Ida Fink, "A Scrap of Time," in *A Scrap of Time and Other Stories*, trans. Madeline Lewis and Francine Prose (New York: Pantheon, 1987), p. 3; and Aharon Appelfeld, "After the Holocaust," in *Writing and the Holocaust*, ed. Berel Lang (New York: Holmes and Meier, 1988), p. 92.

Part of chapter 1, in radically abbreviated form, appeared in "Holocaust Testimonies and Their Audience," *Orim: A Jewish Journal at Yale*, 1, no. 2 (Spring 1986): 96–110; part of chapter 2 appeared in "Interpreting Surviving Testimony," in *Writing and the Holocaust*, ed. Berel Lang (New York: Holmes and Meier, 1988), pp. 26–40.

Designed by Jill Breitbarth
Set in Palatino and Futura types by The Composing Room of Michigan, Inc., Grand Rapids, Michigan.
Printed in the United States of America by Vail-Ballou Press, Binghamton, New York.

Library of Congress Cataloging-in-Publication Data

Langer, Lawrence L.
    Holocaust testimonies: the ruins of memory / Lawrence L. Langer.
        p. cm.
    Includes bibliographical references.
    ISBN 0-300-04966-8 (cloth)
        0-300-05247-2 (pbk.)
    1. Holocaust, Jewish (1939–1945)—Personal narratives—History and criticism. 2. Holocaust survivors—Psychology. I. Title.
    D804.3.L36 1991
    953'. 18—dc20   90-44768 CIP

The paper in this book meets the guidelines for permanence and durability of the Committee on Production Guidelines for Book Longevity of the Council on Library Resources.

10   9   8   7   6

For Sandy
who knows why
and
Noah, Tamar, and Emily
who will

I want to talk about a certain time not measured in months and years. For so long I have wanted to talk about this time, and not in the way I will talk about it now, not just about this one scrap of time. I wanted to, but I couldn't, I didn't know how. I was afraid, too, that this second time, which is measured in months and years, had buried the other time under a layer of years, that this second time had crushed the first and destroyed it within me. But no. Today, digging around in the ruins of memory, I found it fresh and untouched by forgetfulness.

—IDA FINK

By its very nature, when it comes to describing reality, art always demands a certain intensification, for many and various reasons. However, that is not the case with the Holocaust. Everything in it already seems so thoroughly unreal, as if it no longer belongs to the experience of our generation, but to mythology. Thence comes the need to bring it down to the human realm. This is not a mechanical problem, but an essential one. When I say, "to bring it down," I do not mean to simplify, to attenuate, or to sweeten the horror, but to attempt to make the events speak through the individual and in his language, to rescue the suffering from huge numbers, from dreadful anonymity, and to restore the person's given and family name, to give the tortured person back his human form, which was snatched away from him.

—AHARON APPELFELD

CONTENTS

Preface   ix

Acknowledgments   xvii

1   DEEP MEMORY: The Buried Self   1

2   ANGUISHED MEMORY: The Divided Self   39

3   HUMILIATED MEMORY: The Besieged Self   77

4   TAINTED MEMORY: The Impromptu Self   121

5   UNHEROIC MEMORY: The Diminished Self   162

Notes   207

PREFACE

About six years ago, when I first began looking at videotaped Holocaust testimonies, I was watching an interview with a Mr. and Mrs. B., who were on camera together. Each had been in several camps, including Auschwitz; both had lost virtually every member of their families. Their son and daughter are present at the interview too, and at the very end the camera draws back to reveal the entire family sitting together. The interviewer asks Mr. and Mrs. B. what they are left with, what their ordeal has done to them.

Her children sitting next to her, Mrs. B. confesses: "We are left with loneliness. As long as we live, we are lonely." Mr. B., his children sitting next to him, looks down, an utterly forlorn expression on his face, shrugs his shoulders, and whispers barely audibly: "Nothing to say. Sad." Then he shakes his head and weeps quietly as his wife describes how deprived her children were because while growing up they lacked grandparents and relatives to give them the affection and small presents that other children received.

The interviewer then asks the daughter the same question: How does *she* feel about her parents' experience (which, in addition to Auschwitz, included the Lodz ghetto, as well as Dora-Nordhausen for Mr. B. and Bergen-Belsen for Mrs. B.)? The daughter seems to speak from a different world:

> First of all, I think I'm left with a lot of strength, because you can't have parents like this who survived some very, very ugly experiences [a *mammoth* understatement, for anyone who has seen the interview] and managed to build a life afterwards and still have some hope. You can't grow up in a household like that without having many, many strengths, first of all.
>
> And second of all, something that I have as a child of survivors which second and third generation American people don't have is still some connection with the rich Jewish cultural heritage which is gone now. That is my connection.[1]

As if some mocking spirit of irony were supervising the enterprise, the tape runs out at this very instant, severing and silencing the "connection" and leaving the screen blank. The interview never resumes (at least, not until eight years later, when I reinterviewed Mr. and Mrs. B. myself, separately, to give them a chance to tell their stories more fully).

While watching this sequence of moments on the initial tape, I remember thinking: "Wait a minute! Something's wrong here! Either someone's not listening, or someone's not telling the truth!" This was of course a naive response. But what I was reacting to was this: Despite the presence of their children, the parents speak of being lonely and sad. The daughter, if we listen carefully to the tenor of her words, sees her parents as people who have "managed to build a life afterwards and still have some hope," and who have been able to insure for her a "connection with the rich Jewish cultural heritage which is gone now." *She* draws on a vocabulary of chronology and conjunction, while *they* use a lexicon of disruption, absence, and irreversible loss. It took me some time to realize that *all* of them were telling a version of the truth as they grasped it, that several currents flow at differing depths in Holocaust testimonies, and that our understanding of the event depends very much on the source and destination of the current we pursue.

Nevertheless, the longing for connection continues to echo in our needful ears. Too often, unfortunately, it turns out to be a hollow echo, its sound bounding and rebounding off the walls of sealed chambers. If I have discovered anything in my investigation, it is that oral Holocaust testimonies are doomed on one level to remain disrupted narratives, not only by the vicissitudes of technology but by the quintessence of the experiences they record. Instead of leading to further chapters in the autobiography of the witnesses, they exhaust themselves in the telling. They do not function in time like other narratives, since the losses they record raise few expectations of renewal or hopes of reconciliation. This does not mean that witnesses have no future. In spite of their final words, Mr. and Mrs. B. are very much parents to their children (and indeed grandparents to their grandchild, whom they discussed with undisguised joy during the lunch break between their second interviews). But they are also hostages to a humiliating and painful past that their happier future does little to curtail.

Moral formulas about learning from experience and growing through suffering rapidly disintegrate into meaningless fragments of rhetorical consolation as the testimony of these interviews proceeds. When I began to examine them, I was already suspicious of commentaries and memoirs that celebrated the resourceful human spirit in the face of the Holocaust disaster. As I continued to watch them, I felt that my suspicions were confirmed. A heritage of heroism encountered the awful facts of this particular catastrophe and found that the only honest judgment was to declare the confrontation "no combat." When former victims, entreating our sympathetic understanding, insist that the situations in which they found themselves in ghettos and camps were "different," they are making a specific appeal to us to abandon traditional assumptions about moral conduct and the "privileged" distinctions between right and wrong that usually inspire such assumptions. The events they endured rudely dispel as misconception the idea that choice is purely an internal matter, immune to circumstance and chance.

Recently a friend surprised me—I suppose "stunned" would be a more precise term—when he condemned all Jews who worked in any capacity for the Germans in the camps as "collaborators." With a few rare exceptions, nothing could be further from the truth, though I was not sure whether to blame his attitude or his vocabulary. If I use "former victims" rather than "survivors" to describe the witnesses in these testimonies, one reason is to mark my belief that their morally quarantined situation then is still so little understood nearly a half century later. My friend's rebuke was more than a trifle self-righteous, but I wondered at the time whether its origin lay in an area of spiritual repose that would be disturbed by his accepting an alternative point of view. The mind in search of sedatives and antidotes—my friend was a physician—is understandably wary of stimulants whose unpredictable sway may do more to destabilize than to cure.

This is a book I would gladly not have written, if somehow I could have prevented the reality on which it is based from having happened. Writing about Holocaust *literature*, or even written memoirs, as I have done in my previous works, challenges the imagination through the mediation of a *text*, raising issues of style and form and tone and figurative language that—I now see—can deflect our attention from the "dreadful familiarity" of the event itself. Nothing, however, distracts us from the immediacy and the intimacy of conducting interviews with former victims (which I have done) or watching them on a screen. Struggling to identify with the voices of the witnesses, who themselves are struggling to discover voices trustworthy enough to tell their *whole* stories (and not all have the courage or stamina or resources to succeed), I often found myself naked before their nakedness, defenseless in the presence of their vulnerability. Perhaps my own effort to develop a style and form and tone and language to capture the implications of their ordeal, in addition to reflecting a tribute to their raw frankness, represents a desire to find moral and intellectual garb more relevant than my discarded attire. I am still not sure how durable such raiment may be in our post-Holocaust era; but in our age of atrocity (a label certified by the personal evidence in these testimonies), one dons such clothing as one can.

The result is an unfashionable challenge, requiring risks from all participants. From the point of view of the witness, the urge to tell meets resistance from the certainty that one's audience will not understand. The anxiety of futility lurks beneath the surface of many of these narratives, erupting occasionally and rousing us to an appraisal of our own stance that we cannot afford to ignore. A locus classicus of such confrontation appears in the testimony of Magda F., whose husband, parents, brother, three sisters, and all their children were engulfed in the tide of Nazi mass murder. Another brother and sister had emigrated to the United States in the 1920s. She joined them there in 1948. After a while, she says, her brother and sister and their children began to beg her to talk about "it," to tell them the details of what happened to the rest of the family. Magda F. recalls:

And I looked at them and I said: "I'm gonna tell you something. I'm gonna tell you something now. If somebody would tell *me* this story, I would say 'She's lying, or he's lying.' Because this can't be true. And maybe you're gonna feel the same way. That your sister's lying here, because this could not happen. Because to understand us, somebody has to go through with it. Because nobody, but nobody fully understands us. You can't. No [matter] how much sympathy you give me when I'm talking here, or you understand . . . you're *trying* to understand me, I know, but I don't think you could. I don't think so."

And I said this to them. Hoping [they] should never be able to understand, because to understand, you have to go through with it, and I hope nobody in the world comes to this again, [so] they *should* understand us. And this was the honest truth, because nobody, nobody, nobody . . . [2]

A main effect of these testimonies (and, I hope, of this book) is to begin to undo a negation—the principle of discontinuity which argues that an impassable chasm permanently separates the seriously interested auditor and observer from the experiences of the former Holocaust victim. In spite of Magda F.'s misgivings, listening to hundreds of witnesses' stories is a form of "coming to this again" that changes her segregated nobodies into sharing somebodies. "You won't understand" and "you must understand" are regular contenders in the multiple voices of these testimonies; Magda F. is representative, not exceptional.

Once we tear off the convenient mask that makes of these narratives spiritual odysseys leading to an easy familiarity with their content—and no more than 1 or 2 percent attempt to follow this pattern—we are left with the charge of transforming the dreadful anonymity that Aharon Appelfeld speaks of in the epigraph to this book into a "dreadful familiarity." Near the end of her own testimony, Magda F. turns to one of her interviewers (I was the other one) and in genuine amazement exclaims: "You're crying!" They were tears of pity, I am sure; but they may also have been tears of fear and despair, resulting from a direct encounter with the melancholy universe that had consumed most of Magda F.'s family. A statement like "to understand, you have to go through with it," however authentic its inspiration, underestimates the sympathetic power of the imagination. Perhaps it is time to grant that power the role it deserves.

One preliminary issue remains, and that is the reliability of the memory on which these testimonies must draw for the accuracy and intensity of their details. How credible can a reawakened memory be that tries to revive events so many decades after they occurred? I think the terminology itself is at fault here. There is no need to revive what has never died. Moreover, though slumbering memories may crave reawakening, nothing is clearer in these narratives than that Holocaust memory is an insomniac faculty, whose mental eyes have never slept. In addition, since testimonies are human documents rather than merely historical ones, the troubled interaction between past and present achieves a gravity that surpasses the concern with accuracy. Factual errors do occur from time to time, as do simple lapses; but they seem trivial in comparison to the complex layers of memory that give birth to the versions of the self that we shall be studying in this volume.

When human beings ceased to be emissaries or legatees of love and became instead agents or victims of power on such a massive scale, we may have witnessed a shift in civilization's priorities with whose psychological bequest we continue to struggle. The Holocaust threatens to be a permanent hole in the ozone layer of history, through which infiltrate the memories of a potentially crippling past. These testimonies remind us how overwhelming, and perhaps insurmountable, is the task of reversing its legacy.

ACKNOWLEDGMENTS

All the evidence on which this book is based is located in the Fortunoff Video Archive for Holocaust Testimonies established at Yale University in 1982. By October 1989 the collection numbered over fourteen hundred testimonies, ranging in length from thirty minutes to more than four hours, though the average interview lasts between one and two hours. With a few exceptions, the witnesses are interviewed alone, the camera usually focused exclusively on the interviewee. Among those interviewed, in addition to Holocaust survivors now living in the United States (by far the largest group), are former members of the underground, American liberators, persons who grew up in the Third Reich (persecuted or not), and émigrés who left while it was still possible. All witnesses have volunteered for the interview, which is usually conducted by two interviewers who practice a mainly noninterventionist strategy, encouraging the free flow of memory to recapture the interviewees' thoughts and feelings about their experiences. My esteem and admiration go first to all the hundreds of men and women who told their stories before the camera. They made everything possible by their generous permission to be quoted in this book.

I am grateful to the Video Archive for giving me access to the tapes. To the faculty adviser of the Fortunoff Archive, Geoffrey Hartman, I am indebted for encouragement and support in more ways than I am able to mention. Without the help of its former archivist, Sandy Rosenstock, this project would have been stillborn; her astonishing command of the content of the tapes guided me to dozens of invaluable interviews I might have overlooked, and saved me countless hours. To her associate, Joanne Rudof, I am indebted for a patience and generosity that a lesser spirit could not have mustered. All scholars in this field are obliged to acknowledge the contributions of Laurel F. Vlock, a television specialist, and psychiatrist Dori Laub, who with the support of William Rosenberg, head of the New Haven Farband, in 1979 launched the Holocaust Survivors Film Project, which later evolved into the Video Archive. I offer them admiration beyond thanks, for without their persistence and toil the first two hundred interviews would never have been conducted, and hence there would have been no material to stimulate the vision that led to the writing of this book.

My next thanks go to Margot Stern Strom, executive director of Facing History and Ourselves Foundation, Inc., of Brookline, Massachusetts, an educational organization that for the past fifteen years has been developing Holocaust curriculum for use at the precollege level. Under a grant from the Revson Foundation, and in cooperation with the Yale Video Archive, Facing History accepted the challenge of creating a program for making the taped interviews accessible to a general audience. One day in 1984, Margot called to ask if I would be interested in looking at some videotaped interviews with Holocaust survivors and working with them on the project. In the absence of that initial invitation, this book would never have been written. To Margot, former program director, Bill Parsons, and to members of the Facing History staff, especially Mary Johnson, Marc Skvirsky, and Jan Darsa, as well as to the teachers associated with that excellent organization, I am indebted for the opportunities they gave me to measure my ideas against their own insights and expertise.

To William J. Holmes, president of Simmons College, and Priscilla McKee, former vice president, I am grateful for unfailing support, especially in the early stages of my research, when possible outcomes were still in doubt. Their faith did much to spur my own attempts to focus on a manageable and meaningful subject.

A fellowship from the National Endowment for the Humanities provided a year free from teaching and the leisure to concentrate on the demanding task of organizing chaos without tumbling into its chasm.

To Saul Friedländer, of Tel Aviv University and the University of California at Los Angeles, I owe a special debt for some early conversation and exchanges that inspired me to search for a more complex view of my subject. He bears no responsibility for the results but deserves much credit for the generosity of his concern.

To Ellen Graham, my editor at Yale University Press, I am grateful for an unusual sensitivity to the intention and design of my work.

Finally, to my son, Andy, I owe a special acknowledgment, since with a covert desire to intimidate (accompanied by a genuine intention to help), he presented me with my first word processor, then proposed to humiliate me forever by threatening to take it back three months later when it still lay in its carton in my office. Paternal dignity prevailed over technological trepidation, and I entered the modern age. He made my work infinitely easier and more enjoyable, as he has done for my life, together with his sister, their spouses, and their rapidly proliferating progeny.

My wife stands alone: she bears much, and provides all.

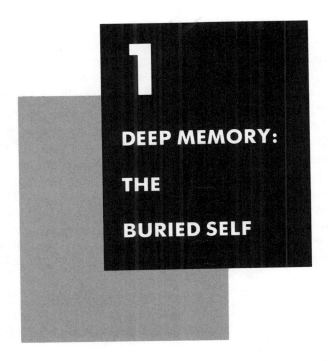

1

DEEP MEMORY:

THE

BURIED SELF

In a recent newspaper editorial, the writer urges his readers to watch the moving documentary *Partisans of Vilna*, to be shown that night on a local educational television channel. He calls the film about opposition to the Nazis in the Vilna ghetto "a tribute to the redeeming power of resistance." He then describes the memorable moment when one of the partisan organization's founders (Abba Kovner) "looks into the camera and recounts how he had to turn his mother away from the barricaded house where she might have found safety." (She did not survive.) Although he does not elaborate, he uses this as an example of the difficult choices imposed on Jewish victims by situations (not created by them) that often required the sacrifice of one life in order to preserve others. The editorial comment following this illustration reads: "Theirs is a story of secular salvation."[1]

1

Sandwiched between a vocabulary ("redeeming" and "salvation") that prods us away from the event toward a consoling future (a vocabulary, one might add, with a distinctly Christian flavor) lies the predicament of a son involuntarily sending his mother to her probable death. Even the most callous imagination could not interpret this as a moment of deliverance, nor am I suggesting that the editorialist is guilty of such insensitivity. Yet Holocaust commentary gives birth to its own involuntary tensions: the habit of verbal reassurance, through a kind of internal balancing act, tries to make more manageable for an uninitiated audience (and the equally uninitiated author?) impossible circumstances like the one Abba Kovner faced. Tributes are cheering; memorials are sad. Language often seems to be the fulcrum tilting us, as in this instance, away from one and toward the other.

Eventually, we must learn to suspect the effect as well as the intent of bracing pieties like "redeeming" and "salvation" when they are used to shape our understanding of the ordeal of former victims of Nazi oppression. Scarcely a volume appears on this subject that is not celebrated as a homage to "the indomitable human spirit." Certainly anyone who managed to live through or, more precisely, to stay alive under the inhuman conditions of the labor, concentration, or death camps deserves some form of special notice. But after having watched hundreds of videotaped testimonies of former victims, I have concluded that developing suitable accolades is neither a useful nor accurate way of responding to them. Such accolades do not honor the painful complexities of the victims' narratives, any more than they reflect the ambivalence of their trials in the camps.

Testimony is a form of remembering. The faculty of memory functions in the present to recall a personal history vexed by traumas that thwart smooth-flowing chronicles. Simultaneously, however, straining against what we might call disruptive memory is an effort to reconstruct a semblance of continuity in a life that began as, and now resumes what we would consider, a normal existence. "Cotemporality" becomes the controlling principle of these testimonies, as witnesses struggle with the impossible task of making their recollections of the camp experience coalesce with the rest of their lives. If one theme links their narratives more than any other, it is the unintended, unexpected, but invariably unavoidable failure of such efforts.

In *La mémoire et les jours*, the fourth and final volume of periodic commentary on her camp experience (published under the general title of *Auschwitz et après*),[2] Charlotte Delbo devotes the opening section of the text to a monologue addressed to an anonymous "you." In this section, much like Primo Levi in his recurrent literary forays into his Auschwitz past, she renews her attempt (consuming four decades) to explain to herself and to us the "unexplainable" implications of having in one's life an "Auschwitz" and an "afterwards," thus dramatizing the temporal rupture mentioned above. She uses the image of a serpent shedding its old skin and emerging with a "fresh and shining" one to illustrate her own difficulty in imitating nature in a gesture of renewal. She departed from Auschwitz, she tells us, with a worn-out skin. At first, it seemed that she would be able to leave its wrinkles behind, though her shedding process was far more gradual than the snake's. The human ritual of renewal meant relearning habits from her "former" or pre-Auschwitz life: how to use a toothbrush, toilet paper, handkerchief, knife, and fork; how to smile, first with the lips, then with the lips and eyes; how to recapture forgotten odors and tastes, like the smell of rain.[3]

Implicit in the procedure of renewal, however, annealed to it with the epoxy of disruptive memory, is the "counter-time" of Auschwitz, where the rain stank of diarrhea and beat down on the camp, the victims, "the soot of the crematoriums and the odor of burning flesh" (11). It intrudes on narrative memory even as Delbo searches for a solvent to detach it from the present. Two voices vie for primacy here, each honest, each incomplete. On the one hand, Delbo admits that it took several years for her new skin to "reorganize" and "consolidate" itself. On the other, she knows that though shedding a skin may leave the snake unchanged, similar results apply to *her* only in appearance. The metaphor of "layers," indeed, leads to buried revelations that eventually explode the comparison: for this former victim, not only memory exists, but the "skin of memory," a hardened shell that she cannot shed and whose impact is now beyond her control. It exerts its force in spite of the passage of time.

For many, Auschwitz permanently destroyed the potency of the sedative we call illusion. "In the camp," Delbo insists, "you could never pretend; you could never take refuge in the imaginary." The crushing reality of the place, the pain, the exhaustion, the cold, that would later congeal into the hardened skin of memory, prevented her and her companions from fantasizing that they were someone or somewhere else. This is a crucial if controversial observation, because in her earlier volumes Delbo speaks of the value of literature in sustaining her during her ordeal. Here she specifically denies that reciting a poem or discussing a book or a theatrical piece while she and her fellow deportees were digging in the swamps surrounding the camp ever led to a successful "doubling" (*dédoublement*) of the self. Such imagining may have preserved her memories of an *earlier* time and furnished a certain security that her mind was still functioning, but "it never succeeded in negating for a single instant the moment that I was living [then]. . . . The reality was there, fatal. Impossible to withdraw from it" (12).

Through a bizarre reversal, survival made possible, and even necessary, the doubling that eluded Delbo during her years in the camps. Endeavors to leave it behind *now* prove as futile as attempts to escape from its reality into an imagined future *then*. But today she has available psychological and verbal strategies for contending with her albatross. The exploded metaphor of the snakeskin returns in a fresh guise, as if it had shed its own earlier implications to reappear with a vividness that is more than metaphorical. Art has been reclaimed and transformed back into the fragment of truth that had inspired it. Asked if she lives with Auschwitz after her return, she replies, "No—I live beside it. Auschwitz is there, fixed and unchangeable, but wrapped in the impervious skin of memory that segregates itself from the present 'me.' Unlike the snake's skin, the skin of memory doesn't renew itself" (13). Indeed, she wishes it to become tougher, fearing sometimes that it may grow thinner and crack, permitting the camp reality to spill out and recapture her. We note that by now the image of renewal has disappeared, together with the original metaphor. Living "beside" Auschwitz activates a comparison far more complex than the natural event of shedding and renewal, with its reflection of experience as a storehouse of consecutive moments in time.

The doubling that Delbo speaks of invalidates the idea of continuity, and even of chronology, that testimonies from former victims *seem* to offer us by the very structure of their narratives. Her language helps us to anticipate the more reflexive and hence less easily recognizable phenomenon that she writes about with such explicit precision. "I have the feeling," Delbo says, "that the 'self' who was in the camp isn't me, isn't the person who is here, opposite you. No, it's too unbelievable. And everything that happened to this other 'self,' the one from Auschwitz, doesn't touch me now, *me*, doesn't concern me, so distinct are deep memory [*mémoire profonde*] and common memory [*mémoire ordinaire*]" (13). Her terms initiate a verbal breakthrough, a vital and refreshing departure from the familiar approach that tries to entice the Auschwitz experience, and others like it, into the uncongenial sanctuaries of a redeeming salvation.

What Delbo calls common memory might not find them so uncongenial; her deep memory, however, would consider them inhospitable. The witness accounts I plan to investigate, as they unfold before our eyes and ears, veer from one to the other, often unaware of the discrepancies introduced by their alternating vision. Deep memory tries to recall the Auschwitz self as it was then; common memory has a dual function: it restores the self to its normal pre- and postcamp routines but also offers detached portraits, from the vantage point of today, of what it must have been like then. Deep memory thus suspects *and* depends on common memory, knowing what common memory cannot know but tries nonetheless to express. The witnesses in these testimonies, most of them less concerned than Delbo with such exact definitions of the self, often appear troubled or exasperated (without knowing why) when the two kinds of memory intrude on each other, disrupting the smooth flow of their narratives. Delbo's distinctions help us understand and interpret their dilemma.

But they also help us to understand and interpret Delbo's own plight when she seeks to illuminate the complex task of "remembering Auschwitz," a plight that, as the rest of her memoir confirms, she might not have been entirely conscious of herself. "I live in a double existence," she confesses, perhaps too schematically. "The double of Auschwitz doesn't disturb me or mingle in my life. As if it weren't 'me' at all. Without this split, I wouldn't have been able to come back to life" (13). But as Delbo will confess later in another context, speaking here is the voice of common memory, whose very reason for being is to confirm the comforting division that she mentions. It is a form of reassurance designed to sedate the surge of deep memory, that constantly threatens to erupt in the course of any survivor narrative. What happens when that sedation loses its potency concerns Delbo, as it will concern us.

"The skin covering the memory of Auschwitz," Delbo writes, "is tough":

> Sometimes, however, it bursts, and gives back its contents.
> In a dream, the will is powerless. And in these dreams, there
> I see myself again, *me*, yes *me*, just as I know I was: scarcely
> able to stand . . . pierced with cold, filthy, gaunt, and the

pain is so unbearable, so exactly the pain I suffered there, that I feel it again physically, I feel it again through my whole body, which becomes a block of pain, and I feel death seizing me, I feel myself die. Fortunately, in my anguish, I cry out. The cry awakens me, and I emerge from the nightmare, exhausted. It takes days for everything to return to normal, for memory to be "refilled" and for the skin of memory to mend itself. I become myself again, the one you know, who can speak to you of Auschwitz without showing any sign of distress or emotion. (13–14)

The cry that awakens her also awakens us to the astonishing realization that Delbo, unwittingly or not, has herself pierced the skin of memory through her description, using the dream as an "excuse" to do so.

It is a virtuoso performance, as the two versions of her self occupy center stage simultaneously, the voice of deep memory struggling to displace the milder tones of common memory as we read, in spite of her insistence that this is not possible. In her next sentence, for example, Delbo argues, "When I speak to you of Auschwitz, my words don't come from deep memory; they come, so to speak, from external memory [*mémoire externe*], intellectual memory, reflective memory." Refining the opposition between deep and common memory, she develops a parallel distinction between what we might call "thinking memory" and what she labels "sense memory" ("*mémoire des sens*") (14). From the point of view of writer and former victim, Delbo is naturally wary of confusing the two. But in fact in her own narrative, and even more in oral testimonies, the two interact and intersect continually, and the challenge to us as audience is to recognize and interpret those moments. On the surface, the difference appears to be one between account and evocation. But more fundamentally, these testimonies invite witnesses to re-create "*me*, yes *me*, just as I know I was" (and "it," just as they knew "it" was) in spite of the monitory other self that is hesitant and skeptical about the whole enterprise.

The problem is compounded by the limited power of words to release the specific kinds of physical distress haunting the caverns of deep memory. Like Primo Levi, Delbo contends that as a result of the camp experience the word as well as the self has achieved a form of doubling: "cold," "filthy," and "gaunt" mean one thing to her and another to the "you" she is addressing. Because a language of Auschwitz has never emerged, an interpreter is constantly at work in the texts of deep memory to remind us of the need to collaborate with all efforts at redefinition. Witnesses themselves are hounded by this predicament—the dual thrust of the words they use. "Otherwise," Delbo concedes, "someone [in the camps] who has been tormented by thirst for weeks would never again be able to say: 'I'm thirsty. Let's make a cup of tea.' . . . 'Thirst' [after the war] has once more become a currently used term. On the other hand, if I dream of the thirst that I felt in Birkenau [the locale of the extermination facilities in Auschwitz], I see myself as I was then, haggard, bereft of reason, tottering. I feel again physically that *real* thirst, and it's an agonizing nightmare. But if you want me to *speak* to you about it . . . " (14). Not surprisingly, Delbo locates the expression of deep memory in her dreams, though we know, even as she knows, that the nightmare she describes is not a metaphor but a reality. Nothing is disguised, and no one is needed to analyze its concealed meanings.

Most videotaped oral testimonies are less explicit; audiences are hence essential to interpret demurrals like the one with which Charlotte Delbo ends the passage cited above. There is value not only in admitting the existence of the two voices of deep and common memory and in learning to recognize what they reveal and conceal, but also in noting when one glides into the other, and the possible significance of those moments. Similarly, there is value in assessing our response to intellectual memory when, for example, it retreats from the principle of verbal doubling and like our editorialist applies current usage such as "redeeming" and "salvation" to the world of Auschwitz; and to sense memory, when it offers its own equivalent of Delbo's "I feel death seizing me, I feel myself die." Former victims, in other words, are not the only ones threatened by the ordeal of oral testimony. As we shall see, the subtle urging of an interviewer, who after all is no more than an emissary of the outsider's point of view, can lead a witness to shift from one form of memory to another, and indeed control and shape the content of each.

One effect of common memory, with its talk of normalcy amid chaos, is to mediate atrocity, to reassure us that in spite of the ordeal some human bonds were inviolable. For instance, a recurrent theme in the oral testimonies is the mutuality that sustained sisters who went through the camp experience together. Common memory recalls family unity as a nurturing value in one's darkest moments—and there is no reason to dispute this. But simultaneously deep memory, often in the same testimony, burrows beneath the surface of the narrative to excavate episodes that corrode the comforts of common memory. Remembering and recording what happened operate on several levels, leaving atrocity and order in a permanently disrupted suspension.

Consider the story of Celia K. and its subversive impact on the framework of normalcy that we as audience bring to these narratives. In 1942, not yet nineteen, she flees the small ghetto where she is living with her mother, brothers, sisters, and her sisters' children to hide in the nearby woods with her younger sister. The Germans approach the woods with loudspeakers and try to entice the Jews to return to the ghetto, promising them work. Unconvinced, but unable to bear the loneliness and uncertainty, Celia and her sister go back, to be greeted by their angry mother shrieking: "I brought you up all these years. Why did you come back? Get out. Get away." Her mother then persuades a Polish peasant to enter the still unsealed ghetto, spirit her daughter out, and hide her on his farm. At great personal risk, he succeeds; he then digs a hole beneath his barn floor, two feet wide, Celia says, and just as long and high as her body was, and from June to October 1942 she stays there alone.

One day, the farmer appears at her hiding place with her younger sister, who joins her in the hole (presumably after it has been enlarged). The entire ghetto had been liquidated; only her sister, eleven or twelve years old, a champion swimmer, was able to dive into the nearby river and escape. They share their cavity in the earth with rats, who chew at their toes. "You just learned not to scream," says Celia, in response to the interviewer's question of how they felt at the time. They remain there until October 1943, sometimes crawling out to stretch their limbs when the barn was empty. One evening near the end of that anxious period, one of her brothers (who were by then fighting with the partisans) appears with the peasant in the barn and brings them a gun. "Now look," he tells them, "this gun is more valuable than anything I have. I am giving it to you and I want you to use it if the Germans ever capture you. You must never, never under any circumstances get caught alive." He then tells them a grisly story of what the Germans are doing to Jewish women caught in that area. "If you know the Germans are going to catch you, one of you must shoot the other and then shoot yourself." And after this fraternal advice, he leaves.

"A few days later," Celia K. continues,

we heard the farmer coming and he said: "Quick, Germans. Be as quiet as you can." We were in this little hole. I don't know what happened. So much water started coming in. We didn't have any air to breathe, and the water was coming up to our chins. I don't know how long we stood it, for three days, four days, five days, I don't know. And then we heard footsteps over us. So I said to my sister: "Now. You kill me first, and then kill yourself." She said, "No, you're the older one. You want to kill me." I said, "No, you're the younger one. You are going to kill me." And she had her gun poised at me already because we heard German [being spoken] and we heard a lot of footsteps. It just so happened they were retreating, leaving the barn, and the farmer gave us three knocks and we knew we were safe. And this was something that I'll never forget in my life. We were drowning.[4]

And the two sisters, their unique form of sibling rivalry temporarily suspended, remain—with what? A feeling of relief? Imperishable terror? Stupefaction, as the subject of their dialogue sinks in? If we can't speak of mutual support, what *can* we speak of here? How do we define the role of the "angry" mother, who sends her daughter away, and the "nurturing" brother, who sanctions the pact of murder and suicide?

The sense of drowning experienced by the sisters in their hole can be interpreted on physical and metaphysical levels, the sheer immediacy of the terrifying moment causing the trapped body to nullify appeal to the equally trapped spirit. Choosing moral duty over self-preservation suddenly appears as an *outmoded* ideal, overridden by a situation that makes *either* of those options irrelevant. In *Modernity and the Holocaust*, Zygmunt Bauman argues that the "lesson of the Holocaust is the facility with which most people, put into a situation that does not contain a good choice . . . argue themselves away from the issue of moral duty . . . adopting instead the precepts of rational interest and self-preservation."[5] Insofar as Bauman is speaking of Germans, collaborators, or bystanders, his observation is pertinent; the confusion and distortion arise when one tries to apply his "lesson," as so many commentators do, to the experience of former victims too. Witnesses themselves, prompted by common memory, sometimes lapse into Bauman's attitude, causing them to judge themselves harshly; fortunately, their deep memory knows better, intuitively perceiving the almost droll understatement of a formula like "a situation that does not contain a good choice."

We need to guard against the misapplication of such formulas.

It would be simple enough, for example, to extend the "meanings" of the story of Celia and her sister by stressing the symbolic dimensions or legendary echoes of their ordeal. The impulse to create illuminating precedents for moments that were sui generis raises the literary specter of Poe-like tales of premature burial or epic accounts of descent into the underworld. But such artificial contexts, like Bauman's moral formula, do little to blunt the private encounter with a kind of death beyond analogy, shorn of redeeming hopes or mythic associations. Nor do they defuse the illusion that personal dignity could be preserved, no matter what the challenge, through the exercise of individual choice.

Sometimes in these testimonies deep memory infiltrates common memory in such a way that the two become tightly intertwined. Anna G., for instance, recalling a scene on the ramp at Auschwitz upon her arrival there, relates it to her own life much later, during the postwar period of "normalcy," suggesting how hopeless is the quest for total immunity from the original ordeal. She tells of a ten-year-old girl who refused to go to the "left" (toward death) after the selection. (Earlier she had explained that the members of her transport from Plaszow, having experienced many "selections" there, had learned to fear their meaning.) Kicking and scratching, the young girl was seized by three SS men who held her down while she screamed to her nearby mother that she shouldn't let them kill her. According to Anna G., one of the SS men approached the mother, who was only in her late twenties, and asked her if she wanted to go with her daughter. "No," the mother replied, at which point the witness observes: "This left a tremendous effect on me."

She admits that at the time in her mind she blamed the mother for not going with her daughter. Then she adds, "Who am I to blame her? What would be my decision in a case like this?" Of course, this is a response available to anyone; but because Anna G. witnessed the episode, she participated in it—or it "participated" in her—with complex results. When her own daughter was born years later, she began to have nightmares, reliving that moment on the ramp. The only difference was that the screaming ten-year-old was replaced by her daughter. Former victims are thus pursued not only by their own earlier traumatic moments but by the traumas of others too. The situation on the ramp had so violated established conventions of motherhood that it assaulted the narrator's perception of herself in that role decades after the event. Deep memory prevents the imagination from finding refuge from such assaults.[6]

Maternity infected by atrocity—the moment becomes a paradigm for the structure of oral testimonies, which seem to flee such conjunctions by depending on chronology even as they are drawn back ceaselessly into their embrace. In the beginning, I was convinced that these testimonies represented fully spontaneous narratives, unmediated by devices analogous to, though not identical with, ones we find in consciously contrived literary texts. But this expectation appears not to be supported by the evidence. As an illustration, take the testimony of Sidney L., born in 1927 in a small town in Poland. His first piece of information is that he was one of nine children—not an extraordinary detail since many of these accounts begin with a recital of prewar family situations. But as his narrative of more than two hours proceeds, this simple fact emerges as the key to its inconspicuous structure.

The testimony is virtually uninterrupted by questions; it appears as a modest story of how Sidney L. survived. And on its most obvious level, the one mirrored by common memory, this is exactly what it is. But its counterflow, its alter ego, as it were, is the rehabilitation through deep memory of the family that has vanished, and the impact of that disappearance on the single surviving member. This explains the first hour of the interview, in which Sidney L. patiently reconstructs his family's prewar life. At first, we wonder why he alludes so often to the differences in age between himself and his siblings, as if he were driven by a need to establish a distinct identity for each one of them. The reason becomes clearer with the outbreak of war, which causes an abrupt, violent, and permanent change in the family's destiny. This in itself, of course, is not unique to the family of Sidney L.; but it leads to an inner dynamic in his narrative that in turn illuminates his dual role as son and victim and his struggle to reconcile the two.

A few days after the Nazi invasion of Poland, still early in September 1939, Sidney L.'s father sends him to buy some tobacco. When he returns, he finds that a stray bomb has left a crater where the family home once stood. He arrives in time to find some men digging out his mother's remains. The bodies of three sisters and two brothers soon follow. His father and a younger sister are wounded, but not mortally. An elder married brother, not living at home, is safe; another brother is uninjured. So by his explicit count, five remain. Although other memories intervene, the next episode he recalls vividly is returning home one day to see two Gestapo men leading his father and married brother (who lived nearby) into a courtyard, where they are put against a wall and shot. The rest of his narrative tells of his experiences until "liberation," one main focus being the fate of his younger sister, whose whereabouts he can trace until early in 1943, when she is deported somewhere and disappears, never to be heard of again. He and his brother are left.

The two of them are the fragments he uses to shore against the ruins of family, community, and the control of his future that these institutions represented. The subterranean theme of his narrative gradually becomes his revelation of the part of his own self that vanishes with the death of each sibling. He and his brother, who plays an increasingly crucial role in his story, pass through various labor camps, are separated for long intervals, but find themselves reunited in 1944 in Bergen-Belsen, where they end up in adjacent compounds of the camp. At this point, he tells us, he had a "vision" that they were both going to survive, an instinctive conviction that their reunion in this camp had a special meaning for the future. He enters into a kind of dialogue with himself, as we witness the process whereby the imagination manufactures the idea of fate in order to protect itself from the ravages of random circumstance. He returns in desperation to what we might call the predictive spirit, a version of common memory that, notwithstanding the contradictory countermomentum of experience, tries to impose a meaningful sequence on the details of one's life. If it turns out to be so, if his reunion with his brother did indeed "foretell" survival for both of them, then he will have retroactive confirmation of his vision.

But events do not confirm that vision, and this furnishes him with the melancholy coda to his narrative. While he is in the infirmary at Bergen-Belsen, his brother is taken away to another labor camp: "I never saw him again." In the closing moments of his testimony, Sidney L. tries to explain how this final disappointment, signifying the total extinction of his family, undermined the sense of continuity in his life: "There were certain things that I believed in [here he gestures with his fist, perhaps in vague protest], and it didn't turn out to be. I was *positive* that I was going to live with my brother till the end of the war." He even *uses* the word "predestined," holdover from the now depleted dictionary of common memory, but only to expose how his family's doom has exhausted its value as a descriptive term for his personal experience.

We are present at the birth of a point of view when near the closing moments of the testimony the interviewer, still caught in the grip of common memory, asks Sidney L.: "Do you think it was your ability to hold onto that idea [that he and his brother were 'predestined' to survive] that got you through to the end?" The question invites simplified closure and reassurance against the unsettling assaults of deep memory, but the witness, drained by the implications of his own narrative, resists the temptation: "I don't know," he replies. "In all these things that happened—I played a very small part in everything that happened. There were very few things that I initiated, or planned out on this. This is how it happened; it took me from here and put me there. . . . It was not my plan, it was not my doing." He defines his moral situation—or the moral paralysis of his situation—when he says: "I was never asked 'Do you want to do such and such?'"[7]

Thus his narrative emerges not as a story of survival, but of deprival—deprival of the members of his family, and hence, in his own eyes, of his personal will. What he calls the power of "it" whittles away at his sustaining belief in kinship until no one is left but himself. Only at the end, if we have been hearing him, do we realize that all along, while he has ostensibly been telling us how he managed to stay alive (the interviewer's question confirms our belief that this has been the substance of his testimony), its *essence* has been the doom of those closest to him who did *not* survive. His conviction that he and his brother were predestined to live is a last attempt to rescue from oblivion some confidence in the continuity of life. Life goes on, of course, but as we shall see, this has an entirely different meaning. We as audience experience an existence defined not merely by its own survival but also by the destruction of others. It is a revelation fueled by the vitality of its insight—and the gloom of its finality. The breach between Sidney L.'s present and his past intensifies the alienation between his narrative and our response. Literate readers can eventually work their way through the pages of a book, no matter what the theme, because the form and style of the narrative are designed to make us complicit with the text. But literacy has little to do with the problem of entering into meaningful intellectual or emotional dialogue with the contents of these videotaped testimonies. As viewers, we have difficulty doing this because the testimonies are not based on common experience or an imaginable past, real or literary. Though eager to participate with sympathetic understanding, we are driven by the nature of the material to the periphery of comprehension. Odd as it may sound, we need to search for the inner principles of *in*coherence that make these testimonies accessible to us.

A written narrative is finished when we begin to read it, its opening, middle, and end already established between the covers of the book. This *appearance* of form is reassuring (even though the experience of reading may prove an unsettling challenge). Oral testimony steers a less certain course, like a fragile craft veering through turbulent waters unsure where a safe harbor lies—or whether one exists at all! The following illustration offers dramatic evidence of the difference between the two forms of presentation, because the witness also has written an autobiographical historical novel about her camp experience. We thus have an opportunity to observe both forms of narrative at work on an identical theme.

In her testimony, Barbara T. draws on the memory of her camp experience *as well as* on the book she has written about it. We become, as it were, auditors and readers simultaneously, forced to pay attention to the disjunction between the two approaches. Asked by the interviewer to describe her arrival at Auschwitz, Barbara T. begins: "It was night, but it was light because there were flames and there were powerful searchlights in the square. The air stank. Some people in the cars had died of thirst, of hunger, of madness. I felt a tremendous thirst. We had no water. And as the doors opened, I breathed in air as if it would be water, and I choked. It stank. And eventually we saw these strange-looking creatures, striped pajamas, who got us into a marching line." Then an odd thing happens. The witness pauses, half-hypnotized by her own narrative, as if returning from a strange place, and apologizes for what she calls her "absence": "I'm sorry, OK, I . . . I . . . forgive me . . . all right . . . I'm going to . . . I kind of was back there." Intensely aware of the exclusive *and* inclusive privacy of that moment, which she inhabits simultaneously alone and in the presence of the interviewer (to say nothing of a potentially larger audience of viewers), the witness struggles to resume her narrative, to plunge back into the present, as it were, but succeeds only for an instant: "Inmates whipped us out of the cattle cars," she says, "and they got us into rows of five."

At this point Barbara T. pauses and asks, "Do you want me to talk about that?" "Yes," the interviewer replies, "I think so." "I would like to read it," the witness responds. "It's easier."[8] She then reaches for her book, which is lying on the table beside her, and begins to read on camera: "we are dragged out of cattle cars, vomited into an impenetrable black night. suddenly torches brighten up a black sky and i clearly see the night: it engulfs a square drenched in searing brilliance by powerful floodlights." She hesitates an instant, skips a paragraph, and resumes her reading: "screams knife the air and i cover my ears with my hands. torches keep licking the sky like rainbows, flaming rainbows, and i quickly close my eyes but i still see the flames through my closed lids and the screams slash through my hands, into my ears, then a horrible stench hits my nostrils, i gasp for air but i choke. i am terrified. i don't know what to do."[9] Certainly this passage is vivid. But it also is transparently literary, alien to the speech rhythms of the oral narrative. Of the many dozens of testimonies I have viewed about arrival at Auschwitz, not one has mentioned anything remotely resembling being "vomited into an impenetrable black night." When one compares this self-conscious striving for stylistic impact with Barbara T.'s *spoken* testimony—"inmates whipped us out of the cattle cars," for example—one cannot escape the uncomfortable feeling that the *book's* idiom may be intrusive on and distracting from the more unencumbered flow of the oral testimony.

Written accounts of victim experience prod the imagination in ways that speech cannot, striving for analogies to initiate the reader into the particularities of their grim world. This literature faces a special challenge, since it must give most readers access to a totally unfamiliar subject. When searchlights at Auschwitz are said to lick the sky like "flaming rainbows," we are invited to use this simile as a ticket of entry to the bizarre deathcamp landscape. The singular *in*appropriateness of an image of natural beauty, symbolizing good fortune and joy, to describe one's arrival at Auschwitz underlines the difficulty of finding a vocabulary of comparison for such an incomparable atrocity. Indeed, the unexpected juxtaposition of literary and oral versions of the same moment of camp experience raises some vital questions about interpreting such testimonies that until now few commentators have sought to confront.

When the witness in an oral testimony leans forward toward the camera (as happens frequently in these tapes), apparently addressing the interviewer(s) but also speaking to the potential audience of the future— asking: "Do you understand what I'm trying to tell you?"—that witness confirms the vast imaginative space separating what he or she has endured from our capacity to absorb it. Written memoirs, by the very strategies available to their authors—style, chronology, analogy, imagery, dialogue, a sense of character, a coherent moral vision—strive to narrow this space, easing us into their unfamiliar world through familiar (and hence comforting?) literary devices. The impulse to *portray* (and thus refine) reality when we write about it seems irresistible. Describing the SS man who greeted her and her mother on the ramp at Auschwitz, Barbara T. writes: "his pale blue eyes dart from side to side like a metronome,"[10] and once again one has the uneasy feeling of the literary *transforming* the real in a way that obscures even as it seeks to enlighten. Yet until now, we have depended almost entirely on *written* narratives of the camp experience to gain insight into the nature of that atrocity.[11]

For the moment, I shall suggest no more than that videotaped oral testimonies provide us with an unexplored archive of "texts" that solicit from us original forms of interpretation. Reading a book that tries to carry us "back there" is an order of experience entirely different from witnessing someone like Barbara T. vanishing from contact with us even as she speaks, momentarily returning to the world she is trying to evoke instead of recreating it for us in the present. Yet her presence before us dramatically illustrates the merging of time senses (so often revealed by witnesses in oral testimony) that *creates* meaning through the very manner of her narrative.[12] A complex kind of "reversible continuity" seems to establish itself in many of these testimonies, one foreign to the straight chronology that governs most written memoirs.

A further distinction may be necessary here. Normal oral discourse—the speech, the lecture, the political address—assumes that the audience is no mystery and that competent presentation and substantial content will rouse and hold an audience's interest. And that is generally true. But the first effect of many of these testimonies is just the opposite, no matter how vivid the presentation: they induce fear, confusion, shame, horror, skepticism, even disbelief. The more painful, dramatic, and overwhelming the narrative, the more tense, wary, and self-protective is the audience, the quicker the instinct to withdraw. Unlike the writer, the witness here lacks inclination and strategies to establish and maintain a viable bond between the participants in this encounter.

To reverse the direction of that initial estrangement, a viewer must find some entry into the realm of disrupted lives and become sensitized to the implications of such disruption. In other words, we should not come to the encounter unprepared—yet we do. We have little choice. It is virtually useless, as we soon discover, to approach the experience from the reservoir of normal values, armed with questions like "Why didn't they resist?" and "Why didn't they help one another?" The first answer is that they did; the second is that sometimes it made no difference; and the third is that, under those circumstances, more often than not they couldn't. All are true, just as each testimony is true, even when the testimonies contradict one another. They impose on us a role not only of passive listener but also of active *hearer*. This requires us to suspend our sense of the normal and to accept the complex immediacy of a voice reaching us simultaneously from the secure present and the devastating past. That complexity, by forcing us to redefine our role as audience *throughout* the encounter, distinguishes these testimonies from regular oral discourse as well as from written texts.

Confrontation with these videotaped testimonies begins in separate narrative and ends in collective memory, though one hardly feels any satisfaction from mastering the "text." Listening to accounts of Holocaust experience, we unearth a mosaic of evidence that constantly vanishes, like Thomas Mann's well of the past, into bottomless layers of incompletion. There is no closure, because the victims who have *not* survived—in many ways, the most important "characters" in these narratives—have left no personal voice behind. They can only be evoked, spoken *about*. We wrestle with the beginnings of a permanently unfinished tale, full of incomplete intervals, faced by the spectacle of a faltering witness often reduced to a distressed silence by the overwhelming solicitations of deep memory.

Witnesses' chronic frustration and skepticism about the audience's ability to understand their testimony is almost a premise of these encounters. Written texts, on the other hand, whether memoirs, fiction, or poetry, are *designed* to avert this possibility—otherwise, one assumes, they would not be published. Indeed, the initial problem surfacing in these oral testimonies with sufficient regularity to call it a "theme" is exactly the opposite: whether *anything* can be meaningfully conveyed. One former member of the Polish underground reports: "If you were not there, it is difficult to describe and say how it was. It sounds very, very, very . . .

I don't know if there is [a] word to describe the nightmare one go through . . . how men function under such a stress is one thing, and then how you communicate and express [to] somebody who never knew that such a degree of brutality [is] existing seems like a fantasy." This witness adds that if he tried to sit with his daughter today to explain what his life was like between 1939 and 1946, she would say to him: "Daddy, you're making all that up."[13] For us as audience, the summons is to induce an involuntary suspension of disbelief, because there is little chance of inspiring a willing one.

How best to do this? How to do it at all? We turn to former victims for insight. One reports that when he was first brought into a crematorium area with a work detail, he did not flinch at the piles of bodies because every day in the Lodz ghetto, from which he had been deported to the deathcamp, he had seen dozens of corpses strewn about the streets. What might seem like fantasy to us became a sign of "ordinary" reality for him, so he could make the adjustment enabling him to accept this "abnormality" as part of his normal daily routine. A similar imaginative transition is required of us, if we are to "hear" the implications of these testimonies, but in the absence of a moral authority, not to mention experiential precedent, to sanction such unions of the normal with the abnormal, we flounder at the point of intersection. Only a collaborative effort can validate the testimony, a transvaluation requiring us to assent to the "normality" of piles of corpses destined for the crematorium. The perplexity of witnesses today at their own moral distance from those moments does little to simplify our task.

One of the most powerful themes on these tapes is thus the difficulty of narrating, from the context of normality *now*, the nature of the abnormality *then*, an abnormality that still surges into the present to remind us of its potent influence. Two time frames converge and then coalesce in the following narrative moment from the testimony of Baruch G., as he tries to explain why, during family celebrations of weddings and bar mitzvahs, he has a sense of being utterly alone, because absolutely no one is there from "his side":

> Loneliness has various aspects to it. I remember after libera- tion, I suffered probably more from the loneliness and the isolation, more than during the Holocaust period . . . . I sup- pose it has to do with the fact that after, the life around you seems to be normal but *you* are abnormal. Well, why? . . . In concentration camps and labor camps, there was a preoc- cupation with survival . . . . But then after what was called liberation—actually, the realization of liberation was not viv- id to me, was not real with me for a long time, but I remember during the years '45, '46, '47, and even up to '48, I would find myself crying, and quite frequently . . . [experiencing] a feel- ing of "Yes, I'm alive, but that's it, the rest doesn't matter."[14]

How can one be alone amid friends and family? The internalized dual existence of witnesses like this one requires of us a respon- sive and reciprocal duality of vision that might grasp what another former victim meant when she said of her Auschwitz past: "I don't live with it. It lives with me." One of the paradoxes emerging from these testimonies is that, although nothing could be more final than the deaths recorded there, nothing could be *less* final either. As a result, the concrete meanings of words like "survival" and "liberation" blur, because they cannot be separated from the doom of those whose "preoccupation with survival" failed. Indi- vidual "successes" are invariably tainted by this conjunction; "I'm alive," to use Baruch G.'s terms, simply lacks the moral resonance of "I survived."

The tension between imposed isolation and the impulse to com- munity, between the revelations of deep memory and the con- solations of common memory, remains unresolved. When Baruch G. speaks drearily of "what was called liberation," when he fails to infuse an expression like "preoccupation with survival" with the moral exhilaration that commentators often attribute to it, when he defines it by implication merely as the tenacity for staying alive one more day, a definition that he knows may appear abnormal from the vantage point of the present—then we are invited to consider the possibility of some words and gestures being welcome and misplaced at the same time. Distinctions between commitment to life and surrender to death dim, while the sharp-edged demarcations separating liberation from confinement grow blunt. A familiar face, as we shall see in a moment, can be a source of awed surprise that mingles with but does not replace one's private pain. Oral testimony repeatedly dramatizes the immediacy of such confusions.

Consider Edith P.'s description of her first days in Auschwitz, not knowing where she is, totally alienated from normal experience by her surroundings, then suddenly thrust back unprepared into the familiar until she is left struggling between disorientation and relief, simultaneously drowned by one and buoyed up by the other:

> You don't think, you don't ask yourself where you are, the only thing that you can think of is that you're hungry, and they don't give you anything to eat, you don't ask yourself where your mother is, where your sister is, you just want to take care of yourself at this point . . . . Everything is closed. Where am I? I never heard the name Auschwitz, I didn't even know I was in Auschwitz, I didn't know what a concentration camp was . . . . And I remember I was standing there after five or six days that we arrived, and somebody tapped me on the shoulder, and I looked at her, and I burst into crying. It was my sister-in-law! There were one million women [an exaggeration, of course], there were about 35 blocks [barracks], one million women looked all alike, no hair, some of them naked—and my sister-in-law says hello to me![15]

Such experiences of mutuality occur often enough on these tapes to tempt one to conclude that proximity to the familiar was itself enough to keep one alive. Certainly it helped, but we would be misreading their evidence if we were to extract from these testimonies some fundamental principle of survival based on such speculations. Edith P.'s immersion in conflicting moods offers a classic example of two time-and-place frames coalescing, neither one negating or affirming the other. When we can perceive the *absence* of logic and the utter *dis*continuity of this moment, we shall be in a better position to realize which premises we need to discard or adjust before we can contend with the so-called inaccessibility of the former victims' experiences.

Edith P. reports the fate of conventional thought in the camps concisely when she insists, "The only thing that you can think of is that you're hungry." Elie Wiesel argued with equal vehemence years ago that man in Auschwitz was a starved stomach. Such definitions grate against our humanitarian ears; they lead down shadowy byways of experience where the soul, spirit, and conscience grope in unaccustomed darkness. Expecting to encounter heroes and heroines, we meet only decent men and women, constrained by circumstances, reluctantly, to abandon roles that we as audience expect (and *need*) to find ingrained in their natures. Ideally, for example, even in the camps you honored the sanctity of your fellow prisoner's bread ration, often literally the staff of life. But in practice, as these testimonies constantly remind us, starvation and the moral sentiment were uneasy bedfellows. A gesture of generosity from the world of the "normal" might momentarily kindle the despondent spirit, but the starved stomach sought other nourishment. One of the most difficult truths for the outsider to grasp is the moral and physical havoc wrought on conscientious human beings by hunger's ceaseless tyranny. This may be the most incommunicable ordeal to appear on these tapes, even though the following testimony strives to convey it with admirably disarming frankness:

> One night I was so hungry, I couldn't sleep . . . . My . . .
> "roommate"—we were five on our . . . bunk—I got very
> friendly with her and she saved a tiny, tiny slice of bread, and
> a piece of margarine for breakfast . . . . And that particular
> night I stole that piece of bread from her, I never admit[ted] it,
> and she got up in the morning, and she was swearing like a
> truck driver . . . . I never admitted that I took it. I was very
> hurt, I was very sore, I was very sorry, because I was hungry
> and she was hungry. But somehow, once we were outside
> . . . there was something always to put in your mouth, but
> that was no solution, you got diarrhea . . . and you were
> dying anyway; once you got diarrhea, that was the end. So
> this wasn't good and that wasn't good: so what choice did we
> have?[16]

One factor in these testimonies threatening our role as audience
is the unpredictable disorder that prevailed in the world of the
camps. Another, perhaps even more threatening, is a requirement imposed by painful moments like this one—the requirement to suspend judgment, to revise our notion of the "good," to
allow the sheer integrity of the narrative and the stubborn honesty
of the narrator to forge before our eyes an ethical designation that I
have elsewhere called "choiceless choice,"[17] but which our witness describes more vividly with her final words: "So this wasn't
good and that wasn't good: so what choice did we have?" Audiences have little difficulty dealing with heroic gestures where
the agent is in control of the choice—episodes of sharing and
support and even of self-sacrifice, all of which occurred in rare
favorable circumstances in the usually hostile camp environment.
Such gestures feed the legends on which the myths of civilizations
have been built. But few witnesses mention them in their testimony, where, unflattering as it may sound, spiritual possibility
turns out to be a luxury for those not on the brink of starvation. To
understand and to sympathize with *un*heroic gestures like Han-

nah F.'s, withholding endorsement or blame but finding instead an admissible frame for them in the moral discourse of our culture—this is one of the burdensome but crucial challenges that still lie before us in this study.

Moral distinctions crumble even further in the following episode from the testimony of Moses S. The reported dialogue, beginning with a perfectly normal gesture, quickly disintegrates into a "logical" sequence whose rules violate our expectations at every turn. The witness does not *tell* the story; he reenacts it. The brusque economy of his narrative, the motions of his arms, as if placing the actors on the stage (and then playing all the roles himself), the brief, staccato sentences, with connectives often omitted, all conspire to reduce the value of verbal effect and to remind us how often terms like "heroic" and "dignified" become orphans in this obscure universe:

> Two boys having one bunk. One said to the other: "Will you watch after my piece of bread? I'm going to the bathroom." He said: "O.K." When he come back, was no bread. Where was the bread?
>
> "I'm sorry. I ate it up."
>
> So he reported to the Kapo [inmate supervisor]. Kapo come along, he said: "What happened?"
>
> "Look, I ask him to look after my piece of bread, and he ate it up."
>
> The Kapo said: "You took away his life. Right?"
>
> He said: "Well, I'll give it back this afternoon, the ration."
>
> He [the Kapo] said: "No, come outside." He took the fellow outside. "Lie on the floor." He put a piece of *Brett* [a small board or plank] on his neck, and with his boots [imitating the action with his hands and feet]—bang! on his neck. *Fertig!* [finished!]

How are we to follow the inner coherence of this exercise in "deductive reasoning," an example of camp "justice" that eludes all traditional conceptions of crime? We grope for a context—and we are not the only ones. Careful examination of this witness's testimony suggests that he intentionally seeks to offend our sense of order, reason, and civilized behavior, so as to break us out of patterns of thought that desensitize us to the implications of his camp experience. His words virtually *dare* us to accept the condition of vulnerability he thrusts upon us.

At one point his wife, who is with him, says: "I think it's time to stop. He's getting upset. We should stop." But he's been perfectly calm throughout his testimony and insists on continuing. He tells a story about two hundred Mauthausen inmates being put in a freezing room in mid-winter, given blankets soaked in cold water, and forced to wrap themselves in the blankets. They all freeze to death. When he finishes, his wife gets up slowly, says, "I can't listen to this any more," and walks off camera. The drama of avoidance initiated by so many of these testimonies thus radiates in many directions, not only toward the audience. Rarely, however, do we find it as intrinsic to the testimony itself as we do here.

Shortly after the wife leaves, one of the interviewers says to the witness, "This is a nice place to stop." Then we hear whispering off camera. Meanwhile, Moses S. is saying to himself aloud, "And more, and more, and more. Do you want to hear more?" One of the interviewers replies: "No. Let's end here." He insists, "One more story." She persists, "No, no. We'll stop here." But he overrides her objection and tells the story of the prisoner choked to death by a Kapo for having eaten his friend's bread. And here the interview ends—but it is the interviewer's choice, not his. Does he see this as a tactic to divert him from the succinct but brutal episodes that pour from his lips in a seemingly endless flow? In his efforts to make *us* witnesses too, Moses S. grows *too* graphic, thus alienating various members of his audience and vividly illustrating their difficulty in becoming active collaborators in the ordeal of testimony.[18]

The shock of insight does not come easily, and to some comes not at all. Younger audiences still persist in asking, "Why didn't they know what was coming?" and "When they did, why didn't they do something about it?" It is perhaps more difficult for Jewish victims to answer those questions than bystanders, but also "easier," in the sense that those who bore the mark of Cain under Nazi racial laws were made powerless from the beginning in ways that others were not. One distinguished historian interviewed on these tapes, who escaped with his family shortly before the outbreak of war, offers some helpful speculation on this issue. We build our expectations of the future, he conjectures, on our familiarity with the past. How could we foresee gas chambers, he asks in effect, when we had never heard of them? The average imagination, in other words, perceives what it or someone else has already conceived. Death we can anticipate; but extermination . . . ? And once one saw clearly what lay ahead, it was too late—at least, for most of the victims.[19]

But what of the bystanders, those witnesses who, like us today, saw from a different vantage point the danger to others that did not threaten them? One of the many invaluable contributions of these testimonies is the foresight of the interviewers in interviewing non-Jews who were associated with but not unduly victimized by the Holocaust experience. Most of these testimonies from non-Jews are as revealing for what remains unspoken as for what is said, and here the interaction between witness and audience is especially intricate and demanding. How shall the bystanders *prepare* to react to the ordeal of the victims, once the wretched truth can no longer be evaded or denied? The *attitudinal* similarities to our own situation vis-à-vis the testimonies need hardly be emphasized, though the summons to possible action is of course thoroughly different.

What options were open to these bystanders? It is tempting to approach this question with an impulse to condemn unilaterally, and I am not sure that this impulse is entirely blameworthy. But the following narrative moment from the testimony of a Jesuit priest, who during World War II was being trained in a seminary in Hungary for missionary work in China, suggests some cautionary limitations to the value of the reductive approach. He is himself numbed by the memory of such inappropriate training, given the pivotal historical circumstances. But as his literal role of the "witness as witness" unfolds, he offers us an authentic glimpse into the choices available to human beings, both victims and bystanders, as the catastrophe descended upon them. Deep memory surges slowly but painfully to the surface as he reconstructs an episode that continues to haunt him.

I suppose we may call it a test of our tolerance to stay with this witness and follow what his eyes saw and what the eyes of his mind recall, and finally to hear how he interprets today, with the greatest distress, his conduct then and what he thinks he has learned from it now. He runs away from a sight too terrible to behold—and in this he is not alone. But under the prodding of a shrewd and alert interviewer, who has detected a crucial omission in his narrative and who casually but insistently brings him back to it, he returns from his flight to confront the essential dilemma of bystander response. To his credit, he does so without the familiar evasions, though his discomfort is apparent, a kind of quizzical self-reflection on behavior he can't approve of today but felt in no position to condemn then—a fascinating counterpart (though incomparably less painful) to the testimony of the genuine victims, similarly trapped between the realities of then and now:

Now my personal encounter was with the railroad station. They built a tall wooden fence there, and nobody was permitted to approach the fence; the word was out that they had machine guns lined up alongside the fence in the street which paralleled the railroad tracks . . . . I did not have permission to sneak up on the railroad station . . . . But I sneaked up to the fence . . . and I found a hole there . . . and that was the day when I saw my train, my deportee train

. . . . It was a cattle train, and right in front of me, just about two tracks from the fence . . . it was opened by an SS soldier. And the impression was terrible because it was terribly packed.

I literally saw what you see in pictures, mothers with children, and people, and old people . . . and one man immediately jumped off, and I always remembered his face because he looked a little bit like my father . . . . I did not hear what he said to the German soldier . . . but his behavior was polite. What I made out, that he was asking for water. And immediately that SS soldier with the club of his rifle clubbed him down, and several times, to insensitivity. Whether he died or was later put on the track [I don't know]. And then I ran away, I was so scared and I was so upset; I never saw anything like this in my life. I simply ran away.

These interviews repeatedly touch exposed nerves that the witnesses themselves did not realize existed, resulting in an immediacy of introspection that could probably be captured nowhere else. Confronted by the interviewer with the question of why he did not say something to *someone* about what he had just seen, the priest seems bemused by his failure to come up with an answer to satisfy himself, to say nothing of his interlocutor. Suddenly before our eyes he is wrestling with the deep memory of his own inaction, which common memory clearly disapproves of today, and he is trying inwardly to explain it to himself before he can explain it to us—and so far, he does not have an explanation.

He is left with the question, which he repeats to himself aloud: "Why didn't I say anything to anyone?" But he is not content with unanswered questions, and the remainder of the interview represents a self-exploration that is as rare as it is illuminating, though meaning here emerges as much from the hearing audience as it does from the self-searching speaker. "What I saw when I looked through the fence," Father S. confesses, "was beyond me, totally beyond my experience." He implies that he lacked the capacity to do anything about what he saw. And he continues, with an air of puzzled but honest futility, "I see it personally as the greatest tragedy of my life that the Jewish people were deported all around me and I didn't do anything." He was, he concludes, "simply unprepared."[20]

Unintentionally, Father S. bequeaths us a pair of images that will pursue us throughout our investigation. The fence and the knothole blockade and invite us simultaneously, excluding us from terrain where we dare not venture and do not "belong" while offering an apparently secure post of observation for our role as witness. But as "what" we witness makes inroads on that fragile security, as "distance" provides less and less defense, we are sucked through that knothole and forced to find our moral bearings shorn of prior visions of the noble human spirit under duress. The constant erosion of those visions by the reality of the narrated experiences finds *us* too unprepared and wondering whether past value systems must be charged with breakdown or delusion.

One of the paradoxes nurtured by these testimonies is that the *prepared* will or intelligence was not necessarily any more effective. When a courageous, resolute, well-intentioned act that we admire results not in rescue but in unexpected and unforeseeable disaster, we as audience have to contend with the collapse of belief in the heroic gesture that defies fate and deifies the will to action. The following testimony is a humbling reminder of this:

I'll never forgive myself. Even if I want it, I can't. I had a brother, he was 16 or 17 years old. He was taller than I, he was bigger than I, and I said to him, "Son, brother, you haven't got no working papers, and I am afraid that you will not be able to survive. Come on, take a chance with me, let's go together." Why did I take him with me? Because I had the working papers, and I thought maybe because I gonna go to the right, I knew people who had their working papers, they gonna go to the right, because the Germans need people in the ghetto, to finish the job, whatever they had to do. He agreed with me. At the same time I said he is built tall, then maybe he gonna have a chance.

When I came to the gate where the selection was, then the Gestapo said to me (I showed him my papers), "You go to the right." I said, "This is my brother." He whipped me over my head, he said: "He goes to the left." And from this time I didn't see any more my brother . . . . I know it's not my fault, but my conscience is bothering me. I have nightmares, and I think all the time, that the young man, maybe he wouldn't go with me, maybe he would survive. It's a terrible thing: it's almost forty years, and it's still bothering me. I still got my brother on my conscience. God forgive me![21]

We can often prepare successfully for the foreseeable, and in fact, as his earlier testimony confirms, this witness did, by escaping first from a labor camp and later from a ghetto roundup that would have meant deportation and certain death. One might even argue that his attempt to save his brother was inspired by his previous successes. But who could have predicted that the assumptions on which he based this attempt would prove fatal? The Jesuit priest who warns us that we must be prepared for the most unpredictable of evils offers sound advice. The witness here who mourns how his perfectly reasonable risk turned into a miscalculation that cost a life presents an insight that is also "correct." In our quest for valid principles of survival, we surface once more with a contradiction, a clash between the value and the futility of choosing wisely and in time. An audience trained in the necessity of moral choice to preserve the integrity of civilized behavior might be dismayed to learn how often in the evidence of these testimonies, as we shall see, that belief in choice betrayed the victim and turned out to be an illusion.

Is such dismay a dead end, or can it be converted into some usable understanding? The intrinsic worth of these testimonies is that, in their abundance and variety and painful honesty, they goad us in the direction of an affirmative answer to that question. But pouring the old wine of a conventional dismay into the new bottles of an *un*conventional one is not necessarily a spiritually edifying experience that audiences to these testimonies will greet with enthusiasm. For example, one of the curses willed by the Nazis to their victims is how deep memory continues to infect their experience of time. This is not a joyful insight—merely an accurate one. The intense, silent, anguished visual drama following the closing words of the previous excerpt—"I still got my brother on my conscience. God forgive me!"—verifies the persisting vitality of the unplaced and unplacatable memory, for the former victim above all, but also for those who allow themselves to become part of the seeing-hearing audience. Who can find a proper grave for such damaged mosaics of the mind, where they may rest in pieces? Life goes on, but in two temporal directions at once, the future unable to escape the grip of a memory laden with grief. "I have children," reports one former victim. "I have my family. But I can't take full satisfaction in the achievements of my children today because part of my present life is my remembrance, my memory of what happened then, and it casts a shadow over my life today."

This attitude, unfortunately, is exemplary rather than exceptional in these testimonies. Their importance will be considerably diminished if we gloss over or disregard that shadow in search of more enlightening brightness. For a writer like Camus, the conclusion that there "is no sun without shadow, and it is essential to know the night"[22] was a preface to lucidity, a contemporary restatement of the tragic view of literature. Echoing hope from within its apparent gloom, it was an invitation to art and creativity, a resolute defense of the human in the face of an indifferent universe. The shadows raised here do not speak of personal tragic conflict, or even of the universe they darken. The moral and emotional chiaroscuro they highlight refer not to contending forces but to a parallel existence. They evoke two adjacent worlds that occasionally intrude on each other but more often imply a life after "death" called survival, and a life within death for which we have no name, only the assurance of witnesses like the following—and she is one among many. Here the problem of hearing grows most arduous, because the reality we are asked to accept is both remote and uncongenial. The passionate earnestness of this woman, who invokes her buried self, rises from sorrowful depths: the murder of her mother, her father, her father's five sisters, her mother's brother and sister and their many children, her cousins. Surviving the camps with her husband, she returns with him to Prague, where in 1952, seven years after the war, he is arrested on Stalin's orders during the Slansky purges and executed as a British spy. So when she says, "You know, we have one good thing from Auschwitz, we survivors," she is not speaking ironically. "We know where we are. We know where we come from. We've come from the bottom, the bottom up." Is the "happiness" she subsequently mentions enriched or restricted by the "bottom" that still clings to her?

> You sort of don't feel at home in this world any more, because this experience—you can live with it, it's like constant pain: you never forget, you never get rid of it, but you learn to live with it. And that sets you apart from other people. Not that you can't enjoy yourself. On the contrary, when I am happy, I'm *so* happy, because I know how horribly unhappy I can be. I know the whole difference. But there is a certain—it's like a music in the background. It's that something is different.[23]

It is certainly tempting, probably possible, and, some might argue, even *desirable* to survey these testimonies ignoring that difference, collecting triumphant moments exhibiting the resiliency of the human spirit, the resourceful will, the intrepid mind, the resolve to survive Nazi oppression. And such moments do exist, though far more rarely than one might expect, often prompted by an anxious interviewer. But a resourceful, intrepid, and resolute audience will recognize that these moments are inseparable from their opposite—a genuine form of chiaroscuro. I am reminded of one witness who ends his testimony by blessing his wife and children for restoring to him his sense of life, and of another who near the beginning of his interview greets us with the unforgettable gesture of unfurling a seemingly endless sheet of narrow adding-machine paper on which he had written, the night before, the names of more than one hundred members of his family killed by the Nazis. These names provide a context for his personal story of survival and cast their shadow over the blessing that appears at the end of the other testimony. Between the list and the blessing lies the perilous territory we must venture into, remembering the obligation to heed both ends of the journey, as well as the ordeal in between.

How best to do this? One final witness in this chapter raises an issue that exacerbates our problem. He returns us to the crucial question of what we communicate when discussing this issue, and how. That depends, in part, on what we have heard, and how. A book, Kafka said, is an axe, to crack the frozen sea within us. But these testimonies are icebergs, to freeze the warm, coursing blood within us—and this constitutes a threat as well as a challenge. Testimonies resting unseen in archives are like books locked in vaults: they might as well not exist. We use books to expand consciousness; we must use these videotapes for the same purpose. But what are we to do with the following paradox?

> We are torn apart and even today we don't want to talk; maybe, you know, it's also a fear . . . of the confrontation between us. It took me a long way of thinking to come and to discuss [this] with you . . . . I come, you know, from conversation that turned [that] way in my mind . . . but would

anybody understand [that]? I don't know. And that's probably the biggest tragedy I face, because I cannot relate or convey my experience to another person and make him, you
know, better . . . through my experience.[24]

Lurking in this statement is a longing that returns us to the vocabulary of redemption and salvation with which we began. The
atmosphere of eschatology hovers over these testimonies through
its very absence. Although they dispel many traditional views of
human nature and motive, moral theory, Enlightenment values,
and the heroic temper, witnesses are not immune to the disparity
between the events they record and their audience's expectations,
or even their own. Most of their stories nurture not ethical insight
but confusion, doubt, and moral uncertainty. This is a new version of tragedy *and* history, each of which demands some idea of
causal sequence to achieve its forms. But when consciousness
expands into a universe so violated that old designations like
tragedy and history lose their force, where and how are we to find
new moorings? These testimonies enact the *issue*, if not its resolution, and in the end this may be their crucial importance. In them,
the cherished voices of continuity, adaptation, and renewal speak
with the authority of their absence, immersing us in a world
whose inhabitants remain adrift even as they clamber ashore.

Near the end of his film *Shoah*, Claude Lanzmann asks Itzhak
Zuckerman, a surviving leader of the Warsaw ghetto uprising, to
comment on the experience. "If you could lick my heart," ventures Zuckerman, "it would poison you." We know of course that
many life-sustaining nutrients also seep from the human heart
and that some of them nourished men and women even during
the event Lanzmann and Zuckerman are speaking of. But we
know as well that this did not stop the annihilation of European
Jewry. We may peer into the deep memory from which a statement like Zuckerman's rises without fear of contamination, because its sources are so obviously complex and private. The nature

of the taint, however, solicits our response; we enter that juncture between venom and antidote where one goes on living in spite of the toxin. If that tentative gesture teaches us something about what it meant to have been a victim of the inhuman during that abysmal period, it also teaches us something about what it means to be human in the post-Holocaust era. We validate the significance of these testimonies by listening to their voices until we hear what Nelly Sachs, in a poem about survivors, called "the mutilated music of their lives." To share this dissonance with a perception built from the ruins of mutilation without being crippled by it ourselves is the summons we face when we embrace the legacy of these testimonies, which bear witness to the simultaneous destruction *and* survival of European Jewry.

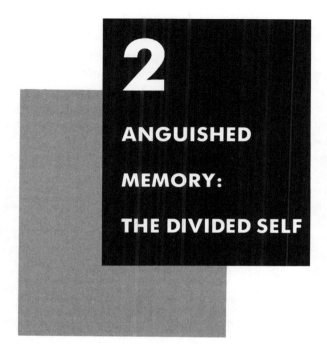

2

ANGUISHED

MEMORY:

THE DIVIDED SELF

To whom shall we entrust the custody of the public memory of the Holocaust? To the historian? The critic? The poet, novelist, or dramatist? To the surviving victim? Candidates abound, all in search of a common goal: the detour that will, paradoxically, prevent us from being led astray. All are in the thrall of what Maurice Blanchot calls the "impossible real." All approach a limit beckoning them across Blanchot's "perilous threshold." In some way, too, with the exception of surviving victims, all are witnesses to memory rather than rememberers themselves. They have an "unstory" to tell, that which, according to Blanchot, "escapes quotation and which memory does not recall—forgetfulness as thought. That which, in other words, cannot be forgotten because it has always already fallen outside memory."[1] Blanchot's style may appear cryptic but, in fact, duplicates the frustrated efforts of language to enclose irreducibly intractable material. The oxymoron of an impossible reality is a small knothole piercing the obstacles.

The impossibility, however, lies not in the reality but in our difficulty in perceiving it *as* reality. It is not surprising to hear witnesses in oral testimonies confess that sometimes they do not believe their own stories. Their effort to recapture through memory what, because of the impossibility of its content, has already (for us) fallen outside memory, risks estranging the audience they seek to inform. In the presence of their anguished memory, we are asked to share less what is recovered than the process of recall itself, the crossing and recrossing of that perilous threshold until the distinctions between entrance and exit blur and fade. "Since the disaster always takes place after having taken place" [as precise a definition of oral testimony as I have seen], Blanchot insists, "there cannot possibly be any experience of it" (28). Thus excluded from the original event, we have the option of withdrawing in silence or of redefining thresholds and the role of memory in helping us to cross them.

Anguished memory, one kind of recall I am investigating in these oral testimonies, imprisons the consciousness it should be liberating. Perhaps this is what Nietzsche, prophetic of the modern age in so much else, meant when he said that "without forgetting it is quite impossible to *live* at all."[2] Witnesses in the testimonies do not search for the historicity of experience, nor do they try to recapture the dynamic flow of events. They are concerned less with the past than with a sense of that past in the present. Unlike those (including surviving victims) who re-create details and images of the event through written texts, they generate narratives less predisposed to remind us that we are dealing with a self-consciously *represented* reality. In fashioning a consecutive chronicle survivors who record their accounts unavoidably introduce some kind of teleology, investing the incidents with a meaning, be it nothing more than the value of regaining one's freedom.

Indeed, as we shall see, some of the most expertly contrived survivor accounts include a commentary on this impulse as part of the substance of their narrative.

Some years ago, in the preface to *Versions of Survival*, I wrote that an "axiom of the narrative mode, from which survivor memoirs are not exempt, is that all telling modifies what is being told."[3] That raised the question of whether an unmediated text on this subject was ever achievable, given the extraordinary nature of the event. And this in turn led to an inquiry into the difference between written memoirs and oral testimony, especially videotaped testimony, which in addition to language includes gesture, a periodic silence whose effect cannot be duplicated on the printed page, and above all a freedom from the legacy of literary form and precedent to which anyone attempting a written narrative on any subject is indebted.

The content of a written survivor memoir may be more harrowing and gruesome than most autobiographies, but such a memoir still abides (some more consciously than others) by certain literary conventions: chronology, description, characterization, dialogue, and above all, perhaps, the invention of a narrative voice. This voice seeks to impose on apparently chaotic episodes a perceived sequence, *whether or not that sequence was perceived in an identical way* during the period that is being rescued from oblivion by memory and language. The most persuasive example of this dilemma that I know comes from the first volume of Charlotte Delbo's Auschwitz memoir, *None of Us Will Return*:

> I stand in the midst of my comrades and I think that if I return one day and want to explain this inexplicable thing, I will say: "I used to say to myself: you must stand, you must stand for the entire roll call. You must stand again today. It is because you will have stood again today that you will return, if you do return one day." And this will be false. I did not say anything to myself. I did not think anything. The will to resist no doubt

lay in a much deeper and more secret mechanism which has since broken; I shall never know.[4]

The teleological imagination of the present narrative voice emerges in the conclusion that "it is because you will have stood today that you will return," while the voice of the skeptical commentator exposes the limitations of trying to clarify *now* what was shadowy *then*. Of course, *both* voices belong to Charlotte Delbo, who impersonates herself as a split observer in search of a point of view, simultaneously looking ahead from Auschwitz (as a victim) to time future when she will try to retrieve the truth of her ordeal (*"je dirai"*) and looking backward from the present (as a writer) in an attempt to recreate a moment held hostage by time (*"je me disais"*).

Although few are as sophisticated as Delbo, all surviving victims who write about their camp experiences must adopt some strategy for providing entry to the reader's imagination into that distant world. Delbo elucidated the paradox of retrieval when she said in commenting on her memoir, "Today, I am no longer sure that what I have written is true, but I am sure that it happened" ("Aujourd'hui, je ne suis pas sûre que ce que j'ai écrit soit vrai. Je suis sûre que c'est véridique").[5] In distinguishing between *vrai* and *véridique*, Delbo illuminates the difference between the abstractness of a recovered truth and the concreteness of an experienced moment. But she also exposes the abyss separating words from the events they seek to animate. The writer strives to narrow that abyss. At a more fundamental level, driven by anguished memory, witnesses in oral testimonies plunge deeper into it even as they venture to escape.

The organic metaphor with its evolutionary corollary that dominated much nineteenth-century thought bequeathed us a vocabulary of purpose, and a mental stance to accompany it, that infiltrates survivor *literature* far more than it influences oral testimony. The results are perplexing. Such invasion reminds us that even memoirs nominally concerned with nothing more ambitious than recording horrible facts cannot escape from traditional literary associations. Some draw consciously on such associations to impose a layer of continuity over the discontinuous interval of the deathcamp universe; others exploit the literary use of language to clarify and emphasize the permanence of the breach. For example, when the young Eliezer, in Wiesel's *Night*, protests, "I did not deny God's existence but I doubted His absolute justice,"[6] the words may be his at that moment, but the voice and the idea belong to Ivan Karamazov, who exclaims to his brother Alyosha, "It's not that I don't accept God, you understand, it's the world created by Him I don't and cannot accept." Thus for the discerning reader the protest against God in Auschwitz radiates out and backward to an established nineteenth-century tradition of dissent. Ivan's sincerity may be questionable (though irrelevant here), but it is worth mentioning that the narrator of Wiesel's second novel, *The Accident*, is struck by an automobile while on his way to see the film version of *The Brothers Karamazov*. A part of Auschwitz's uniqueness is thus inadvertently modified by a literary precedent.

Dostoevsky intrudes on another account of Auschwitz, Viktor Frankl's *Man's Search for Meaning* (perhaps more widely read than any other book on the concentration camp experience). Indeed, Frankl fills his volume with a system of allusion and analogy, chiefly to nineteenth-century figures, in a way that provides a literary subtext for the naked events he intends to describe. It is as if Frankl approached the crumbling edifice of twentieth-century humanism in Auschwitz armed with intellectual and moral props from an earlier era. He is determined to shore up the ruins and to reassure his readers that in fact there has been no irreparable damage to the architecture of thought about the human spirit from Spinoza and Lessing to Nietzsche and Rilke, and up to the present. He cites all of these, in addition to Dostoevsky, Tolstoy, Schopenhauer, Bismarck, and Thomas Mann (together with Ecclesiastes and the Gospel of John). And they *do* reassure. It is comforting to hear from Frankl that Dostoevsky once said, "There is only one thing that I dread: not to be worthy of my sufferings." It is even more consoling to hear Nietzsche's aphorism, "Was mich nicht umbringt, macht mich stärker" ("That which does not kill me makes me stronger").[7] But such a system of allusion and analogy causes our experience of Auschwitz to be filtered through the purifying vocabulary of an earlier time. The wary reader, though perhaps comforted and consoled by such a system, will understand the verbal assertion that has been imposed on a chaotic reality in order to reweld an apparently broken connection between Auschwitz and the literary-philosophical traditions nurturing Frankl's vision.

Primo Levi also uses literary allusion in his memoir of camp experience, but for purposes contrary to Frankl's. Situated in the middle of his *Survival in Auschwitz* is a brief chapter called "The Canto of Ulysses," in which Levi accompanies an inmate named Jean on the daily ritual known as *Essenholen* or *chercher la soupe* (fetching the food). Jean is multilingual, showing equal facility in French and German, referring to the SS *Blockführer* alternately as *"sale brute"* and *"ein ganz gemeiner Hund."* One of Levi's subtexts here is not only that language in Auschwitz sometimes determines survival (since *not* understanding an order has led to the gas chamber) but that words interpreted through what he calls free-world associations can lead to a misconstrual of the Auschwitz experience.

For example, to pass the time during the fetching of the food, Levi recites from Dante's *Inferno* for Jean, then slowly tries to offer a rendering of the passage in French. Can it be coincidence that in the expression "Then of that ancient fire" Levi has difficulty finding an appropriate translation for the Italian *antica*? What indeed do ancient fires have to do with the flames in whose proximity Levi carries on his daily tasks? How, after Auschwitz, shall we connect the "ancient" with the "new" that happened there? No wonder Levi hesitates, suffering, as he says, lacunae in his memory. But it is not Auschwitz that he is forgetting; it is literature, Dante, poetry, the *Commedia*. These have been replaced by a historical event that the traditional term *tragedy* will never adequately describe. Levi then quotes lines from the "Canto of Ulysses" that some might be inclined to take as an affirmation of hope in the desert of the deathcamp:

> Think of your breed; for brutish ignorance
> Your mettle was not made; you were made men,
> To follow after knowledge and excellence.

Or, more literally:

> Take thought of the seed from which you spring.
> You were not born to live as brutes,
> But to follow virtue and knowledge.

But I think the irony of this passage, whose content contrasts so visibly with the setting and the scene, is explicit. For a moment both Levi and Jean, under the compelling sway of Dante's art, forget who and where they are. And this is precisely the point: when literary form, allusion, and style intrude on the surviving victim's account, we risk forgetting where we are and imagine deceptive continuities. It is a dramatic interval in Levi's own text, as Dante's lines seize him with a fervor and transport him for an instant into the literary reality of the poem. For a few seconds, he resembles Viktor Frankl, seeing in Dante "in a flash of intuition, perhaps the reason for our fate, for our being here today."[8] But his fervor quickly abates and, unlike Frankl, he escapes unscathed from the confusion of genres.

Among the babel of tongues seeking to express Auschwitz is the literary voice, but it fades from the text here, never to return. Levi's brief parable has dramatized the seductive powers it exerts over the impulse to embellish one's account of the camp experience. Its disappearance reminds us of Delbo's insistence, mentioned earlier, that "in the camp you could never pretend; you could never take refuge in the imaginary." When we return from Dante's world to Auschwitz, we learn that the babel of tongues is more concerned with eating than with speaking. The momentous question implicit in *Essenholen* or *chercher la soupe* is "what's *in* it?" (not the language, but the *soup*). Levi's multilingual reply rudely replaces Dante's view of Ulysses as an adventurous spirit exceeding God's will (one source of the irony, surely) with Elie Wiesel's definition of man in Auschwitz as a starved stomach. The verbal repast for today, according to Levi's carefully chosen menu of words, feeds the body, not one's penchant for poetry, which belongs to another world and another era: *Kraut und Rüben, choux et navets, kaposzta és répak*—cabbage and turnips. Four versions of survival, without literary echo: language as physical substance, the thing itself.

The counterpoint between literary and historical reality continues to chapter's end, where Levi quotes the last line from "The Canto of Ulysses": "And over our head the hollow seas closed up" (literally, "Until the sea closed over us again") (105). Ulysses' fate is sealed, Dante tells us, "as pleased Another"—that is, by the will of God. But this is hardly a gloss on man's doom in Auschwitz. The *Commedia* records a journey of the human spirit to a divinely conceived, if not predetermined, goal. The Inferno, as we know, is succeeded by a Purgatorio and a Paradiso. However, the chapter following "The Canto of Ulysses" in *Survival in Auschwitz* begins: "Throughout the spring, convoys arrived from Hungary," dismissing the literary subtext and reasserting the primacy of the unwilled voyage to an unchosen destination.

Later versions of the Ulysses legend, shorn of Dante's hierarchical Christian vision, transform his sinner into a model of heroic enterprise. But in both cases, Ulysses is a man of action who creates his fate. What he becomes depends on what he was, what he did. The impact of anguished memory derives from the witness's inability to identify with this principle. Zoltan G., for example, enters into a dialogue with *himself* on this subject, developing a pattern of looking back and listening to his *own* testimony, as if no one else were present. He distinguishes between the self who "does" and the self who is "done to" but cannot reconcile the two roles. Describing the roundups in his town for deportation to Auschwitz, he tries to explain why no one did anything to protest. We had no leaders, he reminds himself; we lacked confidence, were without real choice. But these explanations exasperate rather than satisfy him. He still can't understand why he didn't grab an SS man's gun and shoot some Nazis before they killed him. He insists that, given the opportunity again, he'd do it today. He suffers from a scarred memory, too honest to conceal the original wound, but helpless to heal it. "It bothers me, you know," he confesses, returning to the world of the interview: "Why, why, why" [didn't anyone refuse to obey]?

There is in fact no way to bridge his two identities: discovering this is a chief source of anguish, just as its revelation is perhaps the main drama of the testimonies. You're not "going" to "nowhere," says Zoltan G. of his ordeal; they're "*taking*" you to "nowhere." Meanwhile, he says, the mind cheats itself into believing that "this" is not happening in the twentieth century. Seeing today how layers of normality blanketed them then with false security, he extracts from memory an illustration of the desperate deeds the quest for normalcy might drive one to. He tells the story of a fellow inmate in Auschwitz who one day traded his entire bread ration for a supply of Russian tobacco (which was available from Soviet prisoners of war), smoked it all (thus briefly affirming the pleasure of indulging in familiar habits), then went to the latrine and hanged himself. The momentary illusion of normalcy was nothing more than a prelude to death.

Zoltan G. survived, but the restoration of his identity only exacerbates his memory of his other self, which he describes sadly: "You was too tired to exist. . . . You was indifferent to everything. You was like a vegetable." He ends his testimony with a charge against his persecutors, whom he still hates, which sharply differentiates them from the disabled innocence of the victims: "They did it with knowledge."[9] As informed agents, they direct their own fate (as well as determining the doom of others); in other words, they still inhabit the world of the "normal" from which Zoltan G. has been excluded. Anguished memory is most troubled by that temporary absence, whose reality seems to exist independent of prior and subsequent events.

Former victims cannot say of their journey whose intended end was some form of annihilation that they experienced it "with knowledge." They endured it, some with disbelief, others with despair, still others with determination to hold out as long as they could. Unlike the Passover ritual, which gives Jews an opportunity to celebrate and commemorate their liberation from bondage and to identify with a previous pattern of experience that adds some coherence to their own lives, the ordeal of former victims is anchored firmly, via anguished memory, in its own historical reality, and nothing more. They cannot link their near destruction to a transcendent or redemptive future. Still haunted by the untransfigured actuality of what they recall, they cast about, usually in vain, for some form of escape from its web.

Voices of former victims confirm this dilemma both briefly and at length. Sally H., for example, alludes to her dual self, the one from prewar reality, the other living what she calls the "truth" of the camps. "I'm thinking of it now," she says, "how I split myself. That it wasn't *me* there. It just wasn't me. I was somebody else." And when an interviewer asks, "You didn't try to block it out?" she replies: "I can't. I'm not the person to block it out. I can't. I live it. I have like a panorama in front of me constantly."[10] But she does not mean a majestic panorama like the crossing of the Red Sea; her memory is crowded with disconnected images, like watching a rabbi being forced to walk on the Sefer Torah, or the *picrinoires* in her camp at Skarzysko, whose yellow faces continue to populate her imagination.[11] Instead of integrating past and present, memory here assaults and finally divides the self, leading to Sally H.'s insistence that her two selves are not the same.

A similar but more complex complaint emerges from the testimony of Bessie K., who was a young wife with an infant in 1942 at the time of a selection for work from the Kovno ghetto. Children were of course excluded, but she wrapped her baby in her coat as if it were a bundle and tried to sneak it by the Germans. Unfortunately the baby cried out, and they seized it. "And this was the last time I had the bundle with me," Bessie K. recalls, in a numb and almost trancelike voice. She can not remember details of the subsequent train ride, though the consequences of that awful moment are etched on her memory, as she proceeds: "I think all my life I been alone. Even when I met Jack [her present husband, also a former camp inmate, who is sitting beside her], I didn't tell Jack my past. Jack just found out recently [1979]. To me, I was dead. I died, and I didn't want to hear nothing and I didn't want to know nothing. [Meanwhile, the camera zooms in on Jack's face, a mask of palpable pain.] I didn't want to talk about it, and I didn't want to admit to myself that this happened to me." In a sense, the episode completed her life cycle before it was over: "I wasn't even alive; I wasn't even alive. I don't know if it was by my own doing, or it was done, or how, but I wasn't there. But yet I survived." The separation between agency and event, between the loss of the baby and assigning responsibility for that loss, is a source of lasting confusion ("by my own doing, or it was done, or how").

Bessie K.'s train journey is an emblem of the hermetic ordeal that the Holocaust became for its surviving victims. "The way I felt," she admits, "I was *born* on that train and I *died* on that train." This gives us a clue to the origin of the idea of two selves that Sally H. had alluded to earlier. But the "funeral" for the "dead" self seems interminable, as Bessie K. later adds: "And I had to come out alive by myself. Maybe I did make mistakes. . . . I had a child, I had a family, I had a life. But in order to survive, I think I had to die first. That's what I told our two daughters, and I didn't know the damage what I was doing to them, and to my husband, and to myself."[12] Remembering now her remembering then ("I was *born* on that train and I *died* on that train"), remembering too former attempts to explain to her present family the "impact" of the loss of her earlier family, the witness is left with an intricately interlocking series of memory moments that simply refute pattern or chronology. They create a break in the chain of her life that telling cannot mend.

Would silence be better? Perhaps for us, because it would spare us much pain; but because memory functions with or without speech, it is difficult to see how *not* telling her story could ease Bessie K.'s internal distress. Memory cannot be silenced; it might as well be heard, in an attempt to understand why it must express itself with such disjointed dismay. As historian Yosef Hayim Yerushalmi argues in *Zakhor: Jewish History and Jewish Memory*, it has not always done so. Although Yerushalmi is not specifically addressing the issue of the Holocaust, his remarks shed light on the dilemma we have been considering. The episodes that surface in Bessie K.'s narrative are part of her private memory rather than of Jewish collective memory, with which the circumstances of her situation, *as she experienced them*, permit no connection. The narrow secular context of what she remembers seems to confirm Yerushalmi's contention that the "decline of Jewish collective memory in modern times is only a symptom of the unraveling of that common network of belief and praxis through whose mechanisms . . . the past was once made present."[13] Unraveling, however, seems a tame enough term for the violent, not to say catastrophic disruption of family life that lay at the heart of the belief and praxis supporting the traditions of Jewish collective memory.

Yerushalmi quotes with some skepticism a fellow historian's boast that the "historian . . . is the physician of memory. It is his honor to heal wounds, genuine wounds." He shrewdly qualifies this claim: "Ultimately Jewish memory cannot be 'healed' unless the group itself finds healing, unless its wholeness is restored or rejuvenated. But for the wounds inflicted upon Jewish life by the disintegrative blows of the last two hundred years the historian seems at best a pathologist, hardly a physician" (93, 94). Clearly, Yerushalmi is unwilling to limit the source of the impasse to the attempted annihilation of European Jewry; the historian's broader view differentiates his role and his task from the role and task of the witness in these oral testimonies.

But Yerushalmi is equally dissatisfied with the pathological possibilities of his profession. "Memory and modern historiography," he insists, "stand, by their very nature, in radically different relations to the past. . . . The historian does not simply come in to replenish the gaps of memory. He constantly challenges even those memories that have survived intact." Unlike the former victims whose memories we are examining, the historian tries to recapture a "total past" (Yerushalmi of course is referring here to the "entire Jewish past"), though the "drastically selective" emphasis of collective memory leaves hanging the question of "whether, as a result, some genuine catharsis or reintegration is foreseeable" (94, 95). Content to recapture the fragments that have shattered their past and partially blocked their future, witnesses in oral testimonies dramatize the obstacles to catharsis or reintegration through the necessarily restricted emphases of anguished memory.

The sole mention of the destruction of European Jewry in Yerushalmi's essays on Jewish memory and Jewish history comes in a surprising statement about the inability of the historian's audience to tolerate disagreeable facts. "The Holocaust," Yerushalmi declares, "has already engendered more historical research than any single event in Jewish history, but I have no doubt whatever that its image is being shaped, not at the historian's anvil, but in the novelist's crucible." This is not meant, I suspect, as a compliment to the literary imagination. Jews, Yerushalmi complains, are not prepared to confront history directly "but seem to await a new, metahistorical myth, for which the novel provides at least a temporary modern surrogate" (98). Oral testimony by surviving victims forgoes the responsibility of history to achieve a broader view, as it forfeits the novelist's need to forge, if not a metahistorical myth, then at least an imaginative frame to help the readers chart their way through remote terrain. It etches a lost piece of the past that may be evoked but not restored.

"The choice for Jews as for non-Jews," Yerushalmi concludes, "is not whether or not to have a past, but rather—what kind of past shall one have" (99). The control or elaboration of memory available to historian and novelist, however, is not accessible to the surviving victim, who feels divided by a past that forbids the evolution of an integrated vision. Jacob K., Bessie's present husband, comments incisively on this condition of victimhood: "We perceive life as a precious thing. And then Bessie gives birth to a child and the German takes away the child and kills it. What are we, superhuman, to just brush it aside and say to the world, 'Thank you for liberating us?' And that's all, we wash the hands clean like nothing happened? . . . I can't make peace with that." Once more, we have a split voice entering into dialogue with itself, in futile search for a physician of memory, since the case has nothing to do with illness. Jacob K. continues: "Maybe other survivors can; I don't know. I myself, if you ask me, I can't. And yet I go on, I'm creative, we're both creative, we contribute, we work ["we have two lovely daughters," Bessie interjects], we are happy that we're here in a country that gave us freedom and everything, and we have proved our worth. But this is not the issue. There is another issue, there's a deeper issue. You cannot brush away the pain by giving something else." He explodes the medical image of administering antidotes or healing wounds, a kind of nostalgia for restoring normalcy to a temporarily disrupted life. The deeper issue, the profounder gloom is the normalcy of his memory of the abnormal, because he is convinced that what was done to them represented a consensus, through a combination of active participation and passive indifference, of the world of that time. "Am

I a part of that human community?" he asks at the end of his testimony, staring bitterly into the camera. "I don't think so."[14] His interviewers greet his question with silence.

At once insider and outsider, the surviving victim strives to communicate the quality of that condition to the sympathetic viewer. Many contend that it grows more intractable as they age, as they approach or enter retirement, as the successful completion of careers and raising families leaves more space in their lives for troublesome memories. One surviving victim of Auschwitz is persuaded that her situation is exemplary:

> I feel my head is filled with garbage: all these images, you know, and sounds, and my nostrils are filled with the stench of burning flesh. And it's . . . you can't excise it, it's like— like there's another skin beneath this skin and that skin is called Auschwitz, and you cannot shed it, you know [the similarity to Charlotte Delbo's image of the snakeskin is striking here]. And it's a constant accompaniment. And though a lot of the survivors will deny this, they too feel it the way I do, but they won't give expression to it. I mean I will tell you that it's harder in many ways because . . . because we carry this. I am not like you. You have one vision of life and I have two. I—you know—I lived on two planets. After all, I was—it seems to me that Hitler chopped off part of the universe and created annihilation zones and torture and slaughter areas. You know, it's like the planet was chopped up into a normal [part]—so-called normal: our lives are not really normal— and this other planet, and we were herded onto that planet from this one, and herded back again, [while] having nothing—virtually nothing in common with the inhabitants of this planet. And we had to relearn how to live again. Literally how to hold a fork, how to wash with soap, how to brush your teeth and . . . and we have these . . . these double lives. We can't cancel out. It just won't go away. People will deny

it. I mean, probably a greater number will deny it—these memories—than not. But I will tell you, it's terrible . . . I talk to you and I am not only here, but I see Mengele [she lived in a barrack from which he chose women, including her sister, for his experiments] and I see the crematorium and I see all of that. And it's too much; it's very hard to get old with such— so ungracefully, because that has anything but grace, those memories, you know. It's very hard.[15]

Anguished memory stains the desire for graceful aging with the refuse of annihilation zones and slaughter areas. The rich imagery of this passage, though perhaps not rivaling the novelist's art, verges on a special kind of testimonial art, especially in its evocation of the psychology of what Delbo called dédoublement, or doubling.

"You have one vision of life and I have two": this principle is vividly raised to the level of authentic testimonial art in the following narrative moment, which returns us to one of the primal events in the memory of so many surviving victims, the boxcar journey. The direction here, however, is *from* Auschwitz, the witness being part of a group on their way to a labor site in Germany:

One morning, I think it was morning or early afternoon, we arrived. The train stopped for an hour; why, we don't know. And a friend of mine said, "Why don't you stand up?" There was just a little window, with bars. And I said, "I can't. I don't have enough energy to climb up." And she said, "I'm going to sit down and you're going to stand on my shoulders." And I did; and I looked out. And . . . I . . . saw . . . Paradise! The sun was bright and vivid. There was cleanliness all over. It was a station somewhere in Germany. There were three or four people there. One woman had a child, nicely dressed up; the child was crying. People were people, not animals. And I thought: "Paradise must look like this!" I forgot already how normal people look like, how they act,

how they speak, how they dress. I saw the sun in Auschwitz,
I saw the sun come up, because we had to get up at four in the
morning. But it was never beautiful to me. I never saw it
shine. It was just the beginning of a horrible day. And in the
evening, the end—of what? But here there was *life*, and I had
such yearning, I still feel it in my bones. I had such yearning,
to live, to run, to just run away and never come back—to run
to the end where there is no way back. And I told the girls, I
said, "Girls, you have no idea how beautiful the sun is, and I
saw a baby crying and a woman was kissing that baby—is
there such a thing as love?"[16]

A source of torment rather than profit, Edith P.'s double vision
here reminds us the knothole and fence image we encountered
earlier in the testimony of Father S. The expanded view is simultaneously a diminished view, eroding prior stabilities and increasing the rift between past and present, then and now. We have an
example of memory remembering how memory struggled to recapture its sense of the normal ("I forgot already how normal
people look") combined with a vague hopeless desire to escape
into an uncontaminated future ("to run to the end where there is
no way back"). Rediscovering the beauty of creation only reinforces Edith P.'s own imprisoned state, leading her to question
the very basis of that creation.

This in turn raises some fundamental issues about the nature of
sight and insight, and the possible reversal here of values traditionally associated with them. "Film," writes Carlos Fuentes, "invites us to exercise choice through sight in a world full of material
objects. The way we see is the way we choose, and the way we
choose is the way we are free." But oral testimony of this kind is
not film, which is a cultural form from the normal world, exploit-
ing, as Fuentes argues, a "repertory of possibilities"[17] that in the
scenario we have just heard shrinks and dwindles and finally
vanishes. What I call the cattle-car point of view unsettles the

imagination because it inverts customary expectations: everything Edith P. sees from her confinement mocks the impulse to choice and the will to freedom. "I had such yearning," she says, "to run away and never come back"; but she knows, and her visual representations confirm this, that she draws such yearning from a repertory of *im*possibilities, facing not the quandary of freedom, of unlimited choice, but of its opposite—the quandary of the Auschwitz inmate who was "free" to watch the sun rise every morning but never to see it shine.

This narrative episode evokes for us the challenge of interpreting not only surviving victims' testimony, but the Holocaust experience itself, dramatizing the audience dilemma as few other texts do. Imagine the scene as a painter might perceive it: a station, the sun gleaming on the platform, and that archetypal icon, the mother and child, occupying the center of the canvas. Above the platform, however, hangs a mirror, and in it we see reflected (rendered faithfully by the artist) a boxcar resting on the tracks. Peering through a small barred opening in an upper corner of the boxcar is a woman's face. She gazes at the woman on the platform—who gazes back. Or does she? And we gaze at both, searching for the "real" meaning at the heart of this visual panorama, wondering which is the primary world, which the reflected one: the woman in the boxcar or the mother on the station? The one indeed faces a repertory of possibilities; the other, none. In exercising her "choice through sight," Edith P. reminds herself and us that she "cannot" do what she seems to be doing. *Her* choice of sight is only an illusion, insofar as it confirms the restraints, not the flexibility, of her perspective. Thus we discover that the boxcar and its window have totally different implications for the experience of perceiving than the fence and the knothole. If Edith P. were peering through that knothole, she would see *herself* in the boxcar, not a man resembling Father S.'s father.

Suppose we were to read Edith P.'s testimony in a printed text, instead of seeing it and hearing it from her own lips. I am convinced that the effect would be different (though not necessarily more or less powerful), because the text would be different. Writing invites reflection, commentary, interpretation, by the author as well as the reader. Edith P.'s allusions to mother, child, sun, and love lack lyrical subtexts to enrich their resonance; indeed, we are invited by her testimony to appreciate the poverty of romantic vision when shorn of such ornaments. Oral testimony is distinguished by the absence of literary mediation, so that the material and emotional substance we traditionally identify with the language of "sun," "love," "mother," and "child" has lost its defining contours. To ask "Is there such a thing as love?" is to question the physical and metaphysical basis of the universe we presume to know—and the one Edith P. thinks she may have lost.

Edith P. narrates a pause in her journey, an unfinished voyage that may end with the name but not the experience of liberation. Many surviving victims, perhaps a majority, refuse to finish their narrative with an account of their liberation, though often encouraged to do so by their interviewers. The narrators' imaginations remain chained to memories that have little to do with sequence or chronology. Most *written* survivor narratives, on the other hand, end where they have been leading—the arrival of the Allies, and the corresponding "freedom" of the victims. Oral testimony violates our own need for conclusions, thereby imposing on us an angle of vision wrenching us from familiar assumptions that govern our response to normal narrative.

For example, one of the most unusual written survivor narratives, given the author's work with the *Sonderkommando* (special labor detail) in the vicinity of the killing facilities, is Filip Müller's *Eyewitness Auschwitz*. The title itself (at least of the American edition) invokes the importance of point of view. Yet even Müller's text cannot escape the temptations of teleology or the appeal of representative patterns. Speaking of his fear, as a member of a group engaged in piling corpses in a mass grave, Müller writes: "I tried to recall exemplary men and women down the centuries who were put to death. I remembered that we must all die. Death, I told myself, was, after all, part of our lives and we would have to face it sooner or later."[18] I cannot imagine a sentiment like this intruding on an oral testimony. This is simply not the same voice as the one that transfixes us in Claude Lanzmann's film *Shoah*, in which Müller's haunting accounts of the gas chambers and crematoriums are among the most memorable moments.[19] In this part of the *written* narrative, with a verbal flourish, Müller (with his collaborator) seeks to transform individual doom in Auschwitz into a model of universal history and man's fate in time, thereby affirming a continuity that the deathcamp was determined to divide. Unwittingly, he reminds us that we must establish the authenticity of the voice before we can respond to the reliability of the text.

Oral survivor testimony unfolds before our eyes and ears; we are present at the invention of what, when we speak of written texts, we call style. What is style, as Jonathan Swift reminds us, but the search for proper words in proper places? The question suffers a sea change, however, as anguished memory tries to find proper words for a narrative whose *subject* is improper places like Auschwitz and the other camps. The following excerpt invites us to the birth of a style, but also takes us back to the difficulty of conception, as the witness struggles to develop an idiom consonant with her dark vision of a permanently divided existence— one that bears little resemblance to the integrated strength implied in her interviewer's question:

INTERVIEWER: How do you get the strength? Look, you've been talking and you've been with it for the last two hours or so. Where is your strength? How did you get the strength then? How do you get the strength now? What keeps you?

IRENE W.: To function? . . .

INTERVIEWER: Well, it's not only . . . it's more than functioning.

IRENE W.: To . . . well . . . I often think about it, of course, how there is a sort of division, a sort of schizophrenic division, you know, a compartmentalization of what happened, and it's kept tightly separated, and yet as I said, it isn't. There is this past of daily living that one has to attend to and adhere to, and family and children and their needs and everyday needs and work and so on, and that must not interfere, the other must not become so overwhelming that it will make so-called normal life unable to function. Yet it's always there; it's more a view of the world, a total world view . . . of extreme pessimism [at this word, sudden almost *palpable* breath intake by the interviewer], of sort of one feels . . . of really knowing the truth about people, human nature, about death, of really knowing the truth in a way that other people don't know it. And all of the truth is harsh, and impossible to really accept, and yet you have to go on and function. So it's a complete lack of faith in human beings, in all areas you know, whether it's politics or whatever: you hear one thing and you believe something else. I mean you say, "Oh, well, I know the truth." And . . .

INTERVIEWER [interrupting]: Mrs. W., you are one of the greatest optimists I've ever met.

IRENE W.: [laughing deferentially]: How do you . . . how do you come about to that conclusion [smiling, but not retreating from her position].[20]

If we listen carefully, we hear how this interviewer's response is framed by a vocabulary of purpose, by assumptions about strength and optimism that regulate our image of the heroic spirit. Almost every interpretation of the Holocaust experience, at least on a personal level, requires some acknowledgment of how "so-called normal life" and "the other," as Irene W. refers to them, interact. The interview itself, or this moment in the testimony, is a dramatic reenactment of such interaction, as two verbal motifs and their accompanying attitudes vie for priority. Irene W.'s controlled demeanor, as she struggles unemotionally to distinguish between them, cannot conceal the chilling implications of her remarks. Her subtext, "a total world view of extreme pessimism," encounters "you are one of the greatest optimists I've ever met," leaving one wondering at the psychological interplay of the exchange. Is the interviewer protecting her, or himself, with his consoling interjection? Because Irene W. seems to have managed with such composure the compartmentalized life that she mentioned earlier, there may be some superficial justice to his words. But those words must ignore the deeper probing of anguished memory, which exposes a dreary prospect worthy of the moral bleakness of King Lear's heath.

The interview ends a few moments later in a stalemate, the two perspectives unreconciled. The interviewer, as surrogate for a larger audience, instinctively clings to "optimism" as a shield against a truth that is "harsh and impossible to really accept," one espousing "a complete lack of faith in human beings." Irene W. fails to see the logic leading from *her* language to his—which is perhaps only another way of saying that beyond the verbal style she has given birth to is an inner psychology too elusive and disagreeable to absorb at the moment of hearing it.

The credibility of Irene W.'s experience is not in question, at least not explicitly. But implicitly, how can we separate the challenge of representing it with an undefiled vocabulary from the issue of narrative authenticity? The audience's resistant imagination is at odds with the receptivity demanded by an evolving text. Irene W. has not plucked her private pessimism from the unfeatured air; she offers it after two hours of testimony about her camp experiences, including six months in the *Kanadakommando* (a work detail whose job was to sort out the clothing and belongings of those sent directly to their death) in Auschwitz, where she arrived at age fourteen. Her mother and three younger siblings were sent straight to the gas chambers; her father and older brother went "to the right," but she never saw them again. She and her older sister remained. Although she narrates these details dispassionately, she is firm in her conviction that they are the genesis of the problem she still wrestles with today: how to *talk* about them meaningfully to an audience of outsiders.

She first encountered this dilemma immediately after the war, when she returned briefly to the town of her birth and tried to tell people there what had happened to her family. She remembers thinking that "My family were killed" was totally inadequate, because "killed," she says, was a word used for "ordinary" forms of dying. But to say matter of factly that "My mother and brother and two sisters were gassed" as soon as they arrived at Auschwitz seemed equally unsatisfactory, because plain factuality could not convey the enormity of the event. She was especially reluctant to reduce her family's disappearance to a mere statistic, because she was sure that was how her audience wanted to hear about it. That night, she insists, she could not describe it in that way, but her refusal to speak had nothing to do with the oft-repeated view that perhaps silence was the only appropriate response to such catastrophe. The seeds of anguished memory are sown in the barren belief that the very story you try to tell drives off the audience you seek to capture. Those seeds often shrivel in the further suspicion that the story you tell *cannot* be precisely the story as it happened. Reluctance to speak has little to do with *preference* for silence.

Oral testimony is a living commentary on the limits of autobiographical narrative, when the theme is such unprecedented atrocity. It also reveals the limits of memory's ability to re-create that past. The issue is not merely the unshareability of the experience but also the witness's exasperated sense (not uniformly borne out, as we have seen, by the effects of his or her testimony) of a failure in communication. Chaim E., one of the participants in the Sobibor uprising, who escaped and survived, tries in halting but eloquent sentences to convey his frustration:

> If you take ten people [who] listen to the story and ask them to tell the story back, you would get ten different stories. Why? Because it is not—I'm not so strong in the language to explain it—but even the one which is strong in the language and knows the expressions and has the talent and everything, he still cannot tell the whole story. It is just impossible. The only one what's lived it through knows really what happened. Because the feelings what are involved with this story, they are not the same. You cannot—feelings you can bring, to a certain degree—tell what it is. But you cannot tell how I felt when I found the clothes of my brother, for example [while sorting the garments of those who had just been gassed]. Now if you ask me what I was thinking about, I wasn't thinking at all. I was horrified—things like that you know. But I can tell the story, and it sounds—well, [like] another story. But it is more than the other story. It is more some feelings what you cannot bring out, you know. Or all these kinds of things—what happened.

At this point, the interviewer tries to clarify by interpolating: "You're saying they're alive in you, but there's no language for you to explain it to someone else." Chaim E. replies:

> No, no, no. I try in my best words to bring the picture out of it. But you see, when I . . . I see the picture in *front* of me; you have to *imagine* something. The one that listens has to imagine something. So it has a different picture for me than for the one that imagines it. At least I think so, because sometimes I hear telling back a story that doesn't sound at all the same what I was telling, you see; it doesn't sound the same. It was horrified and horrible, and when you live once with this tension and horrification—if that is the right word—then you

live differently. Your thoughts don't go too far. In normal life, you think about tomorrow and after tomorrow and about a year, and next year a vacation then, and things like that. Here you think on the moment what it is. What happen *now*, on the moment. *Now* is it horrible. You don't think "later."[21]

One of the regrets of anguished memory is its premonition, during the very process of testifying, of the absence of a common ground between *its* reality and our attempts to imagine it. Because they cannot talk back to a *written* text, readers are forced into silent collaboration with the narrative, which tests the inventive capacity of their imaginations by contriving an imaginative vision of its own. In oral testimony, interviewers sometimes assume that role, though the resulting dynamics illustrates one difference between reading about a shaped reality on a page and hearing it in its impromptu form. The following brief excerpt gives us a glimpse of such an interaction, which I hesitate to call a stalemate, because it seems to end with the defeat of the witness, or at least of her language. Here words literally contend with each other for supremacy, offering a stunning instance of the near impossibility of achieving a purely objective oral text. The narrator has experienced *two* deportations to Auschwitz, with stops at Majdanek and Plaszow in between, and the discussion, at the end of her interview, is about how she survived:

INTERVIEWER: You were able to survive because you were so plucky. When you stepped back on the line . . .

HANNA F.: No, dear, no dear, no . . . no, I had no . . . [meanwhile, the two interviewers are whispering audibly with each other off camera about this exchange, momentarily ignoring the witness, who wants to reply]. How shall I explain to you? I know that I had to survive; I had to survive, even running away, even being with the people constantly, especially the second part, the second time, being back in Auschwitz. That time I had determined already to survive—and you know

what? It wasn't luck, it was stupidity. [At this, the two interviewers laugh deprecatingly, overriding her voice with their
own "explanation," as one calls out, "You had a lot of guts!"]
HANNA F.: [simultaneously] No, no, no, no, there were no
guts, there was just sheer stupidity. I just, you know . . .
[more laughter from the interviewers, one of whom now
stands up between camera and witness, blocking our vision,
silencing her voice, ending the interview. Why?][22]

Nothing has been concluded; in fact, the "desired" conclusion,
that Hanna F. survived through pluck and guts, has been undermined by her insistence that she has survived through luck and
stupidity. Words of denial and affirmation leap from the screen,
signifying far more than a dispute between skeptical interviewers
and resolute former victim. No one bothers to ask her how one
survives through "stupidity," as if her remark had been too obviously irrelevant to merit investigation.[23]

We are faced here with a confusion of tongues, a contest of
wills, the audience's desire to preserve preconceived interpretations by searching through the thesaurus of heroic terms for
words like *pluck* and *guts* to confirm such interpretations, while
the narrator—vainly, in this instance, as it turns out—ventures
her own version of survival with a word deleted from that thesaurus: *stupidity*. This is an encounter that is no encounter, because her use of language, as anyone who watches her expression
throughout the testimony can recognize, is memory-specific,
while the interviewers' response is identified with a long tradition
of historical behavior and expectations. *Her* use of language interprets her narrative for her and them; *their* use of language interprets her narrative for them and her. Though certainly not representative of *all* interviews, the confrontation dramatizes the
irreconcilable clash between the differing value-spaces that the
two points of view inhabit.

The conflict between preconceived, culturally nourished moral expectations and their violation is internalized less divertingly and more intricately in the following uninterrupted complex narrative moment from the videotaped testimony of Alex H. It is as if we are in the presence of two contending voices, each seeking independent expression: the first, time- and place-bound by what we might call the chronicle mode; the other, like Charlotte Delbo, struggling to detach "the way it was" from how we think it was (and how he thinks it *should* have been) from the vantage point of the present. The recording memory converges on the will to interpretation; imagining disaster meets traditional moral authority; chronology faces temporal dissolution—and each competes for control of the narrative (and for our intellectual and emotional response to it):

In December 1944, when the war started coming to an end, although we didn't know that, or we did not know to what extent—we were taken out of camp and started off to march—the Russians came near and the Germans took us out from camp and they marched us to other camps. It was terrible cold; we had no clothes. Whoever could not walk they shot. We had no food. It was . . . the real horror story of my camp started in December of 1944.

At night they herded us in some farm . . . a barn. Next morning very early they took us out and we had to march again; we marched for days. And during that march, my brother . . . he could not walk anymore and he was taken from me and shot on the road.

It is difficult to say, talk about feelings. First of all, we were reduced to such a animal level that actually now that I remember those things, I feel more horrible than I felt at the time. We were in such a state that all that mattered is to remain alive. Even about your own brother or the closest, one did not think. I don't know how other people felt . . . . It bothers me very much if I was the only one that felt that way,

or is that normal in such circumstances to be that way? I feel
now sometimes, did I do my best or didn't I do something
that I should have done? But at that time I wanted to survive
myself, and maybe I did not give my greatest efforts to do
certain things, or I missed to do certain things.[24]

Ostensibly, the passage begins as part of a chronological sequence (December 1944), assuming a past, a present, and a
future—in short, temporal continuity ("we marched for days"). It
even assumes continuity in space—we left this camp, and went to
that one. But suddenly, another voice intrudes on the idea that
this is merely a dramatic moment in time embedded in a larger
sequential design. When Alex H. breaks off his narrative to an-
nounce that the real horror story of his camp *started* in December
1944, he introduces a *discontinuity* into his account that detaches it
from his previous efforts at chronology. He shifts from the mode
of *in medias res*—which views the Holocaust as an event sandwiched between prewar and postwar periods—to what we might
call the mode of *in principio*, where, according to most testimony of
surviving victims, the Holocaust has a different beginning for
each witness and provides closure for none. Both modes afflict
Alex H.'s memory, as is evident when he explains: "Actually now
that I remember those things, I feel more horrible than I felt at the
time." The history of morality and the so-called morality of history
educate us about "normal" and desirable behavior in most circumstances. But Alex H. is speaking of what he calls "such circumstances," specifically his inability to help his weakened brother
(he gives details of this traumatic moment earlier in his testimony)
and to prevent the Germans from shooting him. Almost with
desperation, he seeks to establish a retroactive continuity between his repertory of possibilities "now" and the repertory of
impossibilities "at the time." Finding no connection, he remains
in a condition of permanent distress.

Why is this so? His brother's death is a random moment that

surfaces in his narrative several times not as a consummation of logically preceding events but as the creation of anguished memory unappeased, born of Alex H.'s groping efforts to dredge up some of the most agonizing episodes in his Holocaust experience. History demands accuracy, chronology, significance, interpretation; in his role as an agent of history, this witness is provoked to ask "did I do my best or didn't I do something that I should have done?" Remorse and recrimination are part of the moral authority that supposedly governs our lives as social beings. To the question of why moral consciousness seems such an issue now when it apparently was less so then, we might reply that the nature of the interview situation, to say nothing of the passage of time and the former victim's changed circumstances, prompts it.

For example, virtually all videotaped interviews begin in the same way, innocently conspiring to establish an atmosphere of familiarity: tell us something about your childhood, family, school, community, friends—that is, about the normal world preceding the disaster. And most of them end in the same way too, implying a severance between the camp experience and what followed: tell us about your liberation (and your life afterwards). The reluctance of so many surviving victims to see liberation as a form of closure only confirms the need to understand the unorthodox implications of the narrative mode of in principio when responding to their testimony. Asked to describe how he felt at the moment of liberation, one surviving victim declared, "Then I knew my troubles were *really* about to begin," inverting the order of conflict and resolution that we have learned to expect of traditional historical narrative.

During this last fragment of testimony, we observe memory inviting itself to transform a random event into a pattern of sequenced meaning, a process difficult and perhaps impossible to detect on the printed page of a written text. It is as if Alex H. were asking, "How can I tell you, how can I tell *myself*, what I 'remember' about that instant now that I'm back in human society, where fraternal caring is a major measure of civilized conduct?" The search for value contends with the absence of value, giving us a glimpse into the evolution of ethical consciousness at its most elementary level, shaping history out of reality by exposing the illogic of atrocity and trying to replace it with some form of moral continuity. What student of history, inquiring why Alex H.'s brother was shot, would be content with the answer "Because he was too weak to walk"? Far more satisfying to the imagination (though equally inaccurate) is Alex H.'s own hesitant, vaguely guilty response: "Maybe I did not give my greatest efforts to do certain things." This voice from the cultural present, where traditional explanations of ethical and unethical conduct presumably prevail, speaks from in medias res, a world of before and after. His *other* voice, from what I call in principio, is detached from past and present, emerging in what he describes as "the real horror story of my camp." But as Alex H. tells this story, as his memory reperceives the reality on which it is based, he instinctively realizes how uncongenial is the principle of being that he himself has expressed: "All that mattered is to remain alive." This is too primitive a morality for the society he now inhabits—hence the birth of his divided self.

But we are obliged to cross the frontiers within which that principle of being held temporary sway. And even if it represents only *part* of the truth, how do we clear our minds of verbal cant in order to portray it accurately? When Irene W. speaks of knowing the truth as others do not know it; when Hanna F. tries to explain that she survived through "stupidity"; when Alex H. wonders about definitions of "normal" under the circumstances of the death march he endured; and when Edith P., in a desperate, wrenching appeal, asks, "Is there such a thing as love?"—they raise uncomfortable issues that have yet to be explored fully in our post-Holocaust era. Edith P.'s question of course betrays the misery of her own condition; but it also threatens the fundamental integrity of the social and religious fabric of which Western culture is woven. The probings of anguished memory, when (as in these instances) they resist the need to reach comforting conclusions, free our imaginations to examine the rents in this fabric—an unhappy enterprise, at best. Although a negative rejoinder to the question "Is there such a thing as love?" is of course inadmissible, that is precisely why, in facing these testimonies, we must consider the possibility that as a result of the forays of memory, at least for unnumbered potential victims, it might nonetheless have seemed true.

"When the subject becomes absence," writes Maurice Blanchot, "then the absence of a subject, or dying as subject, subverts the whole sequence of existence, causes time to take leave of its order." Although he calls his text *The Writing of the Disaster*, his language applies with equal precision to what we have been examining, the "speaking of the disaster." Lurking behind the apparent subjectivity of these testimonies is the "absent" theme of the disappearance of others, the "un-story" (*"non-recit"*) that we have already mentioned. Blanchot names it "demise writing" (*"défaillance par l'écriture"*); witnesses in oral testimony engage in a form of "demise speaking." They enter Blanchot's "wounded space" to revive with ruined words his "ill-come unknown" (*"l'inconnu mal venu"*)[25]—distant kin, one assumes, to the welcome known. The irony of this revival, however, is the discovery that memory is not only a spring, flowing from the well of the past, but also a tomb, whose contents cling like withered ivy to the mind. For the witnesses, the Holocaust is at once a lived event and a "died" event: the paradox of how one survives a died event is one of the most urgent (if unobtrusive) topics of their testimonies, about which I will have more to say in subsequent chapters.

The oral account of the died event in these narratives is roughly equivalent to Blanchot's idea of demise writing. Such accounts abound in the testimonies. Sometimes they involve one's self; sometimes they involve others. Luna K., for example, begins her story by showing two sets of photographs: of her father and sister, who were murdered, and of her present husband and three children, together with her mother (who survived). While she displays them, she tells us that each of her parents had about ten siblings, none of whom survived. She thus frames her narrative by a visual representation of her loss and her gain, establishing a rhythm that she tries to sustain throughout her testimony. Her mother is the link between the two worlds, because she and Luna K. remained together in Plaszow, Skarzysko, and other labor camps.

Like so many former victims, Luna K. speaks with two voices, though she seems less aware than some of the resulting contradictions. She insists, for instance, on the importance then of cherishing a sense of your own dignity, no matter what the circumstances—of remaining clean and appearing as neat as possible. But one day the German commandant of Skarzysko sees her and says: "You know, you're looking too well, you have it too good. Then you will go to work on picric acid"—and he sends her to join the picrinoires. Dignified appearance thus proved to be a liability at that moment, though since she was not yet sixteen, a sympathetic supervisor assigned her to work away from the toxic materials. This seems to confirm her belief that "if we didn't care for each other, we could have never survived." She insists that not enough attention has been paid to "what loyalties people had" during the struggle to stay alive.

But then, as an *example* of such loyalty, she tells of a group of Hasidic Jews who ran the brush factory where she worked in Plaszow. They declined to work on Yom Kippur, choosing instead to pray. She and the others pleaded with them, fearing for their own safety if the Germans discovered that the output was less than expected—but they refused. The SS learned of the situation, arrived, shot the "malefactors," and began beating and randomly executing some of the others. Earlier, Luna K. had spoken of the importance of learning "what it meant to be quiet" if one wanted to remain safe under these conditions. Her illustration of this requirement during the episode she has been describing is a classic example of the shift of testimony from what one has lived through to what one has died through, though it takes some collaboration on the audience's part to perceive the momentum.

During the shootings in the factory, knowing what it meant to be quiet, Luna K. continues working at her table. An SS man comes up behind her, and she hears a click. She reports that she thought he had taken a cigarette from his case and was lighting it. But she glances at her mother, who is working opposite her, and sees that her face is the color of chalk. It turns out that he had put his gun against Luna's head and pulled the trigger but was out of ammunition—the click had been the sound of the empty chamber. Nobody screamed or said a word, practicing the silence that Luna K. believed was necessary for the preservation of life in the camps. Her own interpretation sees this as a lived event, though her comment invites us to extend her words into more somber realms. "So nobody says anything," she remembers; "it wasn't worth taking my life, so he just walked out. So now you can understand why people were quiet. If my mother said a word, I wouldn't be here today."

In a sense, anguished memory is now transferred from her to us, as we contemplate the companion responses: an "admirable" self-control and a mother staring mutely at her daughter about to be shot—a grim perversion of human response and a concise illustration of what I have called the died event in the experience of former victims. Luna K. interprets her executioner's psychology by concluding that because no one seemed to care about her, he did not think she was worth the bother of putting more bullets into his gun. But her summation of the episode leads us to the verge of further insight: "So this is the complexity of life, this is the complexity of the reality there: that you can't . . . there are no rules."[26] Among the movements concealed by that hiatus is the curious journey of positive words like "caring" and "loyalties," which she had mentioned earlier as evidence of communal support in the camps. The climate of the lived event supports such vocabulary; but the ambience of the died event, as we have just seen, deprives the gift of language of its most cherished attribute—meaning. To imply that a mother's caring and loyalty expressed through silence conveyed to the SS man an indifference that ultimately saved the daughter's life is to draw definitions from the lexicon of *Alice in Wonderland*. It imputes to speech a desperate logic that dissolves when applied to the surface of atrocities like the one we have been describing. Memory itself is not always immune to such misconstruals.

Anguished memory eliminates repose from the reconstituted reality of the died event, which then hovers in a space inaccessible to normal narrative. It has no place of its own. Blanchot calls it "nonexperience." "We feel that there cannot be any experience of the disaster," he says, "even if we were to understand disaster to be the ultimate experience. This is one of its features: it impoverishes all experience, withdraws from experience all authenticity; it keeps its vigil only when night watches without watching over anything."[27] The apparent *non*-sense that often intrudes on Blanchot's playful use of language fulfills a prophecy implicit in many portions of oral testimony: we cannot listen to what we are about to hear with normal ears (any more than we can read written survivor accounts with normal eyes). Like Irene W.'s life, words too are compartmentalized, schizophrenic; remembering disaster subtracts from life and experience even as it adds to them through the very process of recall and narration.

When Blanchot writes that the disaster "withdraws from experience all authenticity," he speaks of *familiar* authenticity; our accounts substitute a different kind of legitimacy, the foundation of which lies in no other reality than its own. Unlike primal episodes such as the Fall of Man or the Fall of Troy—which formed the basis for human morality or the founding of a people, creating a future and hence an entry into history and time—the Holocaust did not offer an opportunity for an evolutionary "afterward." As testimonies constantly show, their progressive narrative collapses under the weight of died events like the one we have just observed. Hearing it, we try to match our sense of authenticity against its logic, only to encounter a failure to connect. During the effort, as Blanchot describes it, the "relation of one to the other ceaselessly comes apart; it undoes every model and every code; it is the nonrelation [non rapport] from which we are not excused" (79). The experience of nonrelation is itself a form of relation, however tenuous; the sense of threatened identity accompanying it reenacts, on a smaller scale (though it does not duplicate), the fragmentation of self, family, community, and harmony with the universe that is the enduring legacy of the catastrophe.

Oral testimonies clarify Blanchot's theoretical speculations as if they had been consciously designed as footnotes to his elusive text. "Dying means: you are dead already," he says, "in an immemorial past, of a death which was not yours, which you have thus neither known nor lived, but under the threat of which you believe you are called upon to live" (65). I shall have more to say later about the need for a word other than "survive" to describe the ordeal of the former victim. To illustrate this idea, and Blanchot's difficult principle, let us consider the story of Magda F., who was born in a part of Czechoslovakia ceded to Hungary by Hitler before the outbreak of World War II. Because of this, she was spared deportation until 1944, when the Germans occupied Hungary, though her husband was sent to a labor camp by his own government, ending up near the Russian front, from which he did not return alive. Magda F. was sent to Auschwitz, then to Plaszow, back to Auschwitz, then to Leipzig, and finally to Theresienstadt, where she remained until the war ended. She returned to Budapest, to learn that her brother, three sisters, parents, and husband had been murdered. Two of her sisters' husbands survived, and she married one of them (his wife [her sister] and two children had also been killed); they came to America and raised a new family.

After speaking fervently about the impossibility of any outsider ever understanding what she is talking about (thus stressing one of the many disheartening features of these testimonies—the *futility* of memory) and of her disinclination to believe her own story, Magda F. abruptly addresses a different issue, dismissing expectations of closure and casting a dreary shadow on the ostensible happy ending of her narrative:

> One thing I forgot to mention. Tommy [her son] was born in Europe. Ellen [her daughter] was born in this country. . . . As they were growing up, how many times, my husband . . . how many times [he] called Tommy "Fred" or called Ellen "Eva." [Fred and Eva were his children by his first wife, the witness's sister, all of whom were gassed.] My daughter told me one day, "Mom, I don't think in Dad's eyes I am Ellen. I am still Eve, and Tommy is Freddie." He looked at them just like the first family what he had. . . . My children did not like that. They felt like my husband liked them better . . . . That was not the truth, but his mind was still, was back in the same story, and in those two children he saw always Tommy—in Tommy he saw Fred, and in Ellen he saw always Eva. I think I covered my story.[28]

She ends her testimony at this point, memory having uncovered a "forgotten" detail that fuses a lived event (renewal through a second family) with the died event (the loss of the first one) in a way that makes them virtually indistinguishable, documenting the literal existence of the divided self. The crucial role of what I have called the died event in the experience of surviving victims now extends its influence over the totally innocent, dramatically illustrating the nonrelation from which we are not excused that Blanchot had mentioned.

It would be hard to find a better example of the absence of an independent time afterward in the narratives that we have been examining. The past of the disaster casts its net over a redeeming future and corrupts its purity, undermining its own oracular value and substituting an incubus containing an insatiable vitality. Magda F.'s second husband, recently dead, invades her testimony with his personal version of anguished memory, complicating the question of identity in an inescapable confusion of roles. The abrupt, violent termination of his earlier role, allowing no emotional or temporal transition, necessitates and in a way *compels* its continuing reality in his imagination, in his behavior, and, as his wife reports, in his speech. Perhaps confusion of roles is an inexact designation, born of our own conventional premises about the self. Anguished memory, in the testimony of surviving Holocaust victims, is inseparably identified with victims who did not survive, dividing the self between conflicting claims—the need and the inability to recover from the loss. Most other disasters seem eventually to encourage conciliatory gestures, balm for the memory, abated pain. This one, if we are to believe the voices in these testimonies, does not.

A concept like "wounded time," similar to Blanchot's idea of "wounded space" mentioned earlier, might help us to understand why. As memory plunges into the past to rescue the details of the Holocaust experience, it discovers that cessation plays a more prominent role than continuity. One surviving victim speaks of emerging from a cocoon, not in order to celebrate a miraculous transformation but to lament the missed and unrecapturable childhood that had passed during his "absence." Another records her amazement, upon returning to her native village in the spring of 1945, at finding the fruit trees in blossom: the rhythms of nature had been oblivious to her form of "demise living," flourishing in spite of it. But her vision of "nature time," instead of healing the scars that had scored the "unnatural time" of her existence during the preceding three years, only irritated them further. The experience of the disaster, Blanchot writes, "obliges us to disengage ourselves from time as irreversible" (78). If we pursue this obligation, we forfeit the immunity from unnatural time that coherence and chronology afford us. But if we are to master the meaning of wounded time, as it afflicts the voices in these testimonies, there appears to be no alternative to immersing ourselves in the shifting currents of its discontinuous flow.

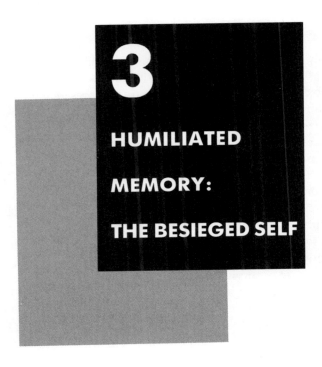

3

HUMILIATED

MEMORY:

THE BESIEGED SELF

If anguished memory may be seen as discontent in search of a form, humiliated memory recalls an utter distress that shatters all molds designed to contain a unified and irreproachable image of the self. Its voice represents pure misery, even decades after the events that it narrates. Neither time nor amnesia soothes its gnawing. After hearing its testimony, we are less prone to dismiss as exaggeration the insistence by many surviving victims that the humiliations they endured in the camps were often worse than death. The details uncovered by humiliated memory dispute the claim still advanced by many commentators that the invincible human spirit provided an armor invulnerable to Nazi assaults against the self.

Nietzsche's legacy (as usual, not completely understood) speaks through the vision of such commentators. Without necessarily endorsing it, Nietzsche defined monumental history as one that "belongs above all to the active and powerful man, to him who fights a great fight." Such a figure "flees resignation and uses history as a means against resignation." This view of history, Nietzsche insists, "disregards causes as much as possible" and concentrates on effects. The monumental view of the past stresses the individual's courage in the face of obstacles. The popular demand for it is an expression of faith in humanity, in the strength of the private will, the resolute deed, the triumph of the spirit. It will live, Nietzsche argues, because "posterity cannot do without it."[1]

But this, as Nietzsche may not have meant to imply, could turn out to be a problem for posterity. He would have perceived instantly how irrelevant the monumental view of history was to the experience of surviving Holocaust victims. Of his historical men he said "Looking into the past urges them toward the future, incites them to take courage and continue to engage in life, and kindles the hope that things will yet turn out well and that happiness is to be found behind the mountain toward which they are striding." Such language frames an expectation while disregarding its genesis—the effect stripped of causes that typifies such figures. Historical men "believe that ever more light is shed on the meaning of existence in the course of its *process*, and they look back to consider that process only to understand the present better and to learn to desire the future more vehemently" (13). It takes no great power of discernment to recognize in this view the reverse of the situation of the witnesses with whom we are concerned; their lives in the camps emerge as a kind of *arrested* process, bereft of meaning and insulated from the future.

Posterity, however, continues to need Nietzsche's language, especially those who tirelessly search for value for the future in the Holocaust experience. Humiliated memory sabotages this quest. It undermines one of the foremost impulses to historical inquiry, which is life-promoting insofar as it mirrors insights from the past that enable us to confront the future with a more informed sense of ourselves as human beings in time. We cling to this rhetorical option—given the grim details of the Holocaust, rhetorical seems the only honest label here—because it rescues us from unmanageable implications. But another option is to embrace, along with Nietzsche, the possibility that "an excess of history is detrimental to life," because with such an excess "life crumbles and degenerates, and finally, because of this degeneration, history itself degenerates as well" (14). The massacre of European Jewry is an excellent candidate for this "distinction." Historical investigation of this subject may serve knowledge (though even this, as historians would be the first to admit, has its limits), but it cannot promote life.

In this regard, humiliated memory negates the impulse to historical inquiry. Posterity not only can do without it; it *prefers* to ignore it. The natural relation of an age, a culture, and a people to history, Nietzsche says, is the desire of knowledge for the purpose of life. Humiliated memory thus forces us into an unnatural relation with the past, because the "knowledge" it imparts crushes the spirit and frustrates the incentive to renewal. Only a radical insincerity, or self-deception, can hear in humiliated memory an expression of monumental history, an affirmative voice, a celebratory spirit. Nietzsche offers us an alternative form of inquiry, what he calls critical history,[2] to compensate for some of the limitations of the monumental excursions into the past. It brings us closer to the revelations of humiliated memory; but because, like its alternative—and indeed, perhaps like all history—it is concerned with *exemplary* attitudes, it too finally leads us to develop distinctions between the kind of knowledge it uncovers and the disclosures of humiliated memory.

Critical history, as Nietzsche defined it, requires a ruthless rejection of all past pieties: his language, if not his intent, helps to define the boundaries of my own investigation. "It is always a dangerous process," he says, "dangerous for life itself," because it is not invariably possible to exempt ourselves from the aberrations we may uncover. "At best," he continues, "we may bring about a conflict between our inherited, innate nature [presumably Nietzsche here means our decent nature] and our knowledge." When knowledge gained through the inquiries of critical history leads to unflattering images of human nature, we are tempted to interpret the past so as to reclaim that nature rather than to confront the significance of its undoing. A potential liability of critical history is thus how it entices one "as it were, *a posteriori* to give oneself a past from which one would like to be descended in opposition to the past from which one is descended" (22). If the monumental vision of the past allows portions of it to be "forgotten and despised, and flow away like an uninterrupted flood" (17), in deference to the heroic aspirations of that vision, its critical counterpart risks rewriting the past when its disclosures appear to profane human nature to the point of indignity.

Humiliated memory records those moments when history failed the individual and left him victim to what Nietzsche called the "blind power of facts . . . the tyranny of the actual" (49). It can retreat to no ideal world of thought as consolation to carry it through the trying times. Witnesses in the testimonies that we shall soon examine would have little difficulty understanding Nietzsche's warning to his overproud contemporaries: "Your knowledge does not complete nature but only kills your own" (50). The dilemma of such testimony is that it is orphaned from the hierarchic imagery dominating Nietzsche's thought and still influencing modern culture. The upward momentum of the invincible human spirit depends for its impact on the stability of the base from which it rises. Nietzsche could not have foreseen how utterly the Holocaust would erode that foundation for the surviving victims considered in this chapter; they did not foresee it themselves. The quest for pinnacles that infatuated the nineteenth-century mind and left a strong imprint on our own ended in the ashpits of Auschwitz and other deathcamps, where upward striving could do nothing to allay the human ruin. When Nietzsche admonished his peers, "Your manner of moving, that is, of climbing as a knower, is your doom" (50), he anticipated one of the gloomiest and most perplexing legacies of humiliated memory.

What future can such knowledge possibly serve? Testimony, and the memory that animates it, part company with history at this juncture, because the raison d'être of historical inquiry is its ability to shed light in two directions simultaneously. Otherwise history becomes mere antiquarianism. Stung by how their experiences have ravaged our commitment to culture, exponents of humiliated memory hold no illusions about the historical value of the *particularities* of their testimony for future generations. They remain dubious that those who cling to outmoded opinions of culture will understand their words. One myth generated by this skepticism is the view that the essential severity of such testimony is inaccessible to "outsiders." We can be sympathetic to this attitude, however, without embracing it. It can be—and has been—used as a convenient excuse for avoiding the subject entirely.

When Nietzsche concludes that "modern man drags an immense amount of indigestible knowledge stones around with him which on occasion rattle around in his belly," he offers us a way of hurdling the barrier of inaccessibility. Indigestible knowledge requires diagnosis to learn why the mind is out of harmony with its nourishment. Moreover, what was indigestible for Nietzsche's modern man might be positively toxic for us—hence the reluctance to ingest. Nietzsche attributes the inability to "swallow" certain evidence to "the remarkable opposition of an inside to which no outside and an outside to which no inside corresponds" (24), eclipsing the digestive metaphor with an intellectual formulation leading directly to our confrontation with humiliated memory.

The excess of knowledge Nietzsche speaks of refers in part to the constant accumulation of scientific information that outruns the capacity of the mind to internalize it, thus preventing the growth of a "higher unity" that is the true sign of a mature culture.

His diagnosis exposes a malady extending well into our own time. The revelations of humiliated memory exhibit a "lower disunity" that has nothing to do with culture; we gain access to it only by suspending temporarily all values associated with that increasingly dim ideal. Because his knowledge "taken in excess without hunger" (24) betrays a surfeit, Nietzsche urges his readers to "devote some thought to the problem of restoring the health of a people which has been impaired by history, to how it may recover its instincts and therewith its integrity" (25). We overcome the obstacle of inaccessibility to humiliated memory by abandoning language such as this and allowing knowledge, we might say, taken in excess *with* hunger, to pour into the vacuum.

That hunger is literal, not metaphorical; physical, not intellectual; personal, not public. Witnesses in oral testimonies are not concerned with restoring the health of a people that has been impaired by history (a problem, ironically, even more pressing for post–World War II Germany than for Nietzsche's German contemporaries); instead, they recall the image of a self insulted not only by history, but also by particular men and women like themselves. No form of integration into an outer public world exists for the inner chaos that disturbs their memory. As audience (and heirs to Nietzsche's quest for a higher unity), we long for such a correspondence to erase the barbaric opposition between what we hear and what we wish to know. But the more we listen, the more evidence we have that the question of inaccessibility may be our own invented defense against the invitation to imagine what is perfectly explicit in the remembered experience before our eyes and ears. Testimony like the following leaps beyond abstract discourse such as Nietzsche's, across thresholds of value-laden vocabulary, to the violation of the self in its most naked guise. Although the hunger from which virtually all victims suffered was unconditionally *un*related to their will (making it a thoroughly *non*-Nietzschean condition), actions resulting from it sometimes led to a diminished self-perception with which the present narrating memory must contend. We must choose our language carefully here. Victims were not *reduced* to certain behavior by their hunger; they were *driven* to it. One term is judgmental, the other is not. But it is clear from the struggle of many witnesses, from their expressions as well as their words, that they inhabit two worlds simultaneously: the one of "choiceless choice" *then;* the other of moral evaluation *now*. Harmony and integration are not only impossible—they are not even desirable.

Description can scarcely do justice to this testimony, whose visible moment lapses into silence as words exhaust their possibilities. Unlike a blank page (or, indeed, a written one), the mobile, anguished face before us duplicates the internalized drama of remembering and evaluating, regarding regretfully the spectacle of a self for which the speaker can find no role in his present existence:

> Of course there are all kinds of difficult periods that you cannot . . . for example, in that camp of Langenstein [a Nazi labor camp] I was so hungry that I don't know what I would have ate. We were sleeping on the floor and next to me was another camp inmate. I don't know how old he was—he looked old. And we just got our ration of bread, and he was already so sick that he couldn't eat that bread. And I was laying next to him, waiting that he should die, so that I can [prolonged pause] *grab* his bread.[3]

In the interval between the "can" and the painstakingly excavated *"grab"* lies an internalized evolution of remorse and humiliation given birth *only* through an audience's collaboration with that agonized instant of searching silence. To call it "inaccessible" is to negate entirely the significance of the confrontation. It proclaims its meaning through its very stillness.

Like what I have called deep and anguished memory, humiliated memory is an especially intense form of uncompensating recall. Instead of restoring a sense of power or control over a

disabling past (one of the presumed goals of therapy—and perhaps of history too), it achieves the reverse, reanimating the gov-
erning impotence of the worst moments in a distinctly non-
therapeutic way. It circles around Nietzsche's "tyranny of the
actual" gropingly, fearfully, but honestly—and this is a major
source of its value. It approaches some uncomfortable truths uncluttered by romantic conjectures. "I want to go back to [talking
about] the ghetto," says Martin L., after a pause in his testimony.
"What do you see in the ghetto?" asks the interviewer. "What
were the Germans doing?" "Killing people," replies the witness,
proceeding to a specific episode, the murder of his friend
Weisskopf, that activates the tumult of humiliated memory.
"They shot him three times," he remembers; then, after an interval, he adds: "When you see a lot of deaths, your mind gets numb,
you cannot do nothing. . . . Your humanity is gone. You're
speechless."

Martin L.'s comment leads in two equally valid directions. Obviously, he means that you cannot do anything, under the circumstances, *then*, at the time it was happening, because you felt helpless and afraid. But you also cannot do anything *now*, because
memory and the process of narrating offer no requital for the
earlier inaction. Hence, for Martin L., though remembering is
difficult, speaking is even more so, because it violates (and thus
reawakens) the condition of speechlessness in which he was left at
the moment of his friend's murder. He appropriates a piece of
Nietzsche's undigested "new" scientific knowledge to illustrate
his meaning. The brain, he says, is a computer that stores everything: "But when you want to 'file out,' the file is missing. You
can't pull it out."[4] Yet he does pull it out, only to discover that he is
still victimized by the blind power of facts, shorn of explanation or
value system, leaving him seized by the emptiness and futility
recorded through his computer image.

That computer has two operators: Martin L. is one, and we are
the other. If the file seems missing for him, what can it be for us?

How are we to imagine its very existence? Humiliated memory is driven by the need to share its contents and its conviction of the impossibility of doing so. If, in writing about the dilemma, we sometimes sound (in Jean Améry's trenchant phrase) like blind men speaking of color,[5] isn't this preferable to excluding color from the universe because we have never seen it? The concept of "you cannot do nothing" is so alien to the self-reliant Western mind (dominated by the idea of the individual as *agent* of his fate) that its centrality, its *blameless* centrality to the camp experience continues to leave one morally disoriented. The very principle of blameless inaction by former victims is foreign to the ethical premises of our culture, where we sometimes confuse such inaction with cowardice, self-indulgence, or indifference.

Dissatisfaction with the ethical premises of our culture riddles the testimony of Pierre T., whose own fate hinged precariously on his ultimate ability to detach himself from those premises. For a long time, he was unable to do this, so humiliated memory evolves only slowly in his narrative. He worked with the underground in France, helping downed Allied flyers return to England and making false papers for Jews, communists, and endangered refugees. He was proud of his Resistance work, until a certain incident gave him his first glimpse into how his way of thinking might be more vulnerable to assault than he originally believed. One day, a German officer was assassinated in the area where Pierre T. lived; Nazi officials announced that unless those responsible turned themselves in, they would execute one hundred hostages chosen at random from "detainees" in surrounding villages.

And in fact this is what happened. Twenty-seven of the hostages were taken from Pierre T.'s town, Chateaubriand. He remembers following on his bicycle the truck carrying the victims to the execution site, hearing the shots, then creeping up to see the nine posts against which they were killed, three at each one. The observation point becomes a kind of metaphorical knothole through which he "views" not only the physical evidence of SS brutality but also the intellectual results of the Resistance work in which he was engaged. At first, he admits, the idea of arrest, torture, deportation, or execution simply was not part of his imagination. When the possibility finally invaded his mind, after friends and associates were picked up by the Gestapo, he still refused to grow alarmed. The romance of secret opposition somehow insulated him against detection and seemed to insure his safety. The executions he witnessed unsettled his security. Then, early in 1944, he himself was seized, imprisoned, questioned, beaten, and eventually deported to Mauthausen.

Pierre T.'s education in atrocity continues here. Instead of celebrating the ethical premises that led him into the Resistance, he deplores the effects of his deportation. "They have made us lose our civilized ways" is his major complaint against his Nazi oppressors. "Gradually, gradually, you become a different person. And you do things that you would *never* think you'd do— and you do it." He worked as a gardener in Mauthausen, an innocent enough occupation, until he discovered that the material they used for fertilizer was human ashes, trucked from the crematorium. This inspires his comment on losing one's "civilized ways," which leads in turn to his account of how the experience depleted civilized words as well.

One day he develops boils all over his body and debates whether to report to the Revier (a primitive medical area or "infirmary" which, paradoxically, existed in most camps), since he has heard that selections (for execution) occur frequently in this place. He tells us that he explicitly refuses to call it a hospital because a "hospital is where they cure and take care of the ill." He finally decides to go, though he recalls how troubled he was then, and still is today, by a choice that is one in name only, since he had no control over the results. He was (and is) even more disturbed by the loss of moral dimension in his life because of the absence of control. He is unable to replace that displaced faculty through some form of justifying explanation, and this is the genesis of humiliated memory in his narrative. In the Revier was a comrade suffering from a facial phlegmon (a painful infected swelling) that caused him to moan constantly. The witness says that he and a friend used to *urinate* on a piece of cloth and apply it as a soothing poultice to relieve the pain. Finally one night three *Kapos* in the barrack, unable to sleep because of the noise, carried the man to a separate bunk, held his legs, and put a pillow over his mouth until he suffocated.

Telling this story is more than a form of testimony, designed to inform others; it is also a self-examination, a futile effort to exonerate oneself of "guilt" concerning a deed for which one bears no responsibility in the context of the event. In a reassertion of moral vigor, Pierre T. views with total disapproval the "different person" who stood by and watched a comrade being killed. Today he asks in despair, in dialogue with himself, "What could I say? What could you do? Nothing! Nothing!" Normally, we might expect a rehearsal like this to clarify choices and help to explain behavior. But in the absence of useful patterns, Pierre T. is left only with a sense of disjunction. "This is what you call hospital?" he asks at the end of this narrative moment. "How could I call that a hospital?"[6] Yet today, he still cherishes the values of healing and helping which that designation implies. The inversion of these values in Mauthausen leaves him alienated from his earlier self.

Perhaps contrary to expectation, surviving victims in these testimonies rarely complain about the loss of spiritual dignity. They suffer from the memory of physical constraints, insults to the body that continue to rankle and exasperate. Speaking of torture, which he experienced personally, Auschwitz survivor Jean Améry writes: "In almost all situations in life where there is bodily injury there is also the expectation of help; the former is compensated by the latter. But with the first blow from a policeman's fist, against which there can be no defense and which no helping hand will ward off, a part of our life ends and it can never again be revived."[7] Leo P., speaking of his own torture at the hands of the Gestapo, was convinced at the time that they intended to kill him and insists that he was not afraid to die. He felt not fear but shame, at being placed in a position where he was unable to assert his physicality. "They could get hold of me and kill me like a piece of cattle," he recalls, though it is not clear whether the source of his humiliation lies more in the results of remembering or in the original situation. If Améry is correct in concluding that part of one's life ends, never to be revived, then we must be content with the effect, which is vivid enough.

Leo P. speculates on the reluctance of some former victims to tell their stories. Though he is uncertain about the reasons, he suggests that for many the experience was too degrading to review. "I was ashamed," he confesses about his own encounter with the Gestapo. "And when I'm ashamed, I don't like to talk about it." Asked what the ordeal has left him with, he replies that some people are beasts, and there's nothing you can do about it, while others will risk their lives for you, and these he respects. But then he adds, "I've also learned that not everyone who is arrested by the Gestapo was a hero. Lots of cowards were arrested and brought to concentration camps."[8] If Pierre T. could respond to this "insight," he would argue that the witness has allowed language to impede his vision of the past. Just as *hospital* deflects our attention from the real nature of brutality in Mauthausen, so words like *hero* and *coward* create an artificial framework for understanding the response of the dishonored body to torture or starvation.

Améry illuminates this distinction with a lucid personal example. One day in Auschwitz a Polish prisoner foreman (*not* a Nazi official, against whom Améry could not have risked a gesture of opposition), who had been a professional criminal, struck him in the face for some trifling offense. That was how he dealt with all the Jews under his command, Améry observes, continuing:

In open revolt I struck [him] in the face in turn. My human dignity lay in this punch to his jaw—and that it was in the end I, the physically much weaker man, who succumbed and was woefully thrashed, meant nothing to me. Painfully beaten, I was satisfied with myself. But not, as one might think, for reasons of courage and honor, but only because I had grasped well that there are situations in life where our body is our entire self and our entire fate. I was my body and nothing else: in hunger, in the blow that I suffered, in the blow that I dealt. My body, debilitated and crusted with filth, was my calamity. My body, when it tensed to strike, was my physical and metaphysical dignity.[9]

Those still in the grip of an irrelevant vocabulary—for which they cannot be blamed, since society has yet to face the implications of acknowledging its irrelevance—might struggle with Améry's notion of a metaphysical dignity residing *in* the body. For Améry, attitude was dispossessed of value by a situation that canceled its power to affirm the self.

Améry's physical gesture, pathetic as it may have seemed in terms of consequences (though it was far more dangerous than he concedes, since he was lucky only to have been thrashed, not beaten to death), collapsed the transcendent into the tangible, fusing them, rejecting what Leo P. had deplored as the well-intentioned naïveté on the part of people who want to believe the best of others (and, one might add, of themselves). He begins by accepting the difficult axiom that in the camp environment to "be a Jew meant the acceptance of the death sentence imposed by the world as a world verdict." Because Pierre T. and Leo P. were non-Jews, they did not have to face this extreme encounter with their personal doom. Améry's fight against humiliated memory is thus complicated by a factor they do not have to contend with. "I became a person," he says, "not by subjectively appealing to my abstract humanity but by discovering myself within the given social reality as a rebelling Jew and by realizing myself as one" (91).[10]

Améry's leisure to work out the implications of this process in a written text illustrates some of the distinctions I have been trying to develop between such documents and oral testimony. Just as his blow against the Polish foreman was virtually unprecedented, so his carefully elaborated assessment of the event reveals his need to come to grips with it in an orderly intellectual fashion. He dismisses heroic intentions but refuses to portray himself in the morally helpless condition that characterizes parallel moments in oral testimony. "When the Kapo drew back his arm to strike me," he confesses, "I didn't stand firm like a cliff, but ducked. And still, I tried to initiate proceedings to restore my dignity, and beyond physical survival that provided me with just the slightest chance to survive the nightmare morally also" (90).

Améry, in other words, retrospectively defines the antidote to humiliated memory, though he would be among the first to admit its scarcity, not to say total unavailability, for most victims in the concentration and death camps. Moreover, the very fact that his memory dredges up this single instance of revolt and clings to it almost as the sole example of possible moral survival convinces even him of how flimsy that shred is. One hesitates—though one is tempted—to see his eventual suicide as an admission of the final triumph of humiliated memory, that is, of the ultimate failure to escape the assaults on the moral self during his Holocaust-determined existence. His essays were an attempt to deliver himself from the sentence of the camps—that the "deprivation of dignity was nothing other than the potential deprivation of life" (89). He had also written, we recall, that "with the first blow from a policeman's fist, against which there can be no defense and which no helping hand will ward off, a part of our life ends and it can never again be revived." Yet his own blow against the Polish Kapo he sees as just such an effort at revival. The contradiction, however, is only superficial; like most surviving victims, Améry too speaks (or writes) with two voices. His writing constitutes the reconciliation or the integration whose success oral testimony dramatically disputes.

Humiliated memory covers a much broader landscape than the realm of the self that Améry investigates. Perhaps this is one reason why witnesses are at a loss to recover from its effects. George S., for example, is unable to separate his own ordeal from the reality surrounding him, and this in turn prevents him from even thinking in terms of a personal recovery. Work and hunger, work and hunger, is how he describes the rhythm of his days in the Lodz ghetto. He was unable to share his bread ration with anyone, he recalls with troubled demeanor: "If I would, then I would die." He tells of mothers concealing their children to avoid a selection. One mother's child was found and taken; she went berserk, and began revealing the hiding places of the other children. The disintegration of basic life supports undermined the very integrity that Améry sought to cling to, especially when the security of one's entire family was at stake. The consequences, as George S. recalls, were devastating, for him and the community as well:

> I was ashamed of the whole thing—it was so shameful. It was so degrading. You were completely turned. Hunger was devastating to the human spirit; it was devastating to the human body, and you didn't know how to function. Families were beginning to—some were even fighting among themselves over a piece of bread. Some were stealing from each other. It was horrible. Some became informers to the Germans for a piece of bread. They thought they would be saved, and [would save] their families. Everybody did what they could, just to save their family.[11]

Lament rather than censure, George S.'s testimony reveals a far more extensive collapse of what we would call dignity than do some of the previous examples, but only to remind us what a privileged word *dignity* is in the vocabulary of atrocity. Some behavior cannot be "undone," its finality being its only legacy. The "shame" that George S. feels as he remembers what he cannot approve of now and couldn't condemn then leaves a permanent scar on his life.

My imagery is probably inexact here: a scar is a reminder of a curable condition, a past injury healed in the present. What we are really speaking of, as the testimony of Leon H. makes clear, is a festering wound, a blighted convalescence. His story of survival is everywhere afflicted by the scourge of his loss and his own remembered inability to hinder it. The infection begins when two SS searching for valuables come to his family's apartment in the Lodz ghetto and force his partially paralyzed mother to tear up some floorboards. Because she moves too slowly, they kick her mercilessly with their boots; she dies a few days later. "That was my anger," he declares, in conjunction with this description. "I am angry at the world. The world stood still, when we were burning." It is not difficult to discern from this scenario, however, a more specific rage, directed first at the gratuitous cruelty of his mother's murderers, and then at himself, for being forced to remain mute witness to that deed. He speaks at length of the anger that remains on his face today; it frightened his children, he insists, as they were growing up.

This generalized hostility against reality is one of the main sources of humiliated memory. It expresses a latent resentment toward a world that had betrayed the individual by promoting values that proved useless in the presence of catastrophe, especially values espousing family loyalty. This is ironically confirmed when Leon H. returns to his apartment in the ghetto one day after having gone to collect some soup to find that the building has been emptied in a roundup during his absence. Instead of hiding, he rushes to the train station to join his father and brothers for deportation—to Auschwitz, as it turns out. Devotion to family unity, which he cherishes, rivals the family's collapse, which he can scarcely bear to describe. As each member disappears, the remaining ones become more precious, his last links to normality. The illusion that he still controlled those links sustained him, though it was shaken on arrival at Auschwitz, when his father, too old to work at fifty-three, was sent to the left, never to be seen again.

His narrative represents in part the consequences of his confrontation with that illusion and the subsequent erosion of his tranquility. The principle of family unity continues to deceive him as he and his older brother are chosen to be sent to a factory at Görlitz. He decides to "take a chance," as he puts it, reaches out unobserved and pulls his younger brother into the group destined for transport, thus "saving" him from probable death in Auschwitz. But one day at Görlitz his younger brother is late for roll call and is beaten so badly that he dies soon after, in his brother's arms. "I cannot forget this," says Leon H. "I'm trying to." His humiliation is evident in his voice as he declares: "Human life was like a fly." Marching from Görlitz as the Russians approach, they stop in a barn where, as he reports, "I ate garbage, whatever I could find . . . . I closed my eyes and swallowed."[12] The decomposition of his present "integrated"[13] self proceeds through the imagery of his narrative, which records a physical vulnerability that, Améry's example notwithstanding, no gesture can protect. Refusing to eat garbage, his brother slowly wastes away, though Leon H. shares his soup with him, while, as he says, the lice ate them both up.

Anyone paying attention to his language will notice the constant shifts from the human to the less-than-human frames of reference, both of which inhabit Leon H.'s memory. As the Russian advance slows, they return to Görlitz, though his brother, too weak to walk, is sent back by truck. "But when I came back [on foot]," recalls Leon H., "I couldn't find him any more." Later he learned that his brother, apparently not deemed worth saving, had been left outside the barracks and had frozen to death. Now he is alone, and the substructure of his narrative becomes clear: his own survival is no transcendence of, but a defeat by, the death of his mother, his father, and his brothers. "How can you live with that?" he asks plaintively. "Everybody was gone from me." His inner distress grows increasingly evident, as he continues: "Since then I couldn't get somebody. I live in torture all these years. Suicide [in tears now] was on my mind. But I had family [meaning his *present* family]; I loved them so much. How do you explain that? How do you tell?" The burden of "that" (the loss of his family and his relation to, his *involvement in*, that loss, as he imagines it through humiliated memory) encounters the reality of "this" (his love for his present family), but only to intensify the disjunction between the two. "I am trying hard," he concludes. "How can you forget? I cannot forgive. I don't know how. . . . I've tried to."

The illogic of juxtaposing contradictory positions—"Since then I couldn't get somebody" versus "But I had family—I loved them so much"—doesn't occur to Leon H. because he has never assimilated the past of which he speaks into the unity of his present life. His disquiet is triggered by his last brother's death, frozen and alone, and he doesn't know how to merge this detail into a continuous narrative. The feeling of incredulity that overwhelms him— "Who will believe? Nobody believes it. Because I don't believe it myself"—insulates the episode from normal adversities and their nostrums. The very mechanism of testimony forbids forgetting, while his resolute "I cannot forgive" confirms the absence of a procedure for pardoning, even if he were searching for such consolation. Forgiveness functions as a relief and a release, disengaging the individual from the trauma of an event hostile to the hopeful future. But we are not even certain (and perhaps neither is he) of the thrust of his use of "forgive." Is it toward himself? The Nazis? The past? History? The world?

His dilemma resembles the astonishing, unsettling experience of training a light on darkness and still seeing only darkness. That violates the laws of physics, as his experience breaches morality's decrees. Whether we speak of his mother, his father, or his brothers, because there is no connection between the victim's life and the victim's fate, humiliated memory is compelled to dwell in a twilight realm that ethical insight can never illuminate. It can thus never be joined to the world he inhabits now. This suggests a permanent duality, not exactly a split or a doubling but a parallel existence. He switches from one to the other without synchronization because he is reporting not a *sequence* but a *simultaneity*. In the same breath, he can speak of loving his present family and of twice considering suicide *after* the war. He can't reconcile his love now with his loss then. "So much pain, so much pain," he complains. "How to get rid of it?"

His apparent monologue is really a dialogue between his two selves: "Even now the joy I have from my children [they are both physicians] . . . I should have been the happiest man in the world. And I'm searching for how—the children were so good. They listened to me." His sense of agency in the raising of his children contrasts sharply with the memory of his impotence in the ruin of his other family. He uses an extraordinary image to explain the impact of that festering wound on his current felicity: "Still a band-aid. I can't feel that I have a full satisfaction of it. No matter how much joy I accomplish now." We have to remember that this is not subjective complaint but objective description. Recall evokes what he cannot revoke.

The division seems to operate on every level, continuing the condition of victimhood far beyond the limits of historical time. "You go back and see a world of plenty here, food and everything," says Leon H., "and I think of starvation all the time. I'd dream of starvation every night. Every morning I get up, I say to them 'O, I'm not there. I'm here.' For me it isn't so easy to live with this kind of a torture." He dwells in a permanent state of anxiety, derived from a deficient moral system that allows no compensating or redemptive response to the anguish that possesses him. Although explanations elude him (as indeed they do us), his search for a suitable language makes his testimony a locus classicus for the kind of futility that is a defining feature of humiliated memory. More clearly than any other form of recall, it recognizes how the Holocaust experience murdered part of the future, even for those who survived it. "We envied the dead ones," he confesses. "At that time when my mother was killed—she died— we were *glad* that she doesn't have to suffer any more." The insufficiency of both "killed" and "died" leaps from his lines, as does the reversal of the natural momentum of being. More than its other versions, humiliated memory is a prison, even though it represents an honest confrontation with an abnormal past that resists normalization. "The rest of my life I'll be suffering," grieves Leon H. "I wish I could heal myself. How?"

Numerous strategies are available to individuals who wish to escape the burden of a vexatious past: forget, repress, ignore, deny, or simply falsify the facts. For reasons difficult to ascertain, what I have called humiliated memory seems immune to these forms of evasion. Leon H.'s chronicle helps us understand why, as it strips away facades to expose an internal maelstrom that cannot settle into a tranquil pool, *even* when it appears to have a reason to do so. Months after his liberation, Leon H. discovers that his sister is still alive somewhere in Germany. He locates her in Regensburg, arriving three days before her impending wedding. A happy occasion, at last! "I knew my parents were gone," he exclaims. "I knew my brothers were gone. My only hope was my sister. It was also very torturous." He cannot separate his sister's marriage from the disintegrated family it reminds him of— a contaminated joy. He speaks of loneliness *beginning* after their arrival in America, of a constant inner pressure and an anger he can neither suppress nor disguise.

Humiliated memory, as his story illustrates, is *prospective* as well as retrospective: "Everything is in *front* of me," he says. "I can't get rid of it. It's like a screen, and everything moves." History is thus prophecy as well as memory, though what it divines resembles a throbbing tooth that fails to respond to treatment. The screen he mentions replays the events of his Holocaust past as reminders of what he sees as his inadequate role in the drama of that time. But he knows that no future "performance" can improve the psychological climate in which he finds himself. Hence, when the interviewer asks if he has any final words, his reply betrays personal depths far more critical than the political surface he seems to address: "Hit back very hard, before you get hit." His message to the world is also a telegram to himself about the "too-late-ness" of a significant portion of his life, and this is for him a source of unending frustration and regret.[14]

Leon H.'s life is not a solitary example of this quandary, though other published testimonies do not often speak of it. The search for lost time is not conducted in Proustian fashion, because the past it uncovers does not fall into an intricate pattern illuminating the present but stops at the remembered disorder as if it were an insurmountable barrier. These insulated moments seem to have been preserved, untarnished by the passage of years. Not surprisingly, they frequently involve what appears to the witness today to be a family obligation unfulfilled. Viktor C., for example, describes the roundup of himself, his wife, and their nine-month-old infant:

> This was summer. Outside there was a bench. So we sat on the bench. My wife [was] holding the kid in her arms. . . . In my head, what to think first of. You want to do something and you know you're in a corner. You can't do *anything*. And when somebody asks me now 'Why didn't you fight?' [voice breaking, tears, a tone and look of utter despair at the moment remembered] I ask them 'How would *you* fight in such a situation?' My wife holds a child, a child stretches out their arms to me, I look at him. . . . Me, a man crying.

He is separated from his wife and son and sent to a labor camp near a steelworks in Czechoslovakia. Later he learns that together with his mother and grandmother, they were deported to Auschwitz, where they were murdered. He volunteers the detail that on the ramp at Auschwitz, as he heard, his wife was selected for work in the camp but refused to leave the baby and so went to her death with the rest of the family. One need not probe very deeply to see the link between his own sense of impotence on that bench and his wife's determination, as it was reported to him and as he chooses to repeat it to us. Although it doesn't alter his earlier-stated conviction that "You can't do *anything*," it intensifies his desperate vision of how what he now calls "the will to *outlive*" thwarted communal efforts to survive.

"Outliving" on its surface level may mean outliving your persecutors but also implies outliving those who did not manage to stay alive. This is one of the most pervasive microbes infecting humiliated memory. Viktor C. offers a stark example. He was transferred from one labor camp to another, always with his brother. At Fünfteichen, a subcamp of Gross Rosen, he was working in the Revier, when his brother was sent there because of an illness. From here, he says, there was no exit for the ill, except as a corpse. He himself was offered a better (and safer) job in the camp but couldn't decide whether to stay with his brother or strengthen his own chance to outlive the others. He calls that enigma his albatross, the resultant wound a hurt that he has tried all his life to heal, without success: "I left him there and I survived [prolonged weeping]. If I forget anything, this I will never forget. I try to justify my act with a practical approach. Can anybody understand it? Can anybody know my pain, my agony . . . that never leaves me? [Sobbing] I can talk maybe calmly or maybe people think calmly about somebody else, although it burns inside—not about this."[15] The total absence of any emotional or psychological chemistry to mix, blend, or fuse the practice of outliving with the principle of fraternal love ignites the inward moral burning that Viktor C. speaks of—an unsanctified eternal flame that memory feeds and nothing can quench.

Transferred to Flossenburg, where he joins a Leichenkommando (corpse detail) whose job was to transport the bodies to the crematorium at Gross Rosen, Viktor C. recalls a particular episode that would have vivid symbolic reverberations, were its literal echo not so devastating. One day he encounters a young boy tearing through the pile of corpses who, when asked what he is doing, replies, "I'm looking for my father." Humiliated memory is a form of response to that frantic search, recognizing as it does the futility of rescuing family "connections" of this sort. It is the most difficult and cumbersome kind of remembering, because it unearths the burden of a way of dying that allows for no ritual of mourning that might appease or console memory. One has but to compare the search for (or escape from) a real or symbolic father that is a mainstay of literary vision with the spectacle of the boy on the mound of corpses to grasp the essential and irreconcilable divergence between the imagined quest and the remembered loss.

Curiously, the return to normality only exasperates this situation. Some time after coming to America, Irene W. learns that a friend's husband has died. She attends the funeral and suddenly realizes that it is the first one she has ever been to, though as a teenager in Auschwitz she had frequent contact with persons dying . Ironically, however, nothing has prepared her for the routines of normal dying. She reports that she didn't know where to stand or what would happen next. "Oddly," she admits, "I left my whole family there to die, but I didn't know how to behave at a funeral."[16] The formal ritual for one dead individual reminds her that for her parents there was neither grave nor ritual for mourning. Their disappearance, she insists, was from a different time and a different world; she wonders how to explain to the mourners today what it must have been like to die anonymously in the gas chambers.

The discrepancy extends beyond modes of dying to what Irene W. describes as the coexistence in her present life of the past event and the present event. Contemporary cultural assumptions, like the funeral ritual itself, promote values totally alien to what Irene W. has in mind. An extreme but trenchant example of that alienation resounds in the words of Bronia K., who participated in the Bialystok ghetto uprising: "We were brought up in too humanistic [a] way. We learned how to love, but not how to kill. And now we have to learn how to kill, how to fight. And it was very difficult."[17] But just as Irene W. cannot use her Auschwitz experience of atrocity to learn her role in the normal drama of dying, so Bronia K. can hardly exploit the lesson of Bialystok in her current life. The precarious coexistence that Irene W. speaks of is less an achievement than an unavoidable necessity, though still a tribute to the remarkable resilience of the human self.

But even that resilience had its limits. At its frankest and most intimate moments, humiliated memory plunges into an erratic universe void of meaning, spiritually adrift, remote from empathetic understanding, bereft of value. Helena B., transferred from Auschwitz to Stutthof, tells of the day when a friend came up to her and said, "You have to help me." In her hand, we are told, the friend is carrying a woman's *foot* (I still recall my brow wrinkling at this testimony, as I winced and thought, "I haven't heard her right"):

> And she had a leg, the bottom part, a *foot* in her hand, like this [gesturing, describing the shape]. One girl was laying there in the hospital, her leg broke off. It froze. And she didn't feel it. She awaked, and she looked, and there was her foot next to her. So she [Helena B.'s friend] said [to her]: "Come, please. Help me to bury it." And after seeing so many deaths, and everything, I couldn't do that. This hit me the worst: that one foot hurt me more than everything there. I just became hysterical.[18]

It is impossible to verify the details of this testimony today, though the precision with which the witness reports the episode suggests a core of accuracy. A doctor in the Revier might have removed the frostbitten foot to prevent the spread of gangrene; or the woman may have already died, the fragile frostbitten foot of her emaciated corpse having become detached through mishandling. Whatever the exact cause, the fragmentation of the physical self conveyed by this stark image remains overpowering. The skeptical mind would like to dispense with such testimony, questioning its authenticity. Such impulses are understandable, duplicating as they do the first responses to Gerhardt Riegner's initial telegrams from Switzerland conveying information about the planned annihilation of European Jewry. By now we should be able to recognize that such skepticism betrays less about the witness than about her audience. Among the many victims of the Holocaust was the classical ideal of the beauty of the human *form*. Humiliated memory testifies to the erosion of that ideal; together with the violation of family unity, it is the least forgettable, the least adaptable, the most disabling (and hence most threatening) of its contributions. Helena B.'s hysteria simply responds to a fragmentation that is without analogy, more than she can manage.

The body can be maimed in many ways, not only through mutilation. The disfigured self that results illustrates the intertwining of the physical and metaphysical that Améry described as one of the legacies of the camp experience. As preface to a vivid example of this condition, Edith P. recalls a moment in a brick factory near her town in Hungary, where she and the rest of her family had been transferred before deportation to Auschwitz. "I still see my mother sitting in that crowded room," she asserts. "It was hot and she was gasping, saying 'I need air.'" As she speaks, the witness clutches at her own throat, panting, exclaiming: "At the time I couldn't understand what was wrong with my mother, because it wasn't that hot, but today I can understand. It was the anguish that was bothering her. She had six children and she couldn't do anything to help them. So *now* I understand." Her father, she adds, sat there for three days and didn't say one word. But in the process of recovering the significance of her mother's physical gesture and the feeling of suffocation it evinced, as she works through her own interpretation of the event, Edith P. exposes the moral paralysis that such a gesture conceals and reveals. Instead of rousing the relief and satisfaction that normally accompany perception, the reenacted moment only intensifies distress.

Throughout her testimony, Edith P. alternates between a fierce insistence that "There's one thing that they didn't do to us. They didn't break our spirit. I was very proud," and frank descriptions of episodes undermining that pride. Neither triumphs over the other; neither cancels the other. But because circumstances in Auschwitz had little respect for individual pride, one's evidence does not always confirm one's conviction. Edith P., for example, tells of an instance when she was suffering severely from dysentery but had enough "humanity" in her, as she reports, to prevent her from relieving herself inside the barracks. She was too ashamed. But she could not go to the latrine, because an order for *Blocksperre* had been issued, a temporary sealing of the barracks while a search was carried out for two missing inmates. She violated the order and left anyway, only to meet a particularly brutal SS woman guard who, learning of her mission, on the spot told her to turn around and gave her ten lashes on the back with her whip. Although she managed not to cry, Edith P. admits that she was humiliated. She explains that the pain was not the problem. "Physical pain you can stand," she says, "but how can you bear the emotional pain?"

Just as her mother's sense of suffocation projected an image of the self thwarted by one's situation—in this case, the mother's instinct and obligation to care for her children—so Edith P.'s public loss of dignity and the attendant emotional pain imply a complex system of motive and effect largely beyond her control. "My body healed," she confesses, "but it never healed my soul, that I had been humiliated this way, in front of my family." (Her sister-in-law and the sister-in-law's three sisters had witnessed the whipping from the barracks.) Decades later (though she makes no allusion to this), the observation that "They didn't break our spirit" seems an irrelevancy rather than a contradiction. Curiously, she had used that expression while describing the natural function of elimination during the boxcar journey to the deathcamp, where victims, though confined, still exerted some control over their conduct. When the "rules" changed in Auschwitz, when Edith P. discovered that shame made no difference because it was not allied to dignity as she had supposed (all of this having nothing to do with her, of course, but with her persecutors), then humiliation replaced pride. Descriptive language is governed in one instance by the self's control over circumstances (however limited), and in the other by its total victimization. Humiliated memory ruefully exposes the difference.

With unusual clarity, Edith P. distinguishes between the common premises that lead to the defense of the spirit and vacant spaces that nurture the possibility, if not the necessity, of what I have called humiliated memory. Much depends on the breakdown of familiar mental categories. After arriving in Auschwitz, she says, "you don't think what goes through your mind. You say to yourself, 'Well, here I am in Auschwitz. And where am I, and what's going to happen to me?'" You lose the ability to think about yourself in the situation in which you find yourself (reminiscent of her mother's experience of suffocation just before deportation—an anticipation of what she is speaking about here). For example, she reflects, one can say "When I get married," or "If I die," or "If someone I love dies," or "If I have a child," or "When I get a job," or "If I have some money," creating certain theoretical probabilities and then imagining oneself into those situations because we know how to think about them—they have precedents in our own or other people's experience. But no one before has ever said "When I get to Auschwitz, I . . . "; therefore, the mind remains blank. There's no way, she maintains, of imagining it in advance or of thinking about it when you're in the midst of it, because mental process functions not in a vacuum but in relation to something that happened previously, that you had felt, thought, read, seen, or heard about.

Thus when Edith P. confesses that in Auschwitz you didn't feel and you didn't think, she is recording not a mental and emotional numbness endemic to the place but a totally foreign atmosphere inhospitable to the responses that normally define a human being. The resultant disunity, which alienates one from one's own nature, remains in memory if not in daily fact a perpetual source of despair, even though it may not dominate one's present life. Edith P. reports with pride how with the infinite patience of her husband as support she managed to reclaim her healthy mind and not be destroyed by what happened. But in virtually the same breath, her eyes turn inward, and though she appears to be looking at the camera, she obviously is back in the hostile climate of her camp experience. She admits that it is very difficult to achieve a healthy mind when you can't prove to anyone that you had a past, who your mother and father were, where you went to school, where you lived, what you did as a child, who your friends were. A past consumed not by time but by violence, by atrocity, floods her memory, as she introduces an image that is the exact antithesis of the restoration that she has just been talking about: "You are totally uprooted."

Just as Auschwitz disrupted her consecutive life in the past, so it continues its influence by disrupting her consecutive narrative in the present. The discontinuous "form" of oral testimony often duplicates the disjunctions of the camp experience itself, thus exposing the witness once more to the status of victim through the very process of overcoming it via narration. Although the chronology of her story has brought her through liberation to America, a family, and the ostensible return to normalcy, Edith P. reverts repeatedly to the wellspring of her existence today by persisting in her attempt to reconstruct for "us" the reality of Auschwitz. And

her description does indeed test our ability to enter sympathetically into her remembering, because it draws from the depths of
memory an ambivalent vision that leaves her *and* her audience
dissatisfied.

In spite of her impressive and at times distinguished eloquence
as a witness, Edith P. stumbles when she asks for the third or
fourth time in her testimony, "Well, how shall I describe to you
how Auschwitz was?" Oddly, she has been doing just that in the
previous few minutes, but the subject has been the mutual support that she, her sister-in-law, and the latter's three sisters were
able to offer one another in the barrack and bunk that they shared.
Language has no difficulty celebrating humanitarian impulse. But
admirable as these efforts were, the witness knows that they do
not reflect the inner reality of Auschwitz. She pauses, looks
down, and for a moment seems to lose her power of speech.
Everything conspires to remind her of her inadequacy to face this
issue. But then she proceeds, as if in pursuit of a controlled *inac-
curacy*, not as a calculated breach of truth, but as a concession to
what words cannot do, an assent to the partial collapse of verbal
power. An audience bred on the assurance that in the beginning
was the word must now adjust itself to a vision uncluttered by that
premise. As Edith P. describes Auschwitz as a "hell on earth," the
look on her face ratifies her belief that she has uttered a commonplace. Then she says, "The days. Let me tell you about the
days," and her subsequent excursion into transformational imagery reminds us how conventional designations deceive, how vulnerable we become when deprived of the security of a precise and
well-honed language: "We got up at three o'clock in the morning
to work, and by 4:00 or 4:30 in the summers the sun was up. I
swear to you, the sun was not bright. The sun was red, or it was
black to me. . . . The sun was never life to me. It was destruction.
It was never beautiful. We almost forgot what life was all about."
We might call this the voice of the denatured self, if by "natured"
we mean the ability to ally ourselves with the positive rhythms of

existence. The reversal of expectation that characterized the Holocaust universe here corrupts the power of observation, though that description seems questionable only if we refuse to allow the tyranny of facts in Auschwitz to destabilize the site from which we view them. From another point of view, Edith P. creates a new impurity of seeing *and* saying, in which black suns remind us of the "black milk" of Paul Celan's celebrated *Todesfuge*.

Humiliated memory, because of the necessarily darker outlook of its utter honesty, entices us into a milieu that seeks to compel our belief despite contrary instincts. The witness herself, in this and most other instances, is not immune to such resistance. Edith P.'s reflections on the days at Auschwitz at first prompt her to question the meaning of all the victims' lives: "You know, we were supposed to be the chosen people. I never believed in that." But this hint of terminal despair is more than she is willing to bear; she weeps, then continues: "But maybe we are chosen because we always stay humanitarians in spite of that. We took care of each other, and maybe we were chosen for that."[19] But it is clear from the skeptical tone of her voice that she is engaged in a desperate struggle rather than a simple declaration of triumph; the subsequent moments of her interview, the closing ones, confirm this.

The teleological thrust of "chosen" echoes more than scriptural authority. It represents what Austrian writer Ilse Aichinger, whose *Herod's Children* (*Die grössere Hoffnung*, 1947) was one of the first fictional efforts to wrestle with the legacy of the Nazi debacle, called "the formation of correlations." One has only to compare the word "chosen" with its synonym "selected" to see how the Holocaust experience has beguiled the search for meaning through language into the practice of deception. Aichinger is wary of this procedure: "No one can demand that I produce correlations as long as they are avoidable. I am not indiscriminate as life is, a better designation for which has also just escaped me. Let's call it *life*, perhaps it deserves nothing better. *Living* is not a special word and *dying* isn't either. Both are assailable, disguising meaning instead of defining it."[20] Like "chosen" and "selected," living and "living" (in Auschwitz) and dying and "dying" (again in Auschwitz) do not mean the same. Aichinger's suspicion of correlations illuminates the (losing) rearguard action that humiliated memory fights to rescue some connection between past and present, thus normalizing the self by revaluing what has been devalued.

If Edith P. succeeds in her resolution but fails in her evidence, she only validates Aichinger's conviction that the heritage from the worst atrocities of the Third Reich sabotaged the formation of such correlations. Near the end of her testimony she certifies, "They wanted us to become animals and I haven't seen one, not one," and for her this reassertion of the human is certainly valid (though it doesn't alter the humiliating mistreatment she received at the hands of the female SS guard). But the chronology she adopts in her narrative, which *ends* in Auschwitz as she tries to define the feeling of uprootedness that she had mentioned earlier, reveals a deeper level of exile from which she cannot escape. Her preserved humanity is no consolation. There's my family, my husband, my children, she concedes, and that's wonderful: "And there's the camp—that other part of my life which I inhabit alone." Such a frank avowal defeats the formation of correlations on which the integrated self depends. Humiliated memory dwells in and on that impenetrable circle of isolation. "In my darkest hours," laments Edith P., "I sometimes wish that the Germans could experience the uprootedness that I feel, the feeling that there's nobody to share with when you have a baby . . . someone you could call up to share your joy or your unhappiness with. And I've had no one." Absence here cancels presence, as she recounts the loss of her parents, all but one of her brothers, her sister, their wives and husbands, their children. We can only conjecture about the extent of its reign. Of its importance, she leaves no doubt. "I want to share it," she concludes, "with someone who knows me *really*. There isn't even a grave to go and cry to. It's not easy to live this way."[21]

What radiates from that "*really*"? Exiled first from normal living or normal dying, and now from normal grieving, Edith P. ends her testimony with the discovery of a permanent estrangement, a missing pattern that might draw her Auschwitz self into a familiar social milieu and give it some meaning in the present. Her manner of telling, her content with its unusual form (like that of many other surviving victims), bears an uncanny resemblance to Hayden White's description of the discourse of the early medieval annalist, though the dissimilarities between that naive method of historical representation and personal Holocaust memories are far greater than the affinities. White writes of these annals: "Everywhere it is the forces of disorder, natural and human, the forces of violence and destruction, that occupy the forefront of attention. The account deals in qualities rather than agents, figuring forth a world in which things happen to people rather than one in which people do things." Up to a point, this is the experience of which the surviving victim speaks. White reinforces the apparent resemblance (though of course not intentionally) when he adds that "the annalist's account calls up a world in which need is everywhere present, in which scarcity is the rule of existence, and in which all of the possible agencies of satisfaction are lacking or absent or exist under imminent threat of death."[22] But the annalist says none of this; White as analyst "reads" the implications from the rigid frame of years on which the annalist hangs the data of his evidence.

The key factor is a responsive and transforming consciousness. At this point, annals become narrative, and narrative makes possible the birth of history for succeeding generations. One aim of history is *inclusion*, in two senses: it assembles the important data of experience, and it makes them accessible to an audience, the awareness of whose consciousness is a premise of the historian's efforts. A major source of despair for humiliated memory is the almost totally *excluding* effect of its revelations, on the witness's own present consciousness, as well as the audience's, at least as the witness perceives it. Thus this is not history as we ordinarily understand it; and though we have the option of rejecting such testimony as a form of history, we also face the challenge of enlarging our notion of what history may be, what the Holocaust has made of it, and how it urges us to reconsider the relation of past to present (in a less hopeful way, to be sure), and of both to the tentative future.

The great feat of the historian is to impose through consciousness an image of narrative coherence to allay what White calls "our nightmares about the destructive power of time" (11). When Edith P. speaks of "that other part of my life which I inhabit alone," she returns momentarily to the state of preconsciousness that the annalist shares. But unlike the annalist, she cannot remain there. Her demand for sequence and continuity emerges in the conjunction of "There isn't even a grave to go and cry to" with "It's not easy to live that way." The presence of a consciousness to *recognize* the disintegration of a bond linking living and dying, and hence of the human and moral forces that constitute our sense of a civilized society, leaves the witness bereft. But *our* perception of the dilemma could be construed as a breakthrough in understanding for us—of the limitations and indeed the fabrications of consciousness, and of the role that the search for "possible agencies of satisfaction" has played in the evolution of public and private systems of order.

Such perception also furnishes insight into how the Holocaust, as reflected in these personal testimonies, has disrupted that role. Humiliated memory is defeated by its own efforts to rescue itself from the cul-de-sac of what I earlier referred to as uncompensated and uncompensatable loss. Consciousness invites us to build exits from this cul-de-sac, transforming personal stories of unredeemable atrocity back into triumphant accounts of survival. As we have seen, even one voice of the surviving victim participates in this endeavor. But humiliated memory, reluctantly, to be sure, exhibits the futility of such attempts. Its discourse runs contrary to the hopes and expectations of the audience and of its own other self. Unfinished chronicle vies with completed narrative history. "The demand for closure in the historical story," Hayden White suggests, "is a demand . . . for moral meaning, a demand that sequences of real events be assessed as to their significance as elements of a moral drama" (21). These oral testimonies may offer versions of closure, but they are such as to undermine the conception of closure that feeds on the need for the realization of prior ethical ideals.

This is strikingly illustrated by the account of Menachem S., whose odyssey of departure and return from his family would seem to fulfill the "elements of a moral drama" that White mentions. When he is five years old, his solicitous parents, anticipating their doom, decide to smuggle him out of the Plaszow labor camp in the hope that some Polish Christian family will give him refuge. They bribe a guard; then, as he remembers, they tie a scarf around his neck and promise to come to get him after the war. Since then, he interjects, apparently sanctioning the idea of moral drama, he's learned that "when you promise something, no matter what happens, what catastrophe . . . if you promise something, you have to do it." Such language, as it turns out, issuing as it does from the voice of normalcy, supplies an *un*reliable guide for hearing the rest of his testimony, though consciousness strains in the opposite direction, longing for "happy endings." The details conspire toward such a conclusion when he adds that at the last moment his mother thrust into his hand her high school identification card with her picture on it. "You keep my picture, so when we meet again . . . " she says, creating a design for closure, for rediscovery and reunion, for continuity and restored normalcy that is built into the expectations of historical consciousness by legends like those of Odysseus and the Prodigal Son.

Then he leaves. Following his mother's instructions, he goes first to a brothel, where presumably she hopes he will find a woman to care for him. From early 1943 until the end of the war, between the ages of five and seven, he joins street gangs of orphaned or vagrant children, living intermittently with various families, particularly with an old woman who had recently lost a grandson, whose identity he assumes. "I was only five," recalls Menachem S., "but I was like 70. Like an old man, I had to rely on myself." The unresolvable conflict between shifting identities is one of the legacies recorded by humiliated memory. Suddenly, in the summer of 1945, he returns to the status of childhood, since his parents miraculously survived as so-called *Schindlerjuden*, Jews saved in a munitions factory, through subterfuge and bribery, by an idiosyncratic Austrian entrepreneur named Oskar Schindler.

The "reunion" between Menachem S. and his parents is a traumatic meeting that violates all traditional notions of closure and afflicts consciousness with an overpowering sense of the *impossibility* of restoring interrupted family unity. His father, more than six feet tall, weighs eighty-eight pounds. His rotted teeth are hanging loosely from his gums. Menachem S. looked at him and didn't recognize him as his father. His emaciated mother did not resemble the woman in the picture she had left with him. "I just couldn't believe that they were my parents," he reports. Although he had waited two years for this moment, "When I was confronted with those disfigured people I just couldn't force myself to make any contact with them." He says that logically he knew they were his parents but emotionally couldn't feel close to them. For some period after that, he called them Mr. and Mrs. S. instead of mother and father, unable to restore continuity to the disrupted story of his life.

Preoccupied, like other surviving victims, with strategies for staying alive, during the war he had relied on a value system with that single focus as its raison d'être. After the war, when he met his parents, as he records, "I had to become a child again, which I resented. . . . Once I was safe again, this is when I disintegrated." The bizarre spectacle of an adult speaking of a seven-year-old child remembering his five-year-old self as an unrecapturable identity reminds us of the complex obstacles that frustrate a coherent narrative view of the former victim's ordeal from the vantage point of the present. Instead of enabling him to attain desirable ends, as the reasoning mind might expect, perceiving the concrete situation he is in confuses those ends, finally invalidating them. Memory functions here to discredit the idea of family unity and to confirm an order of being—or more precisely, a disorder of being—that appears to the witness to have been the unique creation of the Holocaust experience.

The sequel to this encounter in the testimony of Menachem S. is an amusing if painful confirmation of the role of uncompensated loss in the lives of surviving victims. When his own first child, a daughter, was born, he tells us, he went on a buying spree, spending a large sum of money acquiring all kinds of toys for her. Included among them were electric trains and a pedal car, which he put in her room. When his wife returned from the hospital with the three-day-old baby, she asked, "Why did you buy all this?" "What do you mean 'Why did you buy this?'" he replied. "A child needs to have toys." And his wife said, "Yes, but it will take years before she will be able to play with them." "What do you mean?" he objected. "A child needs toys. I just bought some toys." Then he smiles and concludes: "It took me a long time to realize what I was doing—I was finally buying toys for myself!"[23] His main concern today is that his personal anxiety is being transferred to future generations. Although he is speaking of his own children, the subterranean theme is the consequences of a more generalizable wound to social and moral consciousness that time may assuage but not heal. Mind itself is ineffectual in controlling or reshaping the ravages to the self of that earlier period without misrepresenting or misconstruing its effects. Menachem S.'s first meeting with his parents after the war assumes a primal power of terror and estrangement that violates long-established sanctities. Sentimental longings may ignore its implications, but in fact those implications do much to explain why we remain in the grip of this event decades after its apparent demise.

More than any of its other versions, humiliated memory is a content in search of a form. The moments it recalls float in a void because they cannot be connected to a conception of behavior that might establish meaning through analogy. Malka D. is reluctant to tell parts of her story because she cannot bear remembering them herself and refuses to believe that her audience has the capacity to understand her. Nonetheless, she haltingly offers her narration. Because of some irregularity, the SS at Radom took thirty Jews, including her, from the munitions factory where they were working and locked them in a dark cellar without windows. They couldn't see, had no food, and were left fearfully awaiting questioning and torture. At this point, we might imagine a half dozen reasons for their anxiety. But according to Malka D., what troubled them most was the lack of toilet facilities. She seems to tear the words out of the silence that possesses her on this issue; the people were civilized, she says, and afraid to relieve themselves in the presence of others. Finally, she whispers, the men took string and tied it around themselves. "You mean tied their penis?" asks the interviewer, and she replies, "Yes, so urine wouldn't come out."[24]

She is so humiliated by the limits to which the quest for a minimal dignity had driven some men that she can scarcely finish this portion of her testimony. She tells this not to celebrate human ingenuity, or some innate power of resistance to degradation (since most members of this group were tortured and killed) but to lament the condition of helplessness, the absence of control that deprived them of their real natures—or what until that instant she had been taught to believe were their real natures. While they were waiting in the darkness, one woman distracted them by

describing the long tables of food, the singing and the dancing
that would greet them in heaven. It was a great help, Malka D.
concedes, but only as a desperate diversion, not an affirmation.
Memory today offers her no refuge from the desolate conclusion
that human identity and behavior are determined as much (if not
more) by external circumstances as by inner beliefs or values.

Malka D. was "lucky," as she puts it: she was only beaten, not
killed. The process of redefinition, however, extends beyond
words to a larger conception of self that, like Menachem S.'s childhood, disintegrated at a particular point of encounter. Because life
goes on, something must replace that larger and older conception,
a view of what one is capable of doing and enduring that disputes
accepted notions of so-called decorum and restraint. The language with which surviving victims choose to record this perception indicates the imaginative leap necessary to absorb its implications. Magda F., for example, tells how she and another woman
prisoner were made to empty a cesspool filled with human excre-
ment with buckets: "I thought if I don't die now, I never will, and I
thought 'This is the end of my life.' Throwing up, nausea. How
could you do that to a human being? We did it."[25] "We did it" is
spoken not with pride or defiance but with a bitter concession to
an inverted and perverse resurrection or "living through," re-
nouncing a defunct principle of dignity that drowned in the
cesspool still haunting her.

Although the illusory strengths of institutional values like the
family lost much of their vigor,[26] victims clung to them with an
increasingly desperate dependence, in the absence of rituals more
reflective of the deprivations they faced. Malka D. describes marriage ceremonies between Jews in the munitions factory where
she worked, but they seem vain attempts to impose some continuity on a chaotic environment. She admits that she fell in love
herself but won't talk about it: "It's a very painful thing. I met
somebody that was—after three months he was killed." For those
more "fortunate," love and marriage were hardly associated with

rapture: "First of all it had to be quiet. The Germans shouldn't hear. Nobody should see. So it wasn't such a happy event. Everything had to be quiet. . . . And wishing that you should ever meet again, to survive and meet."[27] In spite of the continuing appeal of traditional forms of union, therefore, there is little evidence that they were a match for the systematic assaults on human community that these witnesses testify to.

Unlike rites consecrating hope and the future that prisoners relied on through habit and nostalgia, rituals temporarily endorsing survival were carefully designed by the Germans to humiliate their victims. Others, developed by the prisoners themselves, emerged from the situations in which they found themselves, totally unrelated to values inherited from the prewar era. Witnesses report their ability to adapt to these unprecedented rituals with tones ranging from amazement to enthusiasm to despair, but always too with the latent admission that they are speaking of another self, different from though not necessarily less "authentic" than the one before the camera. Moses S., for example, remembers a roll call in one of his labor camps when the daily portion of food was distributed—a spoonful of cheese, a few ounces of bread, and a slice of wurst so thin that "you could see the sun shine" through it (one wonders if it looked black). The barracks had just been fumigated against lice; because lice were no respecters of Aryan superiority, the SS fumigated regularly in this camp to prevent a typhus epidemic that might eventually infect them. The SS officer in charge of roll call spontaneously invented one of the "survival rituals" mentioned above by announcing: "If anyone would find a [living] louse, you get an extra portion of soup." Moses S. reports, with what can only be described as a gleeful cynicism, that he went out in back of the barracks, dug down, and found a louse. "I looked after it," he exclaims, "like somebody looks after gold!" They returned to roll call, and the SS officer asked if anyone had a louse. Moses S. raised his hand and brought his "treasure" forward. "Schau mir, die muss spazieren"

("Show me, it has to walk"), the officer declared, insisting that a dead louse was worthless. Moses S. then paraded his louse on his shoulder—and the officer sends him for an extra portion of soup. A grotesque tale, but he excavates it as one of his most vital re-collections to convince his audience—and this is a powerful motivation throughout his testimony—that their premises and expectations have virtually no contact with his camp experiences. He almost seems to gain satisfaction from the dismay that he spreads among his interlocutors. He appears intent on eroding their stability until they agree to enter into his reality on *his* terms. His louse story is more than an anecdote; it is a token, an emblem, a sign of his identity in the camps. He confirms this when he explains that in order to insure that escaped prisoners would be recognized, the SS shaved a swath down the center of their skull, which they called the *Laüsestrasse* (or louse road). In the louse episode, Moses S. drafts a bitter but definitive variation on the Nazi slogan "by their vermin shall ye know them," though the wary hearer will recognize that he has initiated nothing, only responded to a condition (hunger) and challenge (louse hunting) created by the SS officer.

Throughout his testimony, Moses S. has been sitting on a couch next to his present wife (his first wife along with their infant had been killed by the Germans—a detail he has included earlier in his narrative). From the beginning, she has protested periodically against prolonging the strenuous ordeal she assumes he is facing, though as she admits at one point, she has never heard some of his most terrible stories herself. Indeed, as her efforts to have him finish increase, and the interviewers support her, he appears even more determined to go on, almost baiting them with the mounting grimness of the incidents he describes. The climax (though by no means the conclusion) arrives in the following episode, which I insert with some hesitation. He presents it so deferentially, so indifferent to its melodramatic not to say barbaric possibilities that in spite of its subject he forces us to consider it as part of the routinized response to constant hunger and oppression that typified the camp experience.

It almost certainly was not; but such events are deeply embedded in humiliated memory, which in this instance is determined to transform the unfathomable into a comprehensible way of behaving given birth by the circumstances of the Holocaust:

> MOSES S.: All right. A few weeks later, the English people came in and bombed the concentration camp [Mauthausen]. And I said, "Yankel, get up, get up, it's no good lying here, you'll be a piece of *gornisht* [nothing at all]." So we got up, and we found a hand from the bombing . . .
>
> INTERVIEWER: A hand grenade?
>
> MOSES S.: No, a hand [at this point, another voice, presumably a family member, interjects: "A human hand"].
>
> MOSES S.: A human hand.
>
> INTERVIEWER: Oh, a human hand.
>
> MOSES S.: Five of us. Divided. And we were eating it. And somebody died, we cut out a piece—we were eating . . .
>
> MOSES S.'S WIFE: Excuse me, I think we have to finish. Too much already.
>
> MOSES S.: Human flesh.

The general disquietude and consternation among the members of Moses S.'s audience, to say nothing of ourselves, is difficult to convey.[28] Although the narrative transition may seem obscure to us, the logic is perfectly clear to Moses S. Just prior to this, he had been describing their rummaging through the garbage outside the kitchen, searching for scraps of discarded food. "We were eating," he said. "It doesn't matter what it is. As long as there was something." And this leads naturally into the above account, a monologue that invites no dialogue, not only because of the interviewers' discomfiture but because the tyranny of this actuality destroys the human scenario and leaves no substitute behind.

The only way out of the inner sanctum of dark revelation, in this and similar moments of testimony, is avoidance. We may call it inaccessible, but what we really mean is that it is not *discussable*. We lack terms of discourse for such human situations, preferring to call them inhuman and thus banish them from civilized consciousness. The rest of Moses S.'s narrative is a stubborn bid to prevent our easy escape from the unsettling details of his ordeal. A few minutes after his disturbing revelation, as his wife still tries to terminate the interview, one of the interviewers seeks to shift his attention by asking, "Where were you when you were liberated?" "Gunskirchen" (near Mauthausen, in Austria), he replies, only to add: "This was the last place where they kept us to die and die and die." Then, as if to appease his offended audience, as well as his offended self, he reenacts what might be construed as a counterbalancing moment of heroic dignity, though it is difficult to see how anyone familiar with his preceding and subsequent testimony could interpret it in this way.

Weak, emaciated, scarcely able to work, he along with other members of his barracks was summoned to a selection during which, for reasons he is unable to fathom today, he suddenly erupted in anger and screamed at the SS doctor (reverting to the original language as he speaks): "Was wollen Sie von uns haben? Wir sind junge Leute. Wir wollen arbeiten" ("What do you want from us? We're young, we want to work" [he was thirty years old at the time]). In fact, his outburst takes the SS doctor by surprise; he orders Moses S. to walk, to demonstrate his physical condition: "Komm, du verfluchte Hund, komm, zeig mir, wie weit kannst du gehen!" ("Come, you accursed dog, show me how far you can walk!"). After bellowing these words, the seventy-year-old witness stands up and with a stoop-shouldered, shuffling gait, much like a Mussulman, imitates his performance from that distant time, taking a few halting steps, *becoming* before our eyes the self he was then. Inexplicably, the doctor decides to send them all back to the barracks, ordering for them an extra portion of food. Moses S. reminds us and himself that he risked his life in that episode: "I saved 250 lives by doing that." But this does nothing to alter his previous conviction that Gunskirchen, where he was liberated, was the place they took you "to die and die and die," nor does he try to generalize a principle of heroic behavior from his tale. It does not signify morally for him because it is an exceptional rather than representative moment in his narrative, with an unexpected outcome, an interval between versions of dying that is the obsessive theme of the closing minutes of his testimony.

To the end, Moses S. resists his wife's determination to have him finish with the interview. Is she a spokeswoman for others beside herself? He also ignores an interviewer's second appeal to "describe that day of liberation," which by now we recognize as a possible plea to free *us* from the burden of the relentless tales of starvation, death by drowning, death by freezing, death by suffocation with which he concludes his testimony. When he finally realizes that they want him to stop, he innocently—or perhaps slyly—asks, "You want me to come again?" Chronology had little importance in his testimony, which has been a drama of transition, as a man possessing a past has been recast almost unnoticeably into a creature possessed by that past, and thereby insulated from his human surroundings. Liberation is displaced, in meaning and fact, by the ordeals preceding that experience, ordeals from whose thrall he cannot be released.[29]

Perhaps Moses S. fails to describe "that day of liberation" because, on the subterranean level where humiliated memory operates, it never arrived. The pain he recollects in tranquility is frozen in time; the heat of memory can reproduce but not melt it. The absence of sequence in his narrative reflects an absence of consequence too. What legend shall we make of the louse that earned an extra bowl of soup, or the air raid that turned up a human hand to be disposed of? What role could they play in a history of the camps or in his personal autobiography? If chronicle is tied to time, and historical narrative organized by "plot" (whether implicit in its events or discovered by the historian), how shall we characterize this kind of oral testimony, which is bound to neither? Unless we revise the language of history (and moral philosophy) to include the "fate" that besieged Moses S. and his fellow victims, they remain exiled from concepts like human destiny, clinging to the stories that constitute their Holocaust reality until some way is found to regard such stories as an expression rather than a violation of contemporary history. This is a difficult task and may be an impossible one, because the price we would have to pay in forgoing present value systems might be too high. "Insofar as historical stories can be completed," writes Hayden White, "can be given narrative closure, can be shown to have had a plot all along, they give to reality the odor of the ideal."[30] The odors discharged through humiliated memory are more noxious; the whiff we receive from it urges us to ask whether the cherished bridge leading from what we know to where we aspire has perhaps fallen into a dangerously rotting disrepair. It raises the further insidious question of whether that bridge may not have been illusory all along.

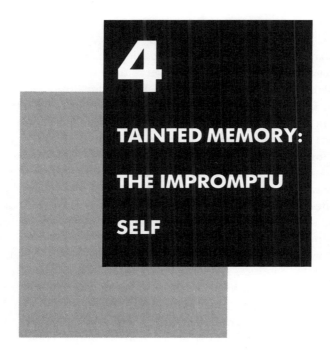

4

TAINTED MEMORY: THE IMPROMPTU SELF

"The disaster ruins everything," Maurice Blanchot begins his paradoxical commentary on *The Writing of the Disaster*, "all the while leaving everything intact." This is the contradiction we still wrestle with nearly half a century after the event. The foundations of moral behavior remain in place, as the goal if not the reality of decent societies, while victims of the Nazi attempt to annihilate European Jewry tell tales of survival that reduce such moral systems to an irrelevant luxury. The luxury, to be sure, remains valid for us, as we continue to strive for what is morally right; but as these tales unfold, in written or oral narrative, the insufficiency of the idea of moral striving as a frame for hearing them, or for understanding victim behavior, becomes ever plainer. When Blanchot says that those whom accounts of the disaster threaten—presumably *us*—remain out of reach, he urges us not to abandon the confrontation but to ask why, and to seek means of narrowing the space that separates us from the event.[1]

Sometimes this seems a futile task, even for surviving victims, who in the process of remembering betray their own difficulty when they use the language of now to describe the experience of then. The situation-based ethics of the camp led to a way of behaving for which we do not have—and probably never will have—a systematic analytic approach. Memory sacrifices purity of vision in the process of recounting, resulting in what I call tainted memory, a narrative stained by the disapproval of the witness's own present moral sensibility, as well as by some of the incidents it relates. Tainted memory is nonetheless a form of self-justification, a painful validation of necessary if not always admirable conduct. The squalid conditions of the camps, so hostile to personal survival, together with the constant threat (and examples) of "unnatural" dying, often unraveled the moral defenses of a more privileged time, leaving victims adrift in the chancy sea of staying alive, among waves they still contend with today.

At the very end of her testimony, Joan B. looks at her interviewer (though she is really addressing all of us) and says: "You see, with a logical mind like yours, or other people who try to think this out, [for] a rule that's being followed, or [for] a certain way that [they] think, [or] had thought out and would do things—there was no such thing. . . . There was no set rule. . . . Just killing, that's all." This is not an accusation but an attempt to clarify a distinction that eludes us. Speaking of her persecutors, she insists that for them improvisation was the rule, though she might just as well have been speaking of herself and her fellow victims. And since, for these latter, improvisation *tests* a situation instead of controlling or defining it, one could rarely anticipate the consequences of an action (or an inaction). Her husband, for example, was sent from Auschwitz to Hamburg, where he

walked the streets barefoot clearing rubble from air raids; he took
pieces of wood and tied them around his ankles to protect his
feet. But the rope began to irritate his ankles, till one foot grew
infected. The infection spread until he couldn't walk, and thus
couldn't work. "They shot him. He was 33 . . . 34, maybe." One
form of improvisation triumphs over another, as for want of a
shoe, a life is lost. In the absence of certain ways and rules to
promote survival, one is left vulnerable to desperate gestures
that have little connection to the moral assurances we cus-
tomarily associate with efforts at self-preservation.

Joan B. also was sent from Auschwitz to Hamburg, to a labor
camp where, because of her prior experience in her parents'
hotel-restaurant, the commandant assigned her to the kitchen as
a cook. She survived there, she says, "because I ate the same
food that he got." But tainted memory soils her tale of good fortune. One of the women in her group was pregnant and eventually gave birth. The commandant came to Joan B. and ordered
her to boil some water. It was just like the films, she declares:
"Boil water. But the water wasn't to help with the act of giving
birth. He drowned the newborn in the boiling water." The ap-
palled interviewer asks, "Did you see that?" "Oh, yes, I did," the
witness imperturbably replies. "Did you say anything?" the dialogue continues. "No, I didn't." Between the expectation of the
outsider and the silence of the insider begins the evolution of a
self-concept that lies at the heart of this chapter. Joan B. sketches
its outlines roughly when, in response to the question of how
she retained her sanity in camp after camp (her back was broken
twice by beatings; she was in a wheelchair for seven months after
the end of the war), she answers: "I had a friend . . . who said
that now when we are here, you have to look straight ahead as if
we have [blinders] on like a race horse . . . and become selfish."
"I just lived, looked," she adds, "but I didn't feel anything. I
became selfish. That's number one." Then she qualifies her anal-

ysis by adding: "Or I should say luck is number one, and that [that is, being selfish] was number two."[2]

The difference between being "selfish" and "self-ish" requires further refinement. The selfish act ignores the needs of others through choice when the agent is in a position to help without injuring one's self in any appreciable way. Selfishness is motivated by greed, indifference, malice, and many other value-laden categories. The former victim who describes self-ish acts is vividly aware of the needs of others but because of the nature of the situation is unable to choose freely the generous impulse that a compassionate nature yearns to express. Hence what one does is detached from any internal system of belief. The result appears to resemble what after the war was popularized under the label of existential choice, which in practice was supposed to *create* value for those disillusioned by the collapse of earlier systems of belief. The self-ish act, however, far from being existential, usually *ignored* or *negated* value because the grim decisions it routinely faced involved death as well as life. Still more paradoxically, it sometimes fostered death even as it supported life.

Some former victims build their distressed testimonies around this principle of being, in the forlorn hope of developing for themselves and their audience a valid basis for their behavior in those days. Myra L. speaks of almost nothing else. She begins with the story of a neighbor in the Lodz ghetto, weak from hunger, who was visited one night by his sister-in-law pleading for help because her husband, the neighbor's older brother, was dying, starving to death. He wanted, she said, a slice of bread. He believed that if he had a slice of bread, it would be enough to keep him alive. And suddenly the witness begins to weep, as she explains that the younger brother replied: "I have no food myself. How can I give him my last slice of bread?" He didn't; the next night, she continues, the older brother died. The younger brother survived. He lives today in the United States, where he and the witness are friends. But between them also exists the unspoken memory of what he deems his failure to respond to his brother's appeal.

Tainted memory cannot purify itself, because it is trapped by a moral design that is virtually useless in helping us understand the episodes that Myra L. describes. Because the moral systems that we are familiar with are built on the premise of individual choice and responsibility for the consequences of choice, we either search for examples supporting such systems, and celebrate them, or ignore and remain baffled and embarrassed by the examples in Myra L.'s testimony. She tells of a mother who hid the corpse of her five-year-old child under the mattress for *five weeks* so she could use the extra rations to keep herself alive. "We had to behave like animals," she complains. "There was no other way to behave." In fact, as these testimonies make clear, she behaved like a human, consistent with the situation-determined ethics that I have been discussing. The witness is not immune to the implications of what she is saying, for she follows this account with the story of a father who sneaked into an SS-controlled hospital where his newborn infant lay and stole the baby, hiding it in the pocket of his coat. We find it much easier to "place" this brave example of paternal concern on an acceptable moral spectrum. But Myra L. sabotages our admiration with her brusque version of the consequences: an SS guard saw him, seized the baby, and smashed its head against the wall "until it fell apart on the floor." Then she stares into the camera, her face convulsed with despair. (As a nurse in the hospital, Myra L. witnessed many scenes that other ghetto inhabitants were protected from.) Courageous gestures like the father's are based on the conviction that the agent is in control of the results of his action. Events proved otherwise.

What can we salvage from the fragments of that wreckage, which signifies far more than the violent death of a single child? Without establishing any *direct* connection, Myra L. lays the groundwork for the emergence of what I call the impromptu self by espousing a principle that will not be universally embraced or acclaimed (and that has, of course, exceptions), but whose large portion of truth is supported by the weight of evidence in these testimonies: "The survival will was so big that nobody was sacrificing himself for anybody else." Her distress is visible as she proffers it. It is evidently an empirical, not an abstract, truth, borne out by the fruitless effort of the father to save his child, as well as by her own experience. At one point, she tells us, the hospital where she worked was cleared of all patients (who would be deported "to the east"), to make room for new arrivals from Germany and Austria. Because she was a nurse, the Germans put her in charge of overseeing the expulsion of some of the patients. She stands by the doorway, helping them come out. A cousin of hers emerges, a short woman, and quickly hides behind the door, hoping to remain unnoticed. But the Germans see her and drag her away, as she cries, "Save me! Save me!" "I couldn't save her," says Myra L. "I also feared that I can be taken instead." Today, however, narrating this episode with the voice of her other, unself-ish self, she muses: "And that's another thing that worked on me—that I couldn't save her." But the voice of the self-ish self instantly replies: "I did not probably want to go for [that is, because of] my cousin," exemplifying her principle that "the survival will was so big that nobody was sacrificing himself for anybody else."[3] The denotative impact of this idea is clear, if unflattering to our moral sensibilities; the practical facts of such plights render the question of retaining one's human dignity a merely theoretical issue. The connotative impact, however, remains troublesome, to witness and audience, because no alternative verbal scheme exists to free the self-ish gesture from the bonds of its unsympathetic "homonym."

The resulting confusion generates some odd strategies. Consider the opening paragraphs of two narratives by former victims, each in quest of a perspective to illuminate the ordeal of remembering. The first, written in 1973, is from a book called *The Victors and the Vanquished*:

> I do not want to write. I do not want to remember. My memories are not simple recollections. They are a return to the bottom of an abyss; I have to gather up the shattered bones that have lain still for so long, climb back over the crags, and tumble in once more. Only this time I have to do it deliberately, in slow motion, noticing and examining each wound, each bruise on the way, most of all the ones of which I was least conscious in my first headlong fall. But I know I have to do it. My future stands aside, waiting until I find meaning in all that has been. I feel as if I had to overcome some almost physical obstacle, and feel drained, breathless from the effort.[4]

This victim is still consumed by her past, a sealed pain, recaptured only through struggle; her vivid imagery confirms Blanchot's conclusion that "there is no future for the disaster, just as there is no time or space [in the present] for its accomplishment."[5] Her experience seems insulated, not only from us but from herself, the self that has survived, entered a new life, and resists the descent to a charnel house that even she may not recognize now. Her consciousness rebels.

The second, written in 1986, is the opening passage of a survivor narrative called *Under a Cruel Star*. The shift in tone will be evident; *this* narrator has found a way out of the abyss:

> Three forces carved the landscape of my life. Two of them crushed half the world. The third was very small and weak and actually, invisible. It was a shy little bird hidden in my rib cage an inch or two above my stomach. Sometimes in the most unexpected moments the bird would wake up, lift its head, and flutter its wings in rapture. Then I too would lift

my head because, for that short moment, I would know for certain that love and hope are infinitely more powerful than hate and fury, and that somewhere beyond the line of my horizon there was life indestructible, always triumphant.[6]

Both the nature and the direction of the language alter, from falling to rising, from pain and anguish to rapture and hope. Authors, of course, have a right to their own mood, temperament, and vision. The problem here is that both paragraphs are by the *same* author, and for the *same* book, the later version, though a different translation, being virtually identical with the former, except for the initial paragraphs. We might say that the first passage confirms Blanchot's notion that the disaster ruins everything, whereas the second affirms its sequel, that at the same time it leaves everything intact. On the one hand, the particular disaster we call the Holocaust denies a future consistent with its violations of the self; on the other, human need requires a future where love and hope reign as motives for human conduct and aspiration in spite of the scope of the disaster. We as audience inhabit both worlds; and if we listen carefully to the testimonies of enough former victims, we learn that they do too. The finality of the change in the written texts that we have just examined exposes and clarifies the frailty of the options available in oral testimony, because the witness there, still dominated by the moments he or she evokes, has little leisure to manipulate responses by redesigning desirable attitudes. Tainted memory seems inconsistent with the rhetoric of hope.

Memory excavates from the ruins of the past fragile shapes to augment our understanding of those ruins. What transforms "shattered bones" into "life indestructible, always triumphant"? The evolution warns us that our encounter with the narratives of former victims demands a wary intimacy with the story far beyond the passive acceptance of details. We cannot know why the author of these two introductory paragraphs decided to change the thrust of her intentions. But we do know that the first version, with its Miltonic plunge into a purely physical abyss, creates tensions for the writer and the reader that the spiritual optimism of the second version avoids. Does a self-conscious literary voice intervene here between the experience and the effect, so that language and imagery obscure even as they seek to clarify? Perhaps; perhaps not. But as we examine definitions and redefinitions of self emerging from victim narratives, we must keep in mind that each one of them represents a combat, more often than not unconscious, between fragment and form, disaster and intactness, birdsong and pandemonium. A hopeful surface story vies with a darker subtext, although—as in this instance—we scarcely recognize that the two voices are the same.

Oral testimonies of former Nazi victims slightly simplify our task, because most of these have neither time nor inclination nor gift to draw on the resources of literary artifice in their narratives. After having watched more than three hundred such testimonies, ranging in length from thirty minutes to seven hours, I have reached the conclusion that the process of recall divorced from literary effort results in a narrative form unlike the written text, equally valuable, rich in spontaneous rather than calculated effects. A member of the Norwegian underground who survived Natzweiler, Dachau, and other camps, who is also writing a book about his ordeal, is asked how his oral testimony differs from his written account. "The book is different because you have more time to phrase your words," he replies. "In a book, you're also trying to be poetic—you're trying to write."[7] This notion of writing as poetic, though perhaps a trifle unsophisticated, nonetheless confirms the role of style in the written memoir—that is, having time to face the conscious choice of phrasing one's words. This is a complex issue, and I mention it here only because it affects, in different ways, the sense of character or self that emerges from written and oral testimonies.

The headlong fall in the first passage quoted above unavoidably (and maybe deliberately) conjures up the image of Satan plummeting into Milton's hell, and this in turn influences our response to the experience of the victim. Such analogies rarely intrude on oral testimonies. When they do, they create a disjunctive resonance, attesting to the *in*sufficiency of familiar analogy. We recall, for example, the story of Edith P., who looks out from the tiny window high up in her boxcar as it pauses at a small station during the journey from Auschwitz to a labor site in Germany and exclaims: "I saw Paradise!"[8] What she saw was a group of people standing on the platform, including a mother and her child, and in the context of her deportation this normal, harmless view, far from Edenic, nevertheless comes to represent for her a vision of Paradise. We witness a metamorphosis of meaning before our eyes, as a commonplace panorama displaces the archetypal idyllic scene, leading in turn to a spontaneous adaptation of familiar formula to an alien situation.

Not all witnesses, however, defer to familiar formulas, leaving the transformation of meaning to the audience's imagination. On rare occasions, memory conjures up striking and original images that approach the poetic intensity of artistic insight. At these moments, we gain a glimpse into the inner recesses of the Holocaust universe where we find the struggle between various versions of the self validated at the deepest levels of consciousness. Paul D., for example, tells of a Greek Orthodox priest in his native Slovakia who agreed to verify that certain Jewish families had converted to Christianity before 1938 (thus exempting them temporarily from deportation), even if they had not, provided parents were willing to have any children in the family actually baptized into the Greek Orthodox faith. Paul D.'s parents consent, and thus secure false certificates, at the price of his "conversion" to Christianity.

This rouses in Paul D. the memory of a dream or a vision he had shortly afterward, which he says he recalls very clearly. Whether or not its details are totally accurate seems irrelevant, because its value as an exemplum remains unimpaired. It's an image, he says, that is "very clear in my mind. I'm on a meadow, and there are Jewish kids playing around me. And at one point they move away from me, and I am alone on this meadow. And God appears before me. And he's a mountain. And God holds in his hands an axe. And he just goes [raising his hands], takes the axe over his head, and with a full swing splits me in half. And I just break [gesturing] into two." At this point the interviewer interjects, "Jew and Christian?" "I think it's more like killing me," Paul D. replies. "Like punishment. It doesn't feel like Jew and Christian. It feels like annihilation." Then he adds, "I tried to be Christian, but it didn't work."9 The vision contains the usual features of orthodox morality, with the stable image of the Lord (as a mountain) presiding over His people moving freely in His presence. Whether God is then displaced by another agent of violence or remains a conventional instrument of punishment, or whether the nature of the universe Paul D. inhabits has been changed by the unorthodox choice forced upon him by a threatening situation, we cannot know. But the "break in two" is consistent with the testimonies that we have been examining, as the violated self seeks to stay alive while conscious of the departures from traditional faith and morality that this requires.

It is indeed a kind of annihilation, a totally paradoxical killing of the self by the self in order to keep the self alive. Subsequently that annihilated self, threatened as in the dream but only dormant, not dead, reasserts its primacy, only to meet resistance from what I call the impromptu self that had replaced it during the ordeal of survival. In its apocalyptic intimations, Paul D.'s dream, filtered through his awareness of future events, foretells the fate of the Jewish children playing around him, for whom no reunion of the divided self will be possible. His experience of their death becomes one of the died events that I mentioned earlier; few surviving victims escape unscathed from the death of others. It is as if there were *two* cosmic orders still contending for supremacy in the mind of the witness. History may have settled the conflict between the two; memory relives the contest, achieving its taint in the process.

Blanchot in his inimitable style sheds some light on this difficult phenomenon: "Dying means: you are dead already, in an immemorial past, of a death which was not yours, which you have thus neither known nor lived, but under the threat of which you believe you are called upon to live; you await it henceforth in the future, constructing a future to make it possible at last—possible as something that will take place and will belong to the realm of experience."[10] Alien death invades the space of survival.

The application of these redefinitions radiates in several directions. To be dead of a death that you have not lived or even known may sound logically meaningless, but the inner structure of testimony after testimony, which reflects incessantly the haunting refrain of the unexperienced death of the missing family member, confirms a sense beyond logic in Blanchot's language. In an era of mass murder, dying is no longer anticipated *or* remembered as a solitary event; the annihilation that Paul D. dreamed of is part of the reality of his *milieu,* and he obviously shares it in his deepest imaginative responses. Many of these testimonies, indeed, serve the function that Blanchot speaks of—constructing a future in which to make possible at least a *beginning* of the sympathetic dying that joins the witnesses to the internal demands of their narratives.

Dying in the past and living in the present are thus inseparable, the threat of the one shadowing the future prospects of the other. Blanchot describes the dilemma as an "impossible necessary death," wondering why these words, and the "unexperienced experience" (*"expérience inéprouvée"*) to which they refer, should escape our understanding: "Why this collision of mutually exclusive terms?" (67).[11] Although he is not speaking here specifically of the Holocaust, his language offers a frame for confronting the dual legacy of normal and abnormal dying (and normal and abnormal living) that surfaces repeatedly in these testimonies. The challenge to us from tainted memory is to see "impossible necessary death" as a conjunction rather than an opposition, and to abandon the fashion of thought that prevents us from gaining entry into its sanctuary.

That conjunction, as Blanchot explains, includes a Hegelian distinction between two kinds of death that opens up crucial avenues to our investigation of tainted memory, even though Hegel could not have been anticipating them when he wrote: "The two deaths were indissociable [*n'étaient pas dissociables*], and . . . only the act of confronting death—not merely of facing it or of exposing oneself to its danger (which is the distinguishing feature of heroic courage), but of entering into its space, of undergoing it as infinite death and also as mere death, 'natural death' [*mort infinie et, aussi, mort tout court, 'mort naturelle'*]—could found the sovereignty of masterhood: the mind and its prerogatives" (68). To kill a past that is already dead is futile; but to enter into its space, as Blanchot asks us to, to let its infinity chip away at our mortality (our immortality too, one might add, as well as our morality), to allow, if one may revise Blanchot, the *unnecessary* to become *possible*—this would carry us well beyond the heroic gestures that Blanchot dismisses to a genuine confrontation with the conception of a dismantled self that the Holocaust has thrust upon us. Blanchot shows little sympathy for those who try to evade the consequent confusion by "the ruse (conveniently) called idealist" (68). But he seems to have great faith in the power of the mind to acquire mastery over that confusion and to reconstruct a version of the self consistent with the death-immersions he speaks of.

The transition is far from simple. The idealist ruse may liberate us from an atrocity-burdened past, but it offers little help to those who wish to move beyond listening, to the disagreeable task of interpretive hearing. Nathan A., for example, crowds his testimony with accounts of gratuitous brutality during roundups and selections at which he was present, but one episode in particular darkens his narrative even as it illuminates the phenomenon of impossible necessary death that Blanchot alludes to. It raises the issue of how *anyone*—victim, witness, participant, or audience— can enter sympathetically into the space of that experience. Nathan A. describes an *Aktion* (a mass execution) in a town in Poland. He and some other young men are taken to the edge of the town where they are made to dig a large ditch. The burial detail then watches as the SS bring the Jewish villagers to the pit by truck, line them up, and shoot them. Some they kill, some they wound, and others, apparently, they miss—but all are thrown into the mass grave.

Nathan A.'s subsequent words leap from the page with the force and audacity of Nietzsche's tyranny of the actual, but they provide no easy channel for us to drift into the reality they record. The stunned imagination seeks a link between mere dying and infinite dying; perhaps for Blanchot assenting to the encounter would itself be the beginning of mastery: "They used to throw the earth on the top, and the earth used to go up and down because they are living people. One—the son bury his mother; the mother was still alive [and called out]: 'Moyshe, ikh leb; bagrub mikh nisht lebedikerheyt' ['Moyshe, I'm alive; don't bury me while I'm alive']. . . . But Moyshe had no choice, because the Germans [don't] give him the choice. And he bury [her] alive." The interviewer is incredulous: "He buried his mother alive?" Nathan A. shrugs his shoulders and remains impassive. Here is more than a clash between mutually exclusive terms, though in a sense the terms of value with which the interviewer reacts to this anecdote intervene between the facticity of the event and its meaningful (and, more threateningly, meaningless) implications. We do not know whether Moyshe survived; supposing he were the narrator instead of Nathan A., what else could we call his act of remembering but tainted memory? The feat of recall transforms a possible if unnecessary death into the impossible but necessary one that

Blanchot speaks of, impossible for our idea of moral order but necessary if we are to consent to the truth of the narrative. Such improvised death sanctions the emergence of an impromptu self as the only form of identity to handle the episode that Nathan A. has summoned from the caverns of memory.

The very form of his testimony, its shifts from successful survival gestures to futile cruel dying, displays the inner conflict that accompanies the birth of this uncongenial but precise image of the self. Unconsciously following Blanchot, Nathan A. offers us a series of mutually exclusive descriptions that more than collide: they enter into each other's space, contaminating the pure division between heroism and villainy that the "ruse (conveniently) called idealist" had hitherto neatly split into separate categories. Together with his father and elder brother, Nathan A. is transferred to a work camp at Budzyn, where during a selection he—only fourteen at the time—is sent to the left while they are sent to the right (to work). We do not know why at this point his memory chooses the sequence that it does, but it dramatizes eloquently how the various spaces of dying intrude on each other and subsequently prove impossible to disentangle.

He first tells how the woman standing next to him—her red hair and green coat remain vivid in his mind—knelt and kissed the boots of the camp commandant, crying "I want to live." "You?" exclaimed the commandant, who then drew his revolver, and shot her in the head. Her blood and brains splattered over Nathan A., staining, we need little prompting to imagine, his self, his memory, and his ensuing story—to say nothing of our own vision of his narrative. Virtually without pause, he begins a "cleansing" action by telling how his father then approached a guard, stood at attention, and announced: "I want to volunteer to go to death with my son." "Take him out," the guard replied, and they both returned to the column on the right. One is tempted to conclude that the woman's irrational terror of infinite dying provoked her end, whereas the action of Nathan A.'s father, inspired by the idea of heroic courage that is able to risk "mere death," saved their lives. But in Nathan A.'s memory, the two moments are inseparable, and this can hardly be accidental. "I call my father—he was a hero," Nathan A. declares, with justification; but the woman's blood continues to stain his memory, and ours.

His odyssey takes him to a Henkelwerke factory in Germany, then to Majdanek, Auschwitz, Gleiwitz, and Blechhammer. His last tainted memory surfaces from Majdanek, where he recalls seeing a vehicle arrive one day near the gas chambers. It is filled with priests and one blond young woman. When the young woman refuses to undress, an SS man begins to tear at her clothing, though she claws his face with her nails. So they tie her up and put her screaming directly into the crematorium. "I saw it," Nathan A. insists spontaneously, as if to appease his own doubts.[12] Although Nathan A. remains silent about the effects of what he has seen, another former victim furnishes us with words that seem to "complete" this portion of his testimony. Although herself a child in hiding in Holland during the war, Julia S. has inherited the legacy of "these people who really have seen the worst," wondering how they can adapt to "new" lives following their experience. "After that," she asks, "what are you supposed to do? . . . You know what I'm saying? You're not supposed to see this; it doesn't go with life. It doesn't go with life. These people come back, and you realize, they're all broken, they're all broken. Broken. Broken."[13] This is an extreme statement in behalf of the impromptu self, helpless in the presence of infinite dying, a kind of violence to the natural course of existence from which one never entirely recovers.

But Nathan A. does not end his testimony on this somber note. Still a teenager at the end of the war, he made his way to Israel, fought in its many wars, was wounded, but clearly reclaimed some of his lost dignity by actively participating in a common effort in behalf of Jewish freedom. This allows him today to establish a precarious balance between the atrocities he witnessed and

endured in the camps and the integrated self that yearns to leave
them behind. But the content of his testimony, which cannot and
indeed refuses to form a hierarchy of values, preferring to jux-
tapose affirmation with negation, the heroic gesture with ruthless
dehumanization, leaves us with an intricate legacy in which infinite death trespasses on natural dying, canceling the balance that
Nathan A. seeks valiantly to sustain.

Devotion to orthodox versions of the self, an inability to pry
oneself loose from these versions, by their own account paralyzed
the will of many former victims. Rarely, however, do we find a
simple opposition between paralysis and action. Oral testimonies
dramatize for us, often implicitly rather than explicitly, the constantly warring impulses of a bewildering series of events. Such
tensions are frequently evident in the witness's manner itself.
Schifra Z., for example, born near Vilna, begins her testimony
with perfect composure, a model of the integrated self. Slowly, as
her narrative unfolds, her facial gestures and head movements,
the stretching of her neck and licking of her lips, her uncontroll-
able perspiring, and deep sighs reveal a woman increasingly possessed by rather than possessing her story. For the rest of her
narrative, she alternates between control and submission, a clear
illustration of the struggle to remain intact in spite of the disaster
at the heart of her testimony.

She was between twelve and thirteen years old when German
troops entered Vilna. She reports that some friendly members of
the *Wehrmacht* who did not believe she was Jewish asked her,
"Why don't you go away from here? Just walk away. Keep walking westward." "I couldn't do that on my own," she tells us. "I
could not beg, I could not steal, I could not take from anyone
anything. I could not go under a false name." It seems she is more
in dialogue with herself than with us as she explains: "I couldn't
see myself walking away." Judgmental moral terminology (beg,
steal, false) and the sense of an inflexible persona combine to
thwart the perception of a self that could respond to the urgency

of the situation instead of to an inner vision of possible behavior. But when the abstract urgency takes on a more concrete shape, her sense of possible personae shifts dramatically.

She learns from a neighbor of the massacre of Jews in Ponary outside of Vilna and recalls thinking: "I will not let them decide when I will die. I will resist that. I refuse to die on their timing. . . . I could not see myself being put up against a wall and shot. . . . If I die, I die on my own terms." Out of context, statements like these resonate with the splendor of heroic determination. But as she re-creates the agony of the slaughter of members of her own family, we learn along with her how provisional was *any* position under those circumstances. Her resolution to choose her own fate dissolves into one more verbal formula as the horror of the situation invades her various defenses. "We were so helpless," she continues, unaware of any contradiction, "in finding your way out, and there was no way out." They had no idea, she says, why they were being killed, when they might be killed, what might happen next, or where to go. They didn't know if it was better to hide in the city, in the surrounding villages, in the forest, in a barn, with others, or alone. She admits now that they simply couldn't see their way ahead and thus were unable to plan the best route to survival.

We encounter in this narrative memories of several versions of the self, from the reluctance to venture into unfamiliar moral terrain through the resolve to resist an imposed death sentence to total uncertainty, a kind of learned helplessness, as Jewish doom imposed by the Nazis replaced the vision of an individual, self-defined fate. Which is authentic? The question confirms the folly of searching for authenticity amid the moral quicksand of atrocity. Schifra Z. herself unwittingly supports this conclusion when she responds to the interviewer's question at the very end about how she feels today, having gone through all this, with the surprising reply: "I believe in the goodness of man." Is this an attempt to restore the apparent order of the pre-Holocaust era, or a private concept of the self that decomposed slowly through the years of her ordeal? Perhaps as an answer to her own homiletic statement, she then adds, again with no apparent feeling of contradiction: "I believe everyone has the right and the responsibility to save his life."[14] The legacy of multiple voices is part of the heritage of survival; any attempt to resolve these voices would seem to betray or falsify that experience.

The "responsibility" of the victim to "save his life" led in unpredictable directions, hardly consistent with pre- or postdisaster ideas of the goodness of man. The "gray zone" that Primo Levi speaks of in the last of his Auschwitz memoirs represents those moments when staying alive could not be practiced as a common pursuit. Neither heroic endeavor nor selfish exploitation satisfactorily defines the options available to the victim. Narrative moments like the following from one of the oral testimonies help us refine our appreciation of how an individual reacts when situation rather than character controls response and the impulses of what I call the impromptu self replace the faculty of moral choice.

Having lost her regular shoes, Hanna F. is left with a dilemma: "Without shoes," she reports, "you couldn't go to work. You were dead." One evening she is standing outside her barrack when she notices a woman who is sitting on the ground and delousing her clothes. Her shoes are beside her. "I was very brave," says Hanna F., who temporarily has been wearing some totally inadequate wooden clogs. She approaches the woman, surreptitiously steps out of her clogs and into the woman's shoes, and then, she concludes, "I walked away."[15] She looks pained while telling this story. She closes her eyes and wipes her lips but does not apologize for the conduct of the impromptu self in the process of staying alive. We, however, would search in vain through familiar dictionaries of moral vocabulary for a definition of "brave" commensurate with the details of this episode. Construing her silence is one form of breaking through the inaccessibility of her ordeal.

Subversive or dismaying as it may sound, the impromptu self of the victim spontaneously detached itself from familiar value systems without apparent anguish. After liberation, that self survives in the narrative as a kind of alter ego, often unfamiliar even to the witness. "When you're hungry," admits one former victim from the Lodz ghetto, "there is nothing else in the world which matters. . . . When you're hungry, it gets to a point where you don't mind stealing from your own sister, from your own father. . . . I would get up in the middle of the night," he confesses, "and slice a piece of bread off my sister's ration. Now I—you would never picture me, and I can't even imagine myself doing that now. But it happened."[16] He is perfectly sensitive, however, to the implications of his narrative. Far from the image of the inviolable self, still our heritage from the romantic era, the impromptu self frequently appears as a *violated* self, in part—a source of chagrin and humiliation to many witnesses—a seemingly self-violated self. One of the most distressing ironies of these oral testimonies is the ease with which, as in this instance, one is tempted to overlook the concealed persecutors, the creators rather than the inhabitants of the Lodz ghetto, and blame the victim's weakness instead.

Witnesses themselves are bewildered by the disequilibrium between the impromptu self, which followed impulse in order to stay alive, and memories of the morally dignified life that was the goal of their prewar existence and continues as their aim today. The chronological sequence on the surface of the testimony, leading through liberation to marriage, family, career, cheers only the naive audience. The subtext of loss exerts its own influence on the narrative. Asked near the end of her account, "Tell me, in your life afterwards have you rebuilt some of the things that you have lost?" Hanna H. sabotages the illusion of continuity by exclaiming:

No, no, everything that happened destroyed part of me. I was dying slowly. Piece by piece. And I built a new family. I am not what I would have been if I didn't go through these things. . . . Life was one big hell even after the war. So you make believe that you go on. This is not something that you put behind. And people think that they can get away from it, or you don't talk about it, or you forgot your fear when you lay in an attic and you know that the Gestapo is a minute away from you. And rifles always against your head. You can't be normal. As a matter of fact, I think that we are not normal because we are so normal.

Like the woman who saw paradise in the spectacle of a mother and child standing on a railroad platform, this former victim frustrates efforts to see survival as a simple chronology of returning from an abnormal to a normal world. Without denying the reality or the significance of her present life, she insists on the discontinuity between it and her past, an unresolved and for her unresolvable stress that nurtures anxiety. After the war, she insists, they weren't allowed to fall apart because "circumstances didn't let us." Just as situation often became a form of necessity in the camps, dictating response far more than fixed principles of character, so here, according to this testimony, postwar life required an abandonment of the impromptu self with all its painful memories. "We had to educate our children," she says, "and we had to guide our children and be nice parents and make parties and everything. But that was all make believe."[17] One of the surprising revelations of these testimonies is the frequency with which such a dual sense of the self emerges, with what we would have considered a solid layer of resistance, reinforced by time, turning out to be only a thin and vulnerable veneer. "Now I am talking here," another former victim says in concluding his testimony, "as if this were a normal thing. Inside my heart burns. My brain boils."[18]

Of course, not everyone expresses this duality. But even contrary accounts of apparently successful adaptation betray some contradiction to the careful hearer. Sigmund W., for example, insists that after coming to America in 1948, he put his camp experiences in a time capsule and decided not to think about them: "I recognized that in order to become part of society I had a choice to make: either to stay a survivor or a prisoner and be in prison for the rest of my life, or try to preserve my sanity by putting this away in my mind and integrating myself into society as if nothing had ever happened. And obviously I chose the latter." Yet, he admits, his wife tells him that for the first *ten* years of their life together, he woke up *every night* screaming. "I am fully unaware of this," he confesses, adding: "So integration into everyday life, I believe, was possible by shutting out the indescribable events that have occurred."

Just before saying this, however, he had shown a gouache portrait of himself made in Paris in 1946 by a friend and barrackmate from the camps, and given to his brother with the observation: "This is how I remember your [brother]" [that is, the speaker in this testimony]. He holds his other self up to the camera, a prisoner in striped uniform and cap, with sallow complexion, an utterly forlorn expression on his face, a blank stare in his eyes. He chooses to present his suppressed self through the portrait, leaving to the viewer the interpretation of the human—or inhuman—condition it represents. And in fact, his strategy is shrewder and less evasive than it appears. He explains his rationale for putting his camp experiences—he was in Blechhammer, Gross Rosen, Buchenwald, Dachau, and several lesser known labor camps—in a time capsule by arguing: "It can only be told, I think it is important to be told, but it cannot be felt, it cannot be experienced. *I* cannot even experience it." He distinguishes between making a record and letting others know what happened, between details and the face in the portrait, or on the most complex level, we might say, between the concreteness of history and the suggestiveness of art.

The appeal of written narrative is based in part on the recognition of affinities, the premise that style and structure can help the imagination to penetrate strange facades, resulting in a shared intimacy with the persons and events portrayed. When witnesses like the one we have just heard insist on the *unshareability* of the experience, or speak of an estrangement even between one's present and past persona, we understand more clearly the crucial role of the impromptu self in oral testimony. That self endured in ways no longer comprehensible even to this witness, who at one point, he tells us, was so weak that he *volunteered* to die (only to be deported to another camp instead).

He speaks of "survival per se" as the "ultimate resistance," of the "will of survival" as the "ultimate feat." Yet, in addition to his own momentary loss of the vaunted will to survival (which led him to volunteer to die), he tells the story of a prisoner who had scooped up some gray powder that had leaked from a split bomb, thinking it was soap. For this act he was publicly *strangled* together with his Kapo and a fellow inmate for attempted insurrection.[19] He makes no effort to connect the two moments in his narrative; but an attentive audience will speculate on the implications of a memory that is never innocent because of the juxtaposition that has just emerged. Oral testimony may not always engage us in the inner workings of tainted memory within the former victim; but it offers some valuable insights into its genesis and consequences, and these in turn help to explain the insistence by witnesses like this one that the gulf between their experience and our sense of it is impassable.

A superficial reading of these testimonies might attribute some of the tensions I have been discussing to what religious systems and psychological theories refer to as guilt. Indeed, many former victims speak with a distress that, in the absence of any other explanation for their feelings, appears to originate in their sense of deeds done or undone that now fill them with guilty regret. In an odd way, we as audience are in a position to assess their experiences from a superior vantage point, because what seems an isolated private ordeal to them is to us part of an emerging pattern of behavior dissociated from choices or failures to act that we commonly identify with guilt. Tainted memory, to be sure, involves a loss of innocence, but in the absence of new cultural or psychological myths drawing on the reality of the camp universe we—together with surviving victims—continue to equate that loss of innocence with its scriptural, Edenic, or Miltonic sources. The evidence in these testimonies, however, indicates that guilt, both as label and concept, is totally inadequate and indeed misleading as a description of the internal discomfort of surviving victims.

In fact, there is no confluence between the loss of innocence reported in the myths and legends of Western tradition and the rupture from those traditions introduced by the stories in these testimonies. Adam and Eve enter into time and through striving and suffering are given instruments to rationalize their loss. As former victims revisit the physical and mental terrain of their losses, they find that neither time nor memory furnishes them with a principle of rationalization. Nothing exists to redeem the moment they recall, and to their dismay, nothing exists to redeem them as they recall it. If one function of narrative is to unify the subjective and objective visions of reality, then their testimonies fail—but, as with guilt, only because in approaching them we defer to traditional terminology of continuity, fusion, and growth. The impromptu self that emerged from the camp situation does not continue to evolve and adapt beyond its perimeters. It loses its raison d'être with the moment of so-called liberation, though as we have seen, it lingers in consciousness as an orphaned incubus long after its apparent demise.

Alex H. struggles with the consequences of this situation. Similar to Nathan A., he sought vindication after coming to America by enlisting in the United States army and served on active duty in Korea. He calls these the happiest days of his life because all the time he was in Germany in the camps he could do nothing to defend himself; now he had a gun and could defend himself and kill the enemy. So strong is his need to purge his impromptu self and restore his integrated self that he goes into seemingly irrelevant detail about battle confrontations that resulted in fatalities, some inflicted by him. Then an introspective mask covers his face, and we are forced once again to construe silence. Finally, he confesses a paradox of his post-Holocaust life: he is unhappy that this should have made him happy. There is, he now realizes, no vindication, no connection, no compensation for the state to which circumstances reduced him during those years.

In July 1983 (the date of his testimony), nearly sixty years old, Alex H. admitted that "all those years in the camps in Germany" were catching up with him, leaving him depressed and feeling that life was no longer worth living: "I feel I have no more fight left in me, and of course my family feels it and they suffer from it." He tries to explain the reasons: "Something good or bad if I *understand* it, it is not as bad even if it is very bad." He can manage it. But his past remains locked in a moral vacuum. Unlike most former victims, however, he seeks to move beyond his discontent, outside the circle of isolated and insulating testimony he is engaging in. He speaks of the possible value of former victims sharing their ordeals with one another, in order to use an insight he has achieved through the process of testifying. "Everybody thinks somehow that certain things happen to him, he is unique," he says. "When I spoke to you [meaning one of the interviewers], I find out there are other people that felt the same way. I feel it would be a great help to have such meetings." But he means much more than sympathetic conversation. We could have these meetings, he adds, "where one could speak out and be reassured that he isn't some kind of a beast or animal."[20] Then he shrugs his shoulders and sighs, a stifled appeal, as it were, from the impromptu self of that time, still wrestling with the conflict between the so-called morality of the camp environment and the morality of contemporary society.

Tainted memory, memory of that impromptu self unrecognizable even through the act of mental recovery, is a monument to ruin rather than reconstruction. This is one of the most melancholy legacies in the subtexts of these testimonies. In another example, throughout his narrative Leo G. hints at the degradation that "transpired" between victims during the worst moments of the disaster but firmly refuses to offer details because "it can't be described." Nonetheless, after more than three hours, the interviewer asks him, "What are you left with today," and to this he readily if allusively replies: "I envy people that can get out of themself for one minute sometimes. . . . They can laugh, enjoy. You know, you see a movie. Anybody in my situation cannot laugh and enjoy, through inside, you know. Only superficially. There's always in the back of your mind everything. How can you, how can you *enjoy* yourself? It's almost a crime against the people that you lost [in his case, mother, father, and six brothers and sisters], that you can live and enjoy yourself." He acknowledges the joy that he receives from his family, his children, their marriages, their accomplishments, but continues, "Enjoyment is cut to the end of my days. I just can't get out of myself."

Self here clearly operates on two levels, separated by an intervening, untranscended loss. The exasperation of this witness at his inability to explain the difference, together with his simultaneous conviction that no one would understand anyway, frames for us but does not clarify the buried dilemma of testifying. Once again, however, the careful hearer may be able to suspect what is troubling him:

> You almost need to educate them for them to understand. If they don't understand it, I don't blame them. They can't. They can't. . . . Talking about it, all this or more, each incident needs so much explaining. It needs explaining to the other person how and why, for them just to grasp it, that you could live through it. That you could live through it consciously without doing anything, without converting your

own person to a different person than you are right now. All
this you lived through, all this you saw, and you go out and
work for money, or you go out and drive a car or whatever
. . . . How could you? . . . It should be as, you know, some
people that turn away from life, because they found it's
senseless, it doesn't add up. And I and the kind of people
that went through it should know that it doesn't add up.
Nothing adds up. It doesn't make any sense. Nothing justi-
fies it. To go on and on after you know what the world is like
or what it was.

He echoes the woman who lamented "I think we are not normal
because we are so normal." If a nostalgia for the heroic spirit that
enabled him and his fellow victims to endure were available, it
would offer him the support he needs to restore continuity to his
existence. What gnaws at his memory is the question of *how* one
lived through it, and then, of how one lived through it *"without
converting your own person to a different person than you are right now"*
(italics added). Obviously, he cannot fall back on a heroic tradition
to transcend this dilemma, because to do so would violate his
sense of nothing adding up. But what else could remove the
obstacles impeding his quest for an image of the integrated self?

The logic of character informing his vision now is neither cause
nor consequence of the humiliation he experienced through more
than three years in Gross Rosen, Dora-Nordhausen, and Bergen-
Belsen. "I couldn't in good conscience tell you even privately
about the horrors on that train," he says about the seven-day
journey in open boxcars to Bergen-Belsen.[21] But other accounts of
such voyages, which include death by freezing and starvation,
and even cannibalism, give us a clue to his reluctance to use the
vocabulary of heroic resistance to justify—or rectify—his ordeal.
His reluctance betrays not only a disinclination to speak about
such things but the absence of an idiom and a context of values to
enable such a discussion.

"Nazism and its effects," writes historian Richard J. Evans, speaking of the current *Historikerstreit* in West Germany, "cannot be made real to people who . . . were born long after the event, if they are presented in crude terms of heroes and villains." If he had added "to people who were born during the event but did not share any of its experiences," he might have been talking of the audiences of victim testimony too. "The nature of the moral choices people had to make," Evans continues, "can only be accurately judged by taking into account the full complexities of the situations in which they found themselves."[22] But it may be easier for historians, with a variety of documents available for research, to reconstruct the moral complexities of Hitler's rise to power and the evolution of the Final Solution, than it is for students of the camp experience, even after a collaborative effort with the victims, to assess the impact on the private (as against the public) self of such an ordeal.

One of the distinctive qualities of oral testimony is its immediacy. Even though witnesses obviously have reflected on their past before their interview, they reencounter the duality of their experience in the process of retelling it. Oddly enough, they say little of their Nazi oppressors once the deportations have begun. They wrestle instead with the dilemma of their own identity and the impossibility of functioning as a normal self in situations so unprecedented and unpredictable. They struggle further with the incompatibility between the impromptu self that endured atrocity and the self that sought reintegration into society after liberation. Both the nature of the villainy and the range of heroic responses during the ordeal elude traditional categories, and this unsettling quandary itself becomes the underground theme of many testimonies. For example, although a concept like "spiritual resistance" has gained increasing popularity among some commentators (including former victims) in their *written* accounts of the disaster, witnesses in the oral testimonies I have seen avoid this expression, or anything resembling it. They demur virtually unanimously when it is raised by an interviewer, as they do when the word *heroic* is introduced. Their responses to such language range from dismay to disdain, in spite of the tempting offer of a verbal way out of their dilemma.

The lesson leading to this refusal was a painful one. Vera B. says that she was lucky in her jobs: in Auschwitz, she was assigned to take care of a group of children, really teenagers between the ages of twelve and eighteen. She took them out to the edge of the camp to play games with them, sing songs, help them to occupy their time. She even performs (in Hungarian) one of the songs they used to sing together. After six weeks, she grew very attached to them. Then one day she appears at the barracks where the children were housed and found the Kapo crying. "What's the matter?" she asks. "During the night they came and took the children and sent them to the gas chamber," the Kapo replies. And Vera B. muses: "If they knew all along they were going to do that, why did they recruit me to take care of the children and play with them for six weeks?"[23] Her perplexity, admirable and naive, helps to give birth to the impromptu self, which narrows the scope of its gestures to instinctive reactions to unexpected situations, gestures that cannot assume (as Vera B. apparently does here) some necessary connection between intention and result.

Those who were willing to abandon such expectations, to forgo traditional forms of assurance or reassurance, were in a better position to understand that short-term opportunities were the only ones still available to them, though even these involved constant risk and the threat of failure. Spiritual resistance is appealing as a concept because it does not require any control over one's *physical* destiny, dwells in a realm detached from the hostile camp environment, and transcends the need to confront its ravages. The impromptu self was less ambitious. Irving F., for example, tells of hiding with his wife, young child, and other family members in a concealed bunker behind a false wall in the cellar of a house. A woman who had not been able to join them tries to gain entrance, inadvertently betraying their bunker to the police. While the police are breaking in, Irving F. climbs alone into a grain oven in the cellar, stretches out on his back, and lies there undetected for several hours. Everyone else is taken away, and he never sees them again.[24]

Eventually, Irving F. made his way to the woods and fought with partisans until Soviet troops liberated the area. After the war, he learned that three of his six siblings had survived. What saved him originally was not a plan, however, but a desperate movement that preserved only him in a roomful of relatives. Had he not done that, he would surely have shared their fate. Would that have helped them? The impromptu self is immune from such judgment, because once the impulse to stay alive begins to operate, the luxury of moral constraint temporarily disappears. Tainted memory then replaces judgment, as it deposes guilt. Retrospectively we may not approve of this situation (any more than surviving victims do)—the internal motives ruling such conduct seem so alien to our own. But we cannot deny their reality; perhaps that explains why we retreat to spiritual resistance—to reestablish a veneer of respectability for situations in which harsh necessity deprives the individual of the familiar dignity of moral control.

Because the impromptu self acted in an atmosphere of total unpredictability, one is not surprised to learn how rarely it acted at all. The Germans capitalized on the psychological paralysis that plagued their victims, besieged as they were by uncertainty. This particularly insidious kind of malice left little flexibility for defensive response. When such responses did occur, as in the following two examples, the circumstances are so singular that they illustrate exceptional rather than widely available opportunities. Leon S. and his wife, both Jewish physicians, were sent by the *Judenrat* (Jewish Council) to a village near Lvov to help fight a typhus epidemic, which the invaders feared as a threat to their own health. While there, the two obtain from a priest false birth certificates, verifying that they are Polish Christians, and they alter their identity papers to make them consistent with these counterfeit documents. Then, with the help of peasants, they manage to relocate under their new identity in eastern Poland. One day they see a notice that the Germans are looking for doctors to be trained to prevent typhus outbreaks. They apply to be "exterminators" (Leon S.'s own word, used with no apparent sense of irony) and after passing a brief training course are told to report to Warsaw for assignment.

What happened next belongs to the category of what I call "crucial moments," situations requiring a split-second response that often made the difference between life and death. Such reactions combine a sense of danger with bluff, bravado, willingness to take a risk, but above all a rejection of normal and familiar deference to authority or apparently insuperable obstacles. The expectation of moral continuity, together with situational constraints, usually inhibits this way of expressing the impromptu self; perhaps because he was already living with false identity papers, Leon S. was able to discard this expectation. When he and his wife detrained in Warsaw, a Pole approached them and said, "You come with me." He takes them across the street to the police station, declaring: "You are Jewish. What sort of papers do you have?" The moment is especially vivid for us, because Leon S. and his wife display those very papers before the camera as they speak.

The policeman examines the wife's papers and says, "This is a good document." Leon S. laughs as he tells this, "because I erased everything [on his wife's papers] and I wrote it up again." He changed the date, erased the name of her religion teacher (a Jewish name), and wrote in the name of a priest. But the policeman, still suspicious of Leon S. himself, says, "Come with me into the other room" and determines that Leon S. has been circumcised. "I have to deliver you to the Germans," he announces. Perhaps because he is already living a disguised life, Leon S. seems not to have suffered the warring tensions that, as we saw earlier, beset a

Schifra Z. The threat activated a flow of adrenalin into the impromptu self that led to instantaneous action in behalf of that self. Its reactions, whether defensive (in the camps) or, as here, aggressive, cannot be calculated in advance or measured against a system of belief. Memory recaptures the moment but does not explain the psychological basis for Leon S.'s uncharacteristic behavior. He smiles and recalls: "Well, I'm not a tame person . . . and I gave [the Polish policemen] a speech. I said: 'You s.o.b.'s, you are Poles. Stalingrad is already fallen. How long will it take for the war to come to an end? How will they view such people as you bastards here, who are delivering Jews to the Germans?'" He explains that he and his wife are doctors (and shows them the official summons to a hospital in Warsaw, incidentally confirming for him and for them his false identity), whose job is to control the typhus epidemic and save people like them. Then Mrs. S. adds, to us: "He let us go." Leon S. removes his watch and puts it in the policeman's hand. And they leave.

One inclined to overestimate symbolic gesture might argue that the climactic dismissal of conventional time in the turning over of the watch was the last in a series of renunciations, beginning with the abandonment of Jewish identity and ending with the rejection of authority, that contains the clue to the genesis of the impromptu self in its most affirmative guise. In Leon S.'s case, there is an additional uncanny reversal of roles that must have influenced his recalled account of his impromptu behavior in that crucial moment. For most of the war, until the Russians arrived in July 1944, he and his wife lived in a small village in central Poland near Lublin, "not far from Majdanek," he reminds us. Then he describes in a curiously detached way his eventual assignment to an exterminating unit orgianized by the National Institute of Hygiene. As he relates it, they went to a house and sealed off a room by closing the windows and stuffing rags and newspapers in the cracks. They then placed a sulphur preparation, made by the Germans, in sand and ignited it so that it gave off smoke. Then they sealed the doors—and that's how they killed the lice! Throughout this part of his narrative, he seems totally oblivious to any resemblance between his work and the doom of the Jews. In spite of his silence on that subject, however, one wonders if so transparent an analogy has really eluded him.

Near the end of his testimony, he and his wife give opposite versions of what their experience has left them with. His wife remains with the memory, as she twice exclaims, of four years of fear, beginning with a fear of being recognized, and then with its consequences. But Leon S. insists, "You want to know the truth? I don't have memories of fear. I have memories of defiance and being prepared for everything." He calls this a "soldier's attitude," restoring his behavior during that crucial moment to a familiar vocabulary and a traditional image. But the episode, as he pictured it, was hardly military as it unfolded, although his spontaneous action then is transformed now into "being prepared for anything." Whether the giving of the watch represents defiance or conciliation is left for the audience to decipher, compounding the difficulty, so evident in these testimonies, of dividing one's trust between the teller and the tale.

Events conspire to favor Leon S.'s gesture of defiance, which should not be mistaken for a model of successful survivor strategy. If the Polish policeman had been a member of the SS or Gestapo, then Leon S.'s outburst would have proved futile, and possibly fatal—if he had dared to attempt it at all. There is no evidence that his good fortune depended on a proper reading of human character or common moral values, or a prevailing spirit of community more basic than the artificial division between Jew and Pole. The motives appear self-ish from every point of view. Moreover, although Leon S. seems exempt from tainted memory as he triumphantly recalls his successful tactic, the opening of his interview establishes a much more somber context for his later life-saving maneuver, incidentally confirming the unusual circular structure of many of these narratives. In the early portion of their testimony, he and his wife show photographs of various family members who were killed by the Nazis, validating their loss even as they attempt to reclaim a semblance of the normal family life that has now disappeared. The failure of the effort, in a stunning example of tainted memory at its most literal level, is dramatized when Leon S. shows a picture of his nephew, a brother's son, and laments: "I don't remember his name. . . . I have never seen him." And there's no one he can ask: his three brothers and sister, their spouses and all their children, were consumed by the catastrophe. The shape of Leon S.'s memory, as it celebrates "being prepared for everything" at the end of his story, lies beneath the shadow of forgetfulness, which he himself had introduced in the beginning. The wary hearer will respond to the dynamic bond joining the two, a bond that qualifies the victory Leon S. enthusiastically attributes to the impromptu self.[25]

That self apparently acts alone, though in reality it is never far removed from the family unit. Even Leon S.'s conduct was intimately allied with the fate of his wife. More often, as we have seen, the impromptu self recalls its responses with grief or humiliation, since its acts annul the legacy of mutual family support. Two episodes from the narrative of Mira B. converge to illustrate the significance of seizing the crucial moment after shedding conventional expectations or restraints. In the Vilna ghetto, where she and her parents and brother share a tiny apartment, rumors of executions in the Ponary woods outside the city had not yet achieved the status of certainty. One day, the Germans appear and take her brother away. She and her mother follow him and the other Jews from the roundup as they are led down the street. Mira B., who has concealed a dress beneath her coat, manages to speak with her brother in Hebrew. "Listen, Mula [Samuel]," she says to him, "we don't know what they are going to do. Go into the bathroom [a public bathroom along the way]. Put on my dress, and come home with me." But he refused, she reports; he didn't believe that they were going to murder him that night, since they had announced the purpose of the roundup to be the recruiting of workers.

Obviously, there is no guarantee that Mira B.'s brother could have followed her suggestion without being detected or that even if he had, he might have rescued himself for more than a few days. But according to his sister, his inability to believe that he was on his way to his death at Ponary inspired his refusal. The illusion that he was still in control of part of his destiny inactivated the impromptu self—and sealed his doom. Later that day, he was led to the ravine with the others (as witnesses testified afterward), where they were all shot. Clearly, when two years later Mira B. and her mother were arrested by Lithuanian police and taken to the local police station before being turned over to the SS, her brother's reluctance was still vivid in her memory.

She describes in elaborate detail the "geography" of the station, illustrating with her fingers on the table as the camera focuses on them: a long corridor with a room at the end on the left, where a Lithuanian guard locks them in. Once inside, she says to her mother: "Listen, they are going to take us from here most probably to Ponary and shoot us; I am not going to carry my body to where they want me to be buried. They will have to shoot me somewhere else, and carry my body." Then she continues: "I'm going to try to run out of here. . . . Promise me, please, if I don't come back, you should know that I am free, that I succeeded. Let's meet tonight." Given her brother's fate, one wonders what she bases her hopeful enthusiasm on as she instructs her mother: "If I don't come back, I want you to get off as they walk you to Ponary. I want you to get off to the sidewalk and try to escape." Her mother promises. She then gives her a friend's address, where she will be able to find her.

The nurturing instinct of community effort in behalf of survival could not have functioned in this situation; we embrace with difficulty the solitary struggle of the impromptu self to stay alive. For her plan to succeed Mira B. must of necessity isolate herself from her fellow victims. She bangs on the door of the room, and when the guard puts his head in to inquire what the problem is, she replies, "I have to go to the bathroom." He asks, "Who else has to go?" When five or six women respond, he leads them all back down the long corridor to a door at the end on the right, which is the entrance to the bathroom. Opposite is the door to the street. Mira B. stands just inside the bathroom doorway, as the women wait their turn. The guard steps inside to learn what is taking so long, looking to the right, and while he does so, Mira B. slips past him and walks out the exit opposite.

Mira B.'s careful description of the external geography of her situation suggests that her internal landscape, cluttered with reasons for not doing what she is about to do, has temporarily gone vacant. Some such condition seems necessary to explain the origins of the impromptu self. She walks slowly down the street, but after a block she hears heavy footsteps behind her. She keeps walking, then decides to stop and turn around. The guard is following her. "Did you have to go after me?" she asks him. No answer. "What do you have against me? What did I do to you?" Silence. "I have Lithuanian friends, very good ones . . . willing to help me now. Do you really want to stop me?" He insists that she return, but she balks: "You can shoot me right here." He then unexpectedly engages her in a long conversation on why (this is his opinion, not hers) the Jews are going so willingly to their deaths, without protesting. But he continues to refuse to release her, until she insists: "I'm not going to go back. You can shoot me here if you want to."[26]

This is a succinct example of the defiance that Leon S. had spoken of, though like him Mira B. is not faced with SS but a young Lithuanian, whose language she happens to speak. After more conversation, after she forces her gold watch on him a second time (which he once more declines to take), he at last sends her off with his blessing. So many contingencies intrude on her plight that it is impossible to assign to a single motive or explanation the success of her plan, tempting though it may be to applaud her spiritual dignity and resolute will. These are universal qualities, lauding the victory of inner virtues over adversity. The self-ish basis of the impromptu self, which requires Mira B. to abandon her mother, or at least to make staying alive a solitary rather than a collective venture, contradicts the social impulses of those inner virtues. Had she remained with her mother through family loyalty, they both would have been shot at Ponary. Staying alive is at best a fragmentary achievement, because she never saw her mother again. Even in its most triumphant guise, the impromptu self seems inseparable from tainted memory. Personal survival lives in the permanent shadow of family loss.

Memory is thus the reverse of redemptive, as the witness plunges into a buried past to rescue the private truths of the event we call the Holocaust. The ultimate experience apparently disengaging atrocity from survival, the so-called moment of liberation, provides some especially dramatic testimony in these narratives. Through the content of their questions, interviewers *invite* witnesses to give detailed accounts of their feelings of joy when they realized that their ordeal was over. We need to understand more about how this psychology of expectation can impose itself on the reality of the situation and gradually forge a myth that would displace the truth. Asked how she felt when liberated, one witness replies: "We were weak. We were starving. We were in a state of apathy. We simply sat and stared into space."[27] Another is more graphic—and more suggestive: "And you know, when I was liberated . . . I was two days on my bed. I not was hungry, I not want dresses, I was [so] sick two days. But at this moment I realize I am alive and I have nobody and I am living." The sudden conjunction of the discontinuous (or impromptu) self that had managed to stay alive with the continuous self (the family member who no longer had a family) receives eloquent understatement here. Terms like *spiritual resistance* and *heroic behavior* dwindle into irrelevancy.

The following brief exchange between an interviewer and this same witness illustrates the kind of well-intentioned but subtle prodding that often results when the normal world encounters the unfamiliar lineaments of atrocity:

WITNESS: I sometimes myself not can believe a person can be so strong. And can lift over so many things.

INTERVIEWER: As you did.

WITNESS: You know, I think I'm normal, and still be normal, and still have children, raise families, and talk and work. [But] something *stimmt nicht*. Something is wrong here. In the chemistry something is wrong.

INTERVIEWER: But you must be very strong and you must have had a will to have survived it.

WITNESS: [Shrugs, looks away.] Look . . .

INTERVIEWER: And you're here to talk about it, and to tell future generations.

WITNESS: I'm strong, I'm strong, *aber* [but] when I tell you I never was doing anything *really* to live . . .

INTERVIEWER: To help yourself . . .

WITNESS: My fate push me, you know, I not help myself.

She then explains, in an apparent attempt to define what she means by "fate," that while she was in Auschwitz her parents (already murdered) came to her twice in dreams and gave her advice that, as she now believes, saved her life. "They came to you when you needed them," the narrator encourages, hopefully. "I need them *now* too," the witness dryly replies, ending the dialogue.[28]

"*Keep watch over absent meaning*,"[29] Maurice Blanchot warns in one of the gnomic fragments from *The Writing of the Disaster*. Our belief in heroic will, deeply etched on the modern sensibility by literary and scriptural traditions from ancient times to the present, intrudes on the need to understand what lies behind the troubled avowal by a former victim that despite her contented present life, something still *"stimmt nicht."* I am reminded of the unsettling, paradoxical discovery by a former deathcamp inmate that one can be alive after Sobibor without having survived Sobibor. When Blanchot distinguishes between "knowledge of the disaster" (*du désastre*) and "knowledge as disaster" (*comme désastre*), he defines the frontiers separating the violated self of the witness from the inviolable self of the audience—of us. It can scarcely be accidental that he begins the passage introducing this distinction by quoting Nietzsche's question, a virtual classical formula, "Have you suffered for knowledge's sake?"[30] The disaster of the Holocaust invalidated forever whatever force that formula once retained, though Blanchot fully appreciates the possibility of knowledge as disaster smiting us and nonetheless leaving us untouched. This would estrange us even further from the testimonies of former victims, the burden of whose stories is the *impossibility* for them of such an eventuality.

Blanchot presses language to its limits in his efforts to prod the imagination into original vision. *Knowledge of the disaster* skirts the subversive essence of the event, whereas *knowledge as disaster* affirms its disruptive impact. But formulation in words is one thing, conversion to insight another matter entirely, as Blanchot himself confesses when he admits that knowledge as disaster often shields us from its implications and "carries us off, deports us [surely a scrupulously chosen term] . . . straight to ignorance, and puts us face to face with ignorance of the unknown, so that we forget, endlessly" (3). Oral testimony is a form of endless remembering, a direct challenge to us to convert our ignorance of the unknown into some appreciation of the disparate, half-articulated tensions that inhabit the former victims' narratives. We gain this appreciation not by transforming words into meaning but by observing the process by which one meaning cancels, neutralizes, or interacts with another as the narratives unfold. Because so many witnesses have a vivid sense of the division resulting from having survived disaster, their testimonies invite us to participate in the painful difficulties they experience when reorganizing disorder. The absence of a complex verbal texture like Blanchot's in their stories highlights the value of his commentary, which stretches language to meet the demanding requirements of atrocity; but it also reminds us of a preliminary and perhaps more urgent need— to abandon the preconceptions that our unstretched language offers to protect our comfortable ignorance. Blanchot follows a bold and innovative verbal path, conjuring the reader's imagination to do the same in its pursuit of the impact of the disaster on the self.

Because oral testimonies do *not* provide us with the kind of constant verbal stimulus that Blanchot or authors of written survivor narratives do, they initiate us into thinking about the disaster with fewer guidelines than a reader is usually provided with. Interviewers' attempts to provoke such frames invariably fail, leaving us with unassimilated texts that demand of us what we might call interpretive remembering. Most written texts flow continuously, compelling us to follow their sinuous turns if we wish to stay mentally afloat. Oral testimonies pause in a variety of ways, one of which is the display of visual icons, like the gouache portrait mentioned earlier, that challenge our capacity for construing silence. Many witnesses, for example (much like Leon S. and his wife), begin or end their testimonies by holding up family photographs, some of them containing a dozen persons or more. Conventional thinking responds to the dignity of the faces before us. But we are prompted to ask by the subtext of the narrative whether the point is to remind us that they once *were* or no longer *are* alive. Is it an effort at rescue or an avowal of loss? Are we gazing at presence—or absence? In fact, oral testimonies offer us both, although the un-story, as Blanchot calls it, raises the issue of how to establish a connection between consequential living and inconsequential dying.

This is the essential dilemma for surviving victims in these testimonies. It may be the insoluble riddle of the Holocaust itself. An underlying discontinuity assaults the integrity of the self and threatens the very continuity of the oral narrative. Perceiving the imbalance is more than just a passive critical reaction to a text. As we listen to the shifting idioms of the multiple voices emerging from the same person, we are present at the birth of a self made permanently provisional as a result of fragmentary excavations that never coalesce into a single, recognizable monument to the past. A last example of multiple voices issuing from the same individual will have to illustrate this idea. They belong to Leo L., who began his encounter with Nazi oppression in a little-known labor camp called Rakhotsky Mlin—the first and the worst, he calls it—followed by Auschwitz, Dachau, Sachsenhausen, Buchenwald, and Ohrdruf. Asked what effect this has had on his life, he replies almost automatically with the language of heroic enterprise: "It makes you a much stronger human being to fight for the right of humanity." But other voices possess him too, because less than a minute later he adds that anyone who went through this kind of atrocity ends up "not being the way you should be." No doubt he means both; can one also *be* both? Earlier in his testimony, he had helped to define the impromptu self by deploring his inability to relate to his own tragedy. The heroic self, by definition, helps to *create* its own tragedy and to live or die by the consequences. Leo L. crystallizes the difference by his last words, the abrupt and forlorn questions that end his two hours of testimony, and that will seem non sequiturs only to those who have not been hearing him and his fellow witnesses: "How did my mother look? When did they take her away?"[31] Unanswered and unanswerable, they remain permanent obstacles to the rebirth of the heroic self in the oral narratives of former Holocaust victims.

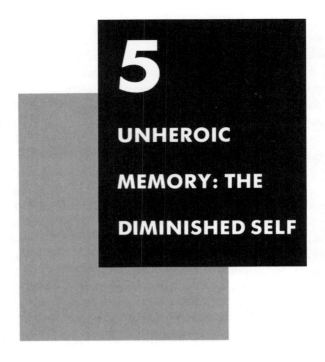

5

UNHEROIC MEMORY: THE DIMINISHED SELF

The ease with which the self adapts its identity to a surrounding situation threatens the notion that spiritual *value* is the primary incentive for human conduct. Hence many Holocaust commentators cling to a grammar of heroism and martyrdom to protect the idea that the Nazi assault on the body and spirit of its victims did no fundamental damage to our cherished belief that, even in the most adverse circumstances, character is instinctively allied to the good. Consider, for example, Martin Gilbert's *The Holocaust*, an epic chronicle based on the testimony of former victims about the fate of the Jews in World War II. Gilbert has unearthed accounts of Nazi atrocities in virtually every ghetto, village, town, and city in Eastern Europe, to add to the more familiar horrors of labor, concentration, and deathcamps. He records them with a ruthless and unsettling resolve not to masquerade the worst, leaving the reader heavy-hearted and bereft. Thus I was not prepared when I reached the last paragraph of his volume. At first incredulous, then perplexed, and finally exasperated, I could not imagine why Gilbert would feel obliged to end with an array of sentiments that he contradicts on almost every other page of his own chronicle. Although the narrative contains more than three dozen detailed chapters describing individual and mass murders across the face of Europe, the final paragraph reads:

> In every ghetto, in every deportation train, in every labor camp, even in the deathcamps, the will to resist was strong, and took many forms: fighting with those few weapons that could be found, fighting with sticks and knives, individual acts of defiance and protest, the courage of obtaining food under the threat of death, the nobility of refusing to allow the Germans their final wish to gloat over panic and despair. Even passivity was a form of resistance. "Not to act," Emanuel [sic] Ringelblum wrote in the aftermath of one particularly savage reprisal, "not to lift a hand against the Germans, has become the quiet passive heroism of the common Jew." To die with dignity was a form of resistance. To resist the dehumanizing, brutalizing force of evil, to refuse to be abased to the level of animals, to live through the torment, to outlive the tormentors, these too were resistance. Merely to give witness by one's own testimony was, in the end, to contribute to a moral victory. Simply to survive was a victory of the human spirit.[1]

Perhaps no more succinct example exists in Holocaust commentary of what I call the grammar of heroism and martyrdom. In spite of its chiefly rhetorical origins, the language of these lines has hardened into a mythology (though I suspect that cliché would be a more exact description) about human behavior during the Holocaust. To test my conviction that the text did not sustain his conclusion, I opened Gilbert's *Holocaust* at random and found the following testimony, from a woman named Lena Berg:

> Every roll call was a selection: women were sent to the gas-chamber because they had swollen legs, scratches on their bodies, because they wore eyeglasses or head kerchiefs, or because they stood roll call without head kerchiefs. Young SS men prowled among the inmates and took down their numbers and during the evening roll call the women were ordered to step forward, and we never saw them again. Maria Keiler, a childhood friend and schoolmate, died that way. She had a scratch on her leg and an SS man took her number. When they singled her out at roll call, she simply walked away without even nodding goodbye. She knew quite well where she was going, and I knew it, too; *I was surprised at how little upset I was* [italics added].[2]

Whatever Ringelblum may have felt in the Warsaw ghetto or his hiding place outside, Lena Berg did not share his point of view from inside a Nazi deathcamp (Majdanek). The paralysis of victim and witness here flows from a profound despair that Ringelblum must have shared at times but chose to ignore when he wrote of the "quiet passive heroism" of the Jews. A multitude of other examples—and this one is not in the least exceptional— would show that Gilbert's scheme for imposing closure does not spring from the personal accounts that comprise the bulk of his history. Indeed, his penultimate line—"Merely to give witness by one's own testimony was, in the end, to contribute to a moral victory"—finds scarcely any confirmation in his text *or* in the much more substantial interviews that form the basis for my own discussion. Once we hear the whole story and not just excerpts, we understand why Lena Berg does not introduce her friend's walking off to be gassed as a martyr's death or her own passivity (and concealed relief at her escape—*this* time?) as a heroic gesture or a form of resistance. To speak of her melancholy narrative as a moral victory is to forfeit one's *own* sense of dignity in the presence of such loss, from which Lena Berg's survival cannot be separated.

Gilbert carefully manipulates his honorific nouns ("will," "defiance," "protest," "courage," "nobility," "resistance," "heroism," "dignity," "victory," "spirit") to neutralize their threatening antitheses ("deportation," "death," "reprisal," "evil"), thus building a monument to hope on the rubble of decay. It is a verbal edifice, without human content, but coming as it does as a peroration, as the reader's last contact with language before closing the book, it leaves an enduring impression, for many perhaps the most memorable one. It restores—or tries to restore—grace to a memory that has been soiled by the spectacle of an abnormal and often humiliated dying, which bears no resemblance at all to the dying with dignity that Gilbert mentions here. His tactic is like strewing violets in Dante's and Virgil's path as they toil downward through the noxious atmosphere of the Inferno; many might welcome this whiff of diversion, but those with a nose for sin (or atrocity) would not be distracted by the misplaced fragrance.

The pretense that from the wreckage of mass murder we can salvage a tribute to the victory of the human spirit is a version of Holocaust reality more necessary than true. Gilbert's citation from Ringelblum (inaccurately quoted) that "not to act, not to lift a hand against the Germans, has become the quiet passive heroism of the common Jew," when examined in context, represents an obviously desperate struggle on Ringelblum's part to rescue some shred of meaning from a hopeless situation. But he hardly sounds convinced by his own reassurances. He speaks frankly of the "complete spiritual break-down and disintegration, caused by unheard of terror which has been inflicted upon the Jews for 3 years." The effect of all this, he continues, disapprovingly, to be sure, "is that when a moment for some resistance arrives, we are completely powerless and the enemy does to us whatever he pleases." To justify what might *appear* to others to be a cowardly surrender, Ringelblum explains, without offering any specific evidence, that "every Jew knew that lifting a hand against a German would endanger his brothers from a different town or maybe from a different country."[3]

If Ringelblum had narrowed the locale of possible reprisal to the immediate vicinity of the potential victims, he would have been closer to the physical and psychological reality reported by witnesses in the testimonies we have been examining. But his need to transform an untenable *situation* into a principle of internal moral behavior led him to conclude, after alluding to the slaughter of three hundred unprotesting prisoners of war (one presumes they were Jewish, though Ringelblum doesn't say so), that "not to act, not to lift a hand against Germans, has since then become the quiet passive heroism of the common Jew. This was perhaps the mute life instinct of the masses, which dictated to everybody, as if agreed upon, to behave thus and not otherwise" (180). Why the instinct to remain alive by suppressing fatal gestures of defiance, even when the lives of one's own family members are at stake, should be regarded as "quiet passive heroism" remains a mystery, unless we share the view, contradicted repeatedly by innumerable former victims themselves, that even in the ghettos and camps one's behavior had to be strictly held to a standard of morality inherited from precatastrophe values. When we view the testimony of these former victims in the nonjudgmental way they deserve and demand, we meet attitudes alien to the myths generated by the language of Gilbert and Ringelblum.

Gilbert writes of "duty" during this era as if the matter were utterly unambiguous. His last instance of individual fate prior to his concluding paragraph is the story of a young Jewish girl from Krakow, Matilda Bandet, who refused to join her friends about to flee to the woods just before an impending "action" because she felt that her place was with her aged parents. She remained,

Gilbert tells us, "to be deported with her parents to Belzec, and to perish with them." Her decision is of course admirable, though made at a time when the *certainty* of dying had not yet been absolutely established. Gilbert chooses to elevate it into a noble model: "In her decision not to leave the ghetto, not to try to save herself, but to stay with her parents, Matilda Bandet showed that very human dignity which it was the German wish totally to destroy."4 Shall we then condemn the *loss* of dignity in her friends who decided to flee? Or her parents, for allowing her to remain, thus needlessly sealing *her* fate in addition to theirs?

In his enthusiasm for the spirit of martyrdom, Gilbert in fact attributes to Matilda Bandet an intentionality that issues more from him than from her. What she apparently said, according to her brother's report decades later, was: "They [her parents] have no means of defending themselves. If I leave them, they will be alone."5 Their precise fate is left to our imagination; Gilbert's language forestalls us from asking whether in Belzec Matilda Bandet (or her parents) might have regretted her decision or greeted her doom with fear, horror, dismay, and despair, thus qualifying the human dignity that Gilbert celebrates. Because as historian he has led us to the edge of more mass graves and the entrance to more gas chambers than we want to remember, the need for reconciliation with a milder reality is overwhelming for us, as it must have been for him. To have left us in the ash pits, as Conrad's Marlow might have agreed, would have been too dark altogether.

But such tact provides insulation, not insight. Like Ringelblum's desperate theory of "quiet passive heroism," it seems a frail conclusion to the chronicle of atrocities that precedes it. Ravaged by the latter, can we really expect to feel rescued and consoled by the former, which seeks to restore us to the world of the familiar, of personal honor and family unity, as if the destruction of European Jewry signified little more than a temporary foray against these bulwarks of civilization? One is reminded of attempts to read into the ending of *King Lear* the triumph of the family reunited under the sanction of Christian love. Understanding here is somehow bound up with the idea of reconciliation, though if the testimony of former victims teaches us anything, it is the permanent *impossibility* of that expectation. The integrity of the testimonies, like the integrity of Shakespeare's vision in *King Lear*, depends on our willingness to accept that harsh principle. Such an acceptance depends in turn on the idea that an unreconciled understanding has a meaning and value of its own, one of the most disruptive being that violence, passivity, and indifference are *natural* and *unsurprising* expressions of the human will under certain circumstances. But as we have learned from living with the immutable possibility, if not probability, of nuclear disaster, the disruptive need not necessarily be destructive.

In spite of their vivid and undoubted intimacy with Nietzsche's tyranny of the actual, both Ringelblum and Gilbert felt impelled to devise a language for softening its impact and diminishing the severity of its implications. One of the most agitating effects of testimonies by former victims is their deliberate undermining of the sentiments enshrined in this language. Recalling Gilbert's tribute to Matilda Bandet, we listen to the voice of Sol R.: "There were many, many times when I was *glad* my father wasn't with me. Really, because it was . . . kids used to steal bread from their fathers and vice versa. Starvation, you know . . . or see your father being beat up, you know. There was really . . . this was going on constantly." One day, during an air raid—it is not clear whether in Mauthausen or Ebensee—a close friend, who always had extra bread, was killed. "He was always loaded with bread and here he was lying dead and I grabbed his bread and I gorged myself, you know." Still in visible distress today as he tells the story, he admits: "I've been choking on that bread ever since."

He is, of course, choking on more than bread. Unheroic memory, like the versions of memory studied in earlier chapters, is disheartened by the subversive realities that it recovers. If we listen carefully to Sol R.'s testimony, however, we hear that even more is involved—a conflict between the values that words signify and the equilibrium of the words themselves. The meanings of family, friendship, and freedom shift so rapidly that the stability of the word vanishes. For example, when American tanks liberated Ebensee, Sol R. says that he and his friend Sam, whom he had been together with from the beginning, clung to each other and cried for the first time—not for joy, but because "now really the truth is going to have to come out. Up until then, it was all speculation that our parents [had] not survived, or my sisters or brothers, or anybody. Now the day of reckoning was coming, and also it was very frightening. . . . So as much as we were happy once that we were getting freed . . . the fact is that we gotta go home and find out."[6]

What they discovered was that in spite of their friendship and their freedom, nothing remained of their families, and this altered the relationship of those words to the reality they sought to convey. The disarmed word leads to what I call the diminished self, a major legacy of which is the insight that the weight of recent history has crushed the absolute firmness of language, and hence the kind of consolatory usage that Ringelblum and Gilbert depended on in our examples. Czech writer Václav Havel explores this phenomenon in detail:

No word—at least not in the rather metaphorical sense I am employing the word "word" here—comprises only the meaning assigned to it by an etymological dictionary. The meaning of every word also reflects the person who utters it, the situation in which it is uttered, and the reason for its utterance. The selfsame word can, at one moment, radiate great hopes, at another, it can emit lethal rays. The selfsame word can be true at one moment and false the next, at one moment illuminating, at another deceptive. On one occasion it can open up glorious horizons, on another it can lay down the tracks to an entire archipelago of concentration camps. The selfsame word can at one time be the cornerstone of peace, while at another, machine-gun fire resounds in its every syllable.

The abrupt change in the political (and hence rhetorical) climate of his native land surely made Havel especially sensitive to the unstable resonance of particular words and how they could be used or misused to support various deceptions. Perhaps in a spirit of diplomacy, but also to suggest that the phenomenon is not exclusively a modern one, Havel turns to the French Revolution as one example of his theme. Unheroic memory is imbued with a spirit of irony, its defense against a reconciliation that it cannot embrace. Havel speaks of the "splendid declaration" that accompanied the French Revolution, then reminds us that it was "signed by a gentleman who was later among the first to be executed in the name of that superbly humane text." He then offers some redefinitions that help to clarify our ironic sense of the diminished link between language and value: "Freedom: the shirt unbuttoned before execution. Equality: the constant speed of the guillotine's fall on different necks. Fraternity: some dubious paradise ruled by a Supreme Being!"[7]

Havel is not the only artist to address this issue. In an essay on "The Condition We Call Exile," Soviet émigré poet and Nobel Prize winner Joseph Brodsky describes exiled writers as "embodiments of the disheartening idea that a freed man is not a free man, that liberation is just the means of attaining freedom and is not synonymous with it."[8] Unintentionally, he offers us a fresh if equally disquieting vista for imagining the condition of former Holocaust victims, as well as for assessing the vocabulary that features their experience. As "freed" men and women, such victims enter into a different kind of exile, which often promises less chance for freedom than the situation Brodsky invokes. For many of them, as Sol R. emphasizes, liberation meant a new and unexpected (hence unfamiliar) form of imprisonment. Survival was synonymous with the recognition of *deprival*. Thus the beckoning future challenging the talent and imagination of the exiled writer was not so readily available to the "freed" victim of the Holocaust.

Words like *survival* and *liberation*, with their root meanings of life and freedom, entice us into a kind of verbal enchantment that too easily dispels the miasma of the death camp ordeal and its residual malodors. As we have seen, in their videotaped testimonies witnesses pay equal homage to what they have "died through," or what has died in and through them, and what they have lived through, though a term like *surmortal* to offset *survival* would only perplex the curious reader. Available vocabulary educes a unified view of the self, which invites us to adapt the Holocaust experience to ideas of heroism *during* the event and a process of *recovery* afterward that are inconsistent with the realities of the disaster.

In his posthumous volume *The Drowned and the Saved*, Primo Levi explores the darker side of this dilemma:

In the majority of cases, the hour of liberation was neither joyful nor lighthearted. For most it occurred against a tragic background of destruction, slaughter, and suffering. Just as they felt they were again becoming men, that is, responsible, the sorrows of men returned: the sorrow of the dispersed or lost family; the universal suffering all around; their own exhaustion, which seemed definitive, past cure; the problems of a life to begin all over again amid the rubble, often alone. Not "pleasure the son of misery," but misery the son of misery. Leaving pain behind was delight for only a few fortunate beings, or only for a few instants, or for very simple souls; almost always it coincided with a phase of anguish.[9]

That phase of anguish appears so often as a continuing concern of former victims that we would be irresponsible to avoid or ignore it. Levi exposes part of the problem when he declares that "one can think one is suffering at facing the future and instead be suffering because of one's past." A far more complex variation on this theme, surfacing repeatedly in the testimony of witnesses, is the notion that one can think that one is *rejoicing* at facing the future and instead be suffering because of one's past. If survivor testimony were modernist fiction instead of remembered stress, we might call the tenacious urge to find joy at the end of the story a kind of narrative lure, a subtle attempt to deflect the reader's imagination toward desirable ends in spite of the disagreeable content of the narrative itself. This seems to be the strategy followed by Gilbert in *The Holocaust*.

Ironically, something of this sort becomes part of our experience of the testimonies too, as a chronology infused with hope vies for our attention with frozen moments of anguish. Unheroic memory hovers between the two, hesitant to concede ultimate authority to either one. The wavering responds to the movement of the narrative, which tells two stories at once, one of life and one of death. Because the witness has survived, we can hardly describe the testimony as the triumph of despair; nevertheless, on the screen we meet so often faces of men and women who because of their memories remain in despair of triumphing that we are left groping for a suitable mental stance. Rejecting nihilism *and* heroism, the diminished self lapses into a bifocal vision, as its past invades its present and casts a long, pervasive shadow over its future, obscuring traditional vocabulary and summoning us to invent a still more complex version of memory and self.

The paradox is neatly expressed in a pair of couplets from the

Buchenwaldlied, or Buchenwald song, that prisoners sang each morning as they marched out to work. Midway through the song appear these lines: "Ach Buchenwald ich kann dich nicht vergessen / Weil du mein Schicksal bist" ("O Buchenwald I can't forget you/Because you are my destiny"), while the song ends with the lines: "Wir wollen trotzdem 'ja' zum leben sagen / Denn einmal kommt der Tag da sind wir frei" ("Nevertheless we wish to say 'yes' to life/Because a day will come when we'll be free"). Between the anxieties (*die Sorgen*) that they bear in their hearts, and the freedom they yearn for exists a tension that may be eased by the hopeful sequence of the "lyrics," but not so easily dismissed in the subsequent testimony about it. The witness who sings this song during his interview tries to explain what a "destiny" like Buchenwald has meant for him: a loss of continuity with the future. Instead of linking episodes, and that part of his nature experiencing them, into a unified continuum, his venture into memory makes him feel like a creature removed from its cocoon too soon. We might call it the enigma of truncated growth, an abortion to time. "So there's no tomorrow, really," observes the interviewer to this witness. "No, there isn't any," he replies. "If you think there is, you're mistaken."[10]

Memory's encounters with a disintegrating time is one of the seminal themes of these testimonies. Buchenwald as one's destiny implies a loss of control of one's fate and hence of the formal attire that once clothed the self with its now compromised dignity. Another witness, Peter C., insists that most of his major postwar decisions lead back to his camp experiences. "It seems to me," he says, "that my life was always decided by other people, while I was in railroad cars, and I'm really living on borrowed time." The metaphor is both a cliché and a revelation: looking back, he sees no continuity from then to now, but rather a fixed frame that has always existed around his postwar life, though he claims he only became aware of that rather recently. No trace of cliché, however, appears in his explanation that "it's very difficult to strike a balance between consciously remembering these things and being possessed by them."[11] Ordinarily, we would expect the process of remembering, through a recovery of images and episodes, to animate the past. But former victims who reencounter Holocaust reality through testimony often discover, as Peter C. tries to demonstrate, a disjunction between "consciously remembering," in order to reveal to us what they already know, and the sense of "being possessed" by moments or events that have never left them. This forces us to alter our traditional notion of testimony, which presumes a chronology or sequence and the act of retreating in time and space to a period and place preceding and different from the present.

Two clocks dominate the landscape of Holocaust testimonies, a time clock (ticking from then to now) and a space clock (ticking from there to here). They seek to sensitize our imaginations to twin currents of remembered experience. One flows uninterruptedly from source to mouth, or in more familiar historical terms, from past to present. The other meanders, coils back on itself, contains rocks and rapids, and requires strenuous effort to follow its intricate turns, turns that impede the mind's instinctive tropism toward tranquility. To vary the analogy and translate it into literary terms: these testimonies include both story and plot. The "story" is the chronological narrative, beginning with "I was born" and ending with "I was liberated" (though some add epilogues about life after liberation). The "plot" reveals the witness seized by instead of selecting incidents, memory's confrontation with details embedded in moments of trauma. The role of the interviewer often appears to be to bring the witness back to the story: "What happened next?" And witnesses are both willing and reluctant to proceed with the chronology; they frequently hesitate because they know that their most complicated recollections are unrelated to time. "Arrival at Auschwitz" is both a temporal and psychological event, tellable and told as story *and* plot: Auschwitz as story enables us to pass through and beyond the place, horrible as it may be, while Auschwitz as plot stops the chronological clock and fixes the moment permanently in memory and imagination, immune to the vicissitudes of time. The unfolding story brings relief, while the unfolding plot induces pain. Like the witness, we struggle to synchronize the two: the most precarious challenges arise when this proves to be impossible.

The ensuing experience of disorientation and reorientation represents a dilemma that witnesses try to share with their audience while constantly feeling frustrated by their effort. Conventionally, liberation meant survival, the beginning of renewal, the end of oppression. The very language we use here is ripe with a spirit of inspiration. But as we listen to the voices in these testimonies, a complex version of existence emerges, which I have called *staying alive* instead of the more consoling and affirmative *survival*. Eva K. struggles to verbalize the enigma of remembering that will not placate but can only disturb, a main source of what I call unheroic memory. "It's something what is behind our mind," she says. "Not a philosoph[er], not a nobody who knows this answer. How can this be—no connection? I not understand this myself. You still like flowers, I like a nice home, I like to look good. My *Schmerz* [pain] is inside." She is seized by the *illogic* of her situation: "Why I am alive I don't know. Maybe this is a punishment. I don't know." Liberation brings not rejoicing but recognition, an epiphany, in a line we have met before in another context: "At this moment I realize that I am alive and I have nobody and I am living." In Majdanek and Auschwitz, she assures us, the future meant only tomorrow, and tomorrow meant death. This sense of time as a continuously impending doom clings to her after liberation, becoming part of the inner pain she speaks of, what Primo Levi might have called her phase of anguish.

The conjunction of "living" with "no one," of "tomorrow" with "death" instead of an unfolding future, confirms the close bond between a defamiliarized vocabulary and the emergence of a diminished self left with the heritage of past discords that cannot be orchestrated into present and prospective harmonies. The parallel currents of Eva K.'s memory, one turbulent and the other calm, never merge. But in spite of her inability to unify the fragments of her being, this witness confesses that she wants her children and grandchildren to "see" what her life has been through an extraordinary device that she has conceived. On her tombstone, she says, she intends to have engraved a forearm with her deathcamp number imprinted on it. An inscription of death on a memorial to the dead? This forearm, from which the fist (symbol of defiance?) has been amputated, this indelible number that cancels the name, what can it signify? Has normal dying been infected by atrocity in this truncated image from a woman who will have been twice committed to death? Less an affirmation than a reminder, the emblem challenges us to understand the quality of lives enfolded by two kinds of dying, the rude disruption of the one imposing a permanent sense of disorder on the interval leading up to the other.

The interaction of self with destiny has been a hallmark of tragic literature since its inception. Imagine Agamemnon, Othello, or even Faulkner's Sutpen echoing Eva K.'s conclusion that "my fate push me, you know. I not help myself."[12] What we might name heroic memory died a difficult death in the Holocaust for many of these witnesses, who are loath to view the will to survive as the last gasp of a superseded idea. Self-esteem is crucial to the evolution of heroic memory; the narratives in these testimonies reflect a partially traumatized or maimed self-esteem, lingering like a nonfatal disease without any cure. Heroic memory is virtually unavailable to such witnesses, because for them remembering is invariably associated with a jumbled terminology and morality that confuse staying alive with the intrepid will to survival. Such remembering replaces the Sisyphean gesture of defiance against a hostile universe with particular circumstances that chip away at inappropriate images of a heroic self. Those circumstances in turn give birth to a diminished self that demands a whole cluster of redefinitions and fresh perceptions, a modernized or modernist view of verbal and moral possibilities and limitations that need not be restricted to Holocaust reality alone.

Naturally not every witness speaks in such explicit terms, but enough voices struggle with the *conception* of a diminished self to furnish evidence for its existence and incentive for its retrieval. Chaim E., for example, arrived at Sobibor on a transport with about one thousand other Jews. The SS chose eighteen of them to work inside the camp; the rest, including his brother, were sent directly to the gas chambers. Asked why he thought he was chosen, he replies without hesitation, "Just random picking." The notion of some connection between individuality and fate had simply disappeared. Ignorant of the nature of the place on arrival, he had relied on the rudimentary assumption that work, no matter how hard, would be manageable: "Whatever it happened, you would still be alive. . . . You didn't picture the extreme." But even this misplaced optimism was a view without illusions, at least as Chaim E. explains it today; it was not meant to convey the idea of a self in command of its situation. Chaim E. then formulates some important redefinitions: "On the other side, you didn't have any choices. You just were driven to do whatever you did. So it is not things that you planned that you do; it's just whatever happened, happened. You don't think. You think on the moment what will happen *this* moment, not what the next moment will happen. Because you're just driven, you do whatever you have to do from *other* people." Implicit in this groping but thoughtful appraisal of a defamiliarized reality is the dismissal of a whole lexicon of safeguards for the security of the integrated self: choice, will, power of deliberation, confidence in predictive certainty. This is not to say that these faculties could not be or never were asserted. They were, as Chaim E. admits; but unheroic memory exposes as an illusion the avowal that they retained their absolute value and meaning even in a deathcamp like Sobibor.

One day, Chaim E. says, a detail of ten Jews was sent with two Ukrainian guards to work in the woods outside the camp perimeter. The workers killed their guards and fled. Several of them were recaptured and sent to their death in the gas chambers. The remaining working Jews in the camp were lined up, and every tenth man was selected for a similar death, as a punishment and warning. "I happened to be number nine," Chaim E. dryly reports, brusquely deromanticizing the will to survive that surfaces so often in Holocaust commentary. "Things like that happened very often," he adds, leaving us to decipher the impact of such episodes on traditional celebrations of the self. He then contributes some further insight into the process of defamiliarization that encouraged the emergence of what I have called the diminished self:

> As I say: we were not individuals, we were not human beings, we were just robots where we happened to eat and we happened to do things. And they kept us as long as we have any function. . . . Now if the function was not good, we don't need you, [we] destroy you. . . .
>
> It is hard really to tell what a feeling that is. You are not an individual. You think you are right, you know all the answers, and you try to find logic and things like that that doesn't *exist* at all. It is one purpose there: that is, to *kill* the people, so that's the purpose there. So all the logic doesn't apply there. It is really hard to explain that, to have this *feeling*. It is easy to *tell*, but the feeling is very hard really to bring over to somebody [that] understands it, what really it means.

The laws of logic (like the rules of morality) are designed to *enhance* life; but because the *purpose* of existence in Sobibor was a particularly grim kind of execution, from which *no one* was exempt through his or her attitude or behavior, unheroic memory brings us face to face with the overwhelming implications of a statement like "So all the logic doesn't apply there." Still imprisoned, perhaps, by conventional rules of morality, one of the interviewers asks Chaim E. whether he or any of the others *resented* the escape attempt, which led to the reprisals he described. He patiently explains that staying alive and the ideal of universal brotherhood were anxious bedfellows in the camp environment, where daily and in fact urgent *immediate* needs effectively crippled such ideals. In Sobibor, you "were" as you were perceived, not as you perceived yourself. Circumstances dissipated the self-confidence and self-esteem that were a sine qua non for protecting the individual from what Chaim E. defines as the robotic life.

Nonetheless, when a transport of Soviet Jewish prisoners of war arrived in Sobibor in the fall of 1943, a small group of the work-Jews in the camp planned a breakout under the disciplined and courageous leadership of one of the Soviet officers. After killing nearly a dozen SS and Ukrainian guards, members of the group fled to the nearby woods with hundreds of others, most of whom were shot during the attempt or recaptured and executed shortly thereafter. Fewer than seventy-five made good their escape and managed to survive the war. One of the leaders of the rebellion was killed by Poles in his apartment *after* reaching safety. The Sobibor episode, like the Warsaw Ghetto uprising, is often pointed to as an example of valiant resistance against insuperable odds, an assertion of human dignity in spite of Nazi attempts to crush it. One collection of brief accounts of the breakout by surviving participants is even subtitled "Martyrdom and Revolt," thus linking the episode to a spiritual reality that finds absolutely no echo in Chaim E.'s testimony.[13] A defamiliarized event is drawn by a familiar vocabulary back within the perimeters of heroic memory, with its dependence on the idea of a controllable future. But anyone who *hears* Chaim E.'s language will recognize the implications of his demurral—summoning us to a reversal of such

traditional attitudes: "You were not thinking for tomorrow because tomorrow's thoughts were bad. Today was already better
than tomorrow." Martyrdom has more immortal profiles.

Resistance, as Chaim E. defines it, was a thoroughly practical
matter, having nothing to do with the welfare of the spirit. There
had been much talk of escape from the beginning, he admits, but
nothing was done until someone arrived with sufficient courage—his own word—to take responsibility for the operation. One
of the first tasks was to poison a German *Jewish* Kapo (who was
"holier than the Pope" in fawning on the SS), because they feared
he would betray their plans. "We did the right thing," Chaim E.
insists soberly, but not happily, in a clear exhibition of unheroic
memory; "we couldn't do differently." He joined two others in the
stabbing to death of one German officer, but his action was literally an impromptu deed, because at the last moment he replaced
the man who had been assigned the job but was unable to fulfill it.
He specifically disclaims any heroic intentions, which might have
been inspired by a private or public vision of the self that remained
intact. Of Sobibor, Chaim E. says simply, "Your idealistic things
didn't have any place there." The self-ish motive prevailed: "Only
the survival for your skin, that's what counted. Because that's the
only thing you could do. The others didn't affect at all."[14]

This bleak view seems confirmed by events subsequent to the
escape, since in the woods one group whose members had seized
weapons before their flight used them to threaten fellow es-
capees, warning them to take off on their own. Chaim E. and
Selma (with whom he fled and hid—she later became his wife)
were among those unarmed and forced to separate from the
armed group. The spirit of community, like spiritual dignity and
so many other values that cluster about the idea of a heroic self,
seems to be a privileged motive. The more we examine the details
of episodes like the one Chaim E. recounts, the more we learn
how easy it is to expropriate them for rhetorical uses while ignoring the contradictory impulses that animate them.

Resistance is one of those key words whose resonance is muted by conflicting claims for its definition. The rhetorical force of its romantic associations often overrides the brutal details that deromanticize the incident as it unfolds. The breakout at Sobibor, which required a group cooperation lasting only until the undisciplined rush toward the fences, was in any event exceptional rather than representative. Luna K. offers a view of resistance that, though its emphasis differs from Chaim E.'s, proves even more limiting in the camp situation because it is associated with the external environment rather than inner principle. Only retrospectively, as memory infiltrates the past with an analysis that transforms what was probably vague then to what seems lucid now, do we get a glimpse of the anxieties that stifled the impulse to resist.

Luna K. reminds us that under the Nazi system, resistance was virtually always allied to the threat of reprisal. Not all former victims would agree that the ensuing dilemma was as conscious and deliberate as she makes it sound; but few would deny its portentous role in the demise of the so-called heroic self:

> The one very, very important part . . . it's a question of the whole idea of rebellion and understanding. What was it, and what were the repercussions for rebellion? When you talk about rebellion and resistance and so forth, every single individual who felt that he wanted to perform an act of resistance was an individual who had to make a conscious choice right then and there, that he not only will commit the rebellious act, but he along with himself will take with him scores of people. So it was not a question, "I'm not going to obey it, therefore you can shoot me," but it was "I'm not going to obey it, you can shoot me and another hundred people." And who wanted this kind of responsibility?

I suspect that this testimony is more successful in defining the *situation* determining the boundaries of resistance than the internal psychology of individual victims, which according to other testimonies varied far more widely than Luna K. is willing to admit. Yet she distinguishes clearly between the martyrdom that is an option for the still-intact self and the complex assaults on that self that she observed in ghetto and camp. "You know," she says, "it's very easy to say 'All right, I will be the victim and I will go to the forefront so you can be free'" (a succinct portrayal of the heroic self, though it is doubtful whether even such a resolute and unambiguous gesture is as easy as she maintains); it was far more troublesome, she continues, to say "I will go to the forefront, therefore I'm condemning you to death together with me. And that kind of responsibility was a very, very difficult thing to face."[15] Whether conscience or fear was the more powerful inhibiting motive in such instances, the result is an example of the diminished self, incapable of finding a natural moral response to the unnatural human condition in which it finds itself. The luxury of such responses during this period reveals how much even they depend on situation rather than merely on an internalized system of values—a threatening and in some ways a treacherous possibility for students of moral philosphy.

The psychological consequences of the Nazi strategy to fragment identity by allying it with disunity instead of community is confirmed by Joseph K., who recalls placards posted in his town listing the names of ten residents who would be summarily executed if there were any attack on a German. Heroic endeavor, whether as resistance or sabotage, thus could become not only potential suicide but, as Joseph K. insists, a version of murder. He is less certain than Luna K., however, that prior knowledge would *necessarily* inhibit action. After all, he concedes, the potential hostages were usually strangers, and their sacrifice would have to be measured against the importance of the act of resistance. In excavating such impossible realities, unheroic memory suffocates the fertile concept of identity that we cherish as we listen.

Joseph K. offers an example, in an effort to explain to his interviewers a dilemma as alien to him today as it is to them. If a Gestapo man were abusing his father, he could vent his anger. He could, in fact, even injure the Gestapo man. But the punishment meted to him would be negligible compared to the knowledge that he would be causing the death of ten innocent men. Going to his father's defense, he insists, viewed from the premises established by the Nazis (and which, like it or not, had replaced filial devotion, which now appears as a privileged value, not a spontaneous feeling), would not be resistance but a "foolish act." Part rationalization, perhaps, but part redefinition too, his words reflect a wounded identity, which I call the diminished self, trying to come to terms with memories of the need to act and the simultaneous inability to do so that continue to haunt him today.[16]

Because this need to act issued from an agent who was *never* in control of the consequences, the ensuing drama resists all efforts at interpretation using traditional moral expectations. In a milieu where living was dying, where existence was a death sentence worse than anything that even Camus was ever able to imagine, where today seemed *always* better than tomorrow because freedom was unthinkable and death a certainty, the self functioned on the brink of extinction, and we are left with a series of personal histories beyond judgment and evaluation. The challenge is to enter this world to reverse the process of defamiliarization that overwhelmed the victims and to find an orientation that will do justice to their recaptured experience *without* summoning it or them to judgment and evaluation. Even when resistance and sabotage occurred, they could not be acclaimed, and rarely were, by the actors themselves, as gestures of heroic defiance.

The story of Max B. is the clearest example I know of the legitimacy of these generalizations. Because of an engineering background, he was assigned to a telephone repair detail in Dora-Nordhausen. This gave him an entrée to certain offices, one of which contained a waste basket full of sketches for a V-2 rocket. Armed with this information, he devised a plan to sabotage relays in the guidance system, befriended a Ukrainian who headed a *Kommando* (labor detail) working on the tail section of the rocket, and recruited him as a coconspirator:

> I gave him instructions what to do—how to switch the wires around. . . . One day, we marched in from the camp to work, and we didn't go right to the assigned Kommando. They lined us up . . . in the tunnels, and I see that the whole Kommando that was working on that particular project what I tell them what to do [that is, to sabotage the relays], they had little sticks put in their mouths and steel wire in the back [of their heads], and their hands behind them with wires, tied up. And they lined them all up in front and they said: "Those people commit sabotage . . . and they gonna be hanged now, in front of you. Listen, if something gonna happen again like this, you gonna go the same as they're going."
>
> Can you imagine that time mine feeling? Only one word from that guy, I could be with them. But luckily enough, I told him: "Listen, if I'll go, you'll go, everything will stop. If *you* go, I'll be still here, and I'm gonna advise other Kommandos what to do."[17]

Opportunities for celebrating martyrdom and heroism abound in this episode: the initial decision, which involves more than marginal risk, given the possible consequences; the silence of the Ukrainian, which saved Max B.'s life; the dilemma of Max B., whether to admit his complicity or survive to continue the sabotage. But they are motives that *we* impose on the text, because the testimony does not even hint at these issues. Instead, it steers us away from our value-laden vocabulary to the self-ish definition of self that came to constitute the raison d'être of so many former victims.[18]

Undeterred by the fatal results of his first foray into sabotage, Max B. tries again, convincing another Kommando to open the sealed relays and urinate into them. They too are caught and publicly hanged. "Then I said to myself," the witness concludes, "'OK, Max, it's enough. You survived so long, let's put a stop on it, because I don't want to take any more chances.'"[19] The temptation to interpret his words within the familiar frame of guilt and responsibility is strong, but for men and women under an irrevocable death sentence—and those who experienced the unmanageable daily conditions of Dora-Nordhausen could hardly think otherwise—the failure is situational rather than human. Sabotage seeks to retrieve identity by controlling the future; memory, via Max B.'s testimony, confirms for us Joseph K.'s conviction that underneath its heroic guise it concealed an invitation to suicide and a totally unintended variation on murder.

These are, of course, as I suggested, the interpretations of retrospective memory. Witnesses remain divided between the knowledge that during their ordeal they were deprived of moral agency by their circumstances and their present need to see themselves then and now as the responsible agents of their own destiny and of those around them. Consider the unresolved dilemma of Abraham P. His moment of arrival at Auschwitz on a transport from Hungary with his parents and four brothers is embedded in his memory, separated from time and chronology by an unpreparedness that he still cannot explain. "That very same day there were so many things have happened to us," he declares. "We really couldn't sort them out, and I'm still trying [nearly forty years later] to sort out that day." His parents are sent to the left (to their death), while he, two older brothers, and a younger brother are sent to the right. Abraham P. recalls:

I told my little kid brother, I said to him, "Solly, gey tsu Tate un Mame [go to poppa and momma]." And like a little kid, he followed—he did. Little did I know that I sent him to the crematorium. I am . . . I feel like I killed him. My [older] brother, who lives now in New York . . . every time when we see each other he talks about him. And he says, "No, I am responsible, because I said that same thing to you. And it's been bothering me too." I've been thinking whether he reached my mother and father, and that he *did* reach my mother and father. He probably told them, he said, "Avrum hot mir gezugt, dos ikh zol geyn mit aykh [Abraham said I should go with you]." I wonder what my mother and father were thinking, especially when they were all . . . when they all went into the crematorium [that is, the gas chamber]. I can't get it out of my head. It hurts me, it bothers me, and I don't know what to do.[20]

The impasse is almost prototypical, so often do similar testimonies occur. The dramas they reenact are both fragmentary and complete. We might call the driving force behind them a kind of moral energy in pursuit—but the pursuit is futile. It is futile because the core reality, the inherent theme, the inner conflict, is forever stigmatized by the absence of antagonists against whom yesterday's victims and today's witnesses might direct that energy. We cannot imagine a Hamlet without a Claudius, an Antigone without a Creon, an Ahab without a Moby Dick. But in his narrative as he reconstructs it, Abraham P.'s "enemy" is "to the left" and "to the right," an enemy he doesn't even identify until after the catastrophe; whereas for Joseph K., the "enemy" is a placard listing the names of potentially doomed hostages; and for Max B., anonymous voices that he describes as "they," threatening reprisal. The heroic self cannot flourish in such a vacuum; unheroic memory salvages what it can, often transferring to itself unwarranted personal responsibility in order to forestall the unhappy (but accurate) dénouement that the drama of the victims was played out on a stage where guilt and innocence had no meaning.

Heroic memory searches for a moral vision, a principle supporting the idea of the individual as responsible agent for his actions. After all, Abraham P. *did* advise his brother to join their mother and father, thereby "condemning" him to certain death. How can we tell Abraham P. that both the quest and the principle are *irrelevant* to his narrative? His effort to rescue his brother from oblivion, and to reclaim him for a moral universe, founders on the capricious essence of Auschwitz and the Holocaust, where left equalled death and right equalled not life but only the temporary postponement of death. Retroactive perception helps us to understand why he is still trying to sort out the moment of arrival at the deathcamp. Bizarre as it may seem (but also a compliment to his present integrity), he prefers to accept the possibility of his own blame for his little brother's death rather than to embrace the law of systematic caprice that governed the selection process. As memory seeks to recapture the details of what happened *as* it happened, inappropriate guilt intrudes to obscure the inner chaos implicit in Abraham P.'s confusion. That inner chaos does not reveal itself voluntarily but needs to be mined by an attentive audience as a corollary to the will to survival that *appears* to be the climactic insight of these testimonies.

Unlike the witness in video testimonies, the *writer* afflicted with the chaos attending the futile pursuits of memory has available a form of closure that invites order, if not consolation. For example, Buchenwald survivor, novelist (*The Long Voyage, What a Beautiful Sunday!*), and scriptwriter (*Z, The Confession,* and *La guerre est finie*) Jorge Semprun wrestles endlessly in his fiction with the problem of how memory reconstitutes past atrocity in the present. The narrative structure in *What a Beautiful Sunday!* allows him to impose a perspective on the camp experience that is unavailable to the oral witness. The narrator in this novel, himself a Buchenwald survivor, listens to his friends (also camp survivors) talk about their ordeal and registers dissatisfaction with what we might call their equivalent of video testimony: "I listened as he recounted to me, awkwardly, interminably, with the prolixity natural to that sort of narrative, his life in the camp, the life of the camps. Sometimes, when it became too confused, when it went off in all directions, I wanted to chip in. But I could say nothing, of course. I had to preserve my anonymity." Listening to another friend speaking about Mauthausen, he feels similarly troubled: "Perhaps that isn't the problem for them, recounting convincingly the life of the camps. Perhaps the problem for them is quite simply that they have been there and survived." The fact of having survived thus *interferes* with a convincing portrayal of the events, and although Semprun does not say so at this point, the palpable reason appears to be the one we have encountered repeatedly in the testimonies we have been examining. Memory can be a soothing comfort as well as an avenue to a caustic reality. "The memory is the best recourse," Semprun's narrator later observes, "even if it seems paradoxical at first. The best recourse against the pain of remembering, against the dereliction, against the unspoken, familiar madness. The criminal madness of living the life of a dead man."[21]

Semprun the writer has available an *art* of language that allows verbal formulation to organize and provide a perspective for the paradoxes that assail the "mere" oral witness. An expression like "living the life of a dead man" raises to the level of consciousness a contradiction that plagues the testifiers while remaining only implicit in their narratives. What I have called the experience of survival and deprival achieves the status of imaginative vision in Semprun's description of coming back from the camps as a "return from the lethal adventure of life." When Semprun's narrator concludes that "there is no such thing as an innocent memory. Not for me any more,"[22] he gives artistic legitimization to the concept of tainted memory that infiltrates so many of these videotaped testimonies.

Once we discard the moral implications hovering over the idea of "taint," we have only the immediate testimonies to help us in the empirical efforts to define it here. If heroic memory is allied to moral grandeur, noble intention, pure purpose, logic would expect unheroic memory to reflect a taint whose source was their opposites—the common, the ignoble, the impure. And though witnesses often *feel* driven to present portions of their testimony within this framework—in the absence of any other viable moral system—they *know* that it does not apply. As audience, we sit in the presence of unheroic memory as it dredges up the anguish of loss with guilty demeanor and grieving conscience, though neither satisfies the need to understand or to gain reconciliation with the past.

Examples of this dilemma abound. Although a category like "innocent memory" may appear to be a literary idea, patient listening to testimony allows us to translate it into a practical application and definition: the penalty for survival is the loss not of innocence but of the *memory* of innocence. Liberation brought neither joy nor happiness to Leon W.: "It was an existence, that's all it was. . . . Because too many things happened afterwards. You know, finding out that my family is all gone." The forward momentum that might inspire one to celebrate the restoration of innocence meets a reverse impulse that invites one to regard ruin, and this encounter contaminates memory. A painful confusion penetrates Leon W.'s words as he tries to explain: "I've got something always in the back of my mind which is like a double existence. . . . I live life before and life now [and that life before] is something entirely different from what we have now, and I don't think I can ever forget that."[23] The problem with the doubling hinted at here is that it is totally *unsuccessful*: the diminished self, to which fragments of disaster still cling, is one result. In the years after the war, in a vain attempt to erase from memory the "life before" in the camps that devoured his family, Leon W. refused to talk about it; but the corrosive inroads of unheroic memory are evident in his distress nearly thirty-five years later.

Even more explicit is the voice of Martin R., for whom death by atrocity became (and remains) an *inner* reality even though external events failed to confirm his expectations. Sent to Bergen-Belsen from a Silesian work camp as Russian troops approached, then to a nearby town to clean up the rubble from air raids, he remembers bodies everywhere, "piled up like merchandise." He was convinced that he was doomed to an identical end: "You know you're going to die. Your brain is telling you you're through, you're dead. You're just walking, but you're dead now. Because I was sure I am dead now." His shifting of tenses reflects the problem of narrating in the present events suspended in the limbo of unheroic memory, where the rhythms of chronology disintegrate together with the anticipations of survival. Another persona emerges to echo in the present with quivering vitality a voice that normally would have receded with time: "Now I know I'm gonna die because inside me, inside me tells me something: 'You're dead!' There's nothing there. Just to collapse and die. And waiting. . . . " The sense of a "missed destiny," an uncompleted doom, haunts that persona, splitting the witness's identity and leaving both him and us searching for a principle of psychological reunification.

"Arrested development" is a familiar phenomenon, but what are we to make of its converse, "arrested destruction"? Martin R. recalls dragging huge numbers of corpses into mass graves. "And you're scared to come close," he says, "because you think you're gonna fall in yourself." You push in dead skeletons, "and you see yourself in that skeleton. That's how you're gonna be dumped too." He associates these images with the murder of his parents; Auschwitz and the gas chambers and what he calls "that" death frequent his dreams. Ironically, his not having died in a similar manner represents for him a bizarre failure of "logic," of the "intended" conclusion to his life. The failure leaves a hiatus that unheroic memory only highlights. Asked by his interviewer, "When did you feel it was over?" he offers a brutally succinct reply: "I didn't feel over *anything!*"[24] The darker side of these testimonies, the one where memory functions not as a relief but as an irritant, exposes a permanently unfulfilled possibility, a disastrous one, to be sure, that hovers over the witness's imagination like a threatening stormcloud. A literary phrase like Semprun's

"returning from the lethal adventure of life" assumes richer personal meaning in the context of testimonies like this one, which
"liberate" only further imprisoning contingencies from the past.

Consider the witness who, after three hours of testimony, suddenly starts to speak of his fear of marriage and setting up a home
after the war. "A home," he defines, "is something that you lose."
The dual pattern of survival-deprival looms through his words:

> I was working hard, and also I was trying to forget myself,
> forgetting the past. It came back to me like a recording in my
> head. After we got married, for the longest time—we were
> already then in a family way, and things were looking up to
> me. During the day I was working, working hard and study-
> ing and trying to get ahead and establish myself, and at night
> I was fighting the Germans—really fighting. And the SS
> were after me all the time, and I was striving to save my
> mother and my sister [both gassed in Auschwitz]. And I was
> jumping off from building to building and they were shoot-
> ing at me, and each time the bullet went through my heart.

His dreams (or nightmares) thus "fulfill" the destiny denied to
Martin R., nullifying the arrested destruction that the accident of
survival frustrates, though of course this proves no consolation to
George S., who admits that his family didn't know how to handle
his waking up screaming every night. Finally, after complaining
about pains in his chest, he was hospitalized. Doctors found nothing physically wrong with him.

Life on a pendulum swinging from past to future continues for
this witness. The timepiece of his existence ticks in two directions.
He devotes the penultimate moment of his testimony to his
daughter, a medical student who takes her parents on a tour of the
labs at her university. She shows them a jar containing a brain
preserved in formaldehyde and says, "This is a human brain; treat
it with respect." But her father says that he associates the image
with the Germans, who brutalized their victims by humiliating

their bodies. Trapped between heir and heritage, how is he to declare allegiance to this emblem of reason and dignity when he cannot erase the memories of a taint that nothing can purify? Although he is admittedly proud of his daughter's accomplishments, his last words identify him as the "only survivor of the W. and S. [that is, his mother's and father's] families."[25] Disruption as well as continuity dominate his thoughts, as he searches for a connection between generations. The most fitting conclusion he can find after nearly *six* hours of testimony is an homage to his perished relatives.

George S.'s daughter is certainly not mistaken to respect the human brain and the dignity implicit in that image. But her father speaks from a depth of experienced knowledge that seems unavailable to her—at least until she joins us as audience to her father's testimony. The burden of insight bestowed on us by such evidence imposes some mournful responsibilities, far beyond a reconsideration of the instinctive praise we confer on the mind and intelligence of man. Portions of certain testimonies convey a quality of parable, as they clarify for us the nature of the challenge. Heda K., for example, tells a story reflecting the transition from heroic resolution to unheroic memory that I have been examining. "It was an accident if you survived or not," she begins. "But the only thing you could contribute was not to be sorry for yourself, not to give in, not to let them hypnotize you into believing that you are something inferior." Her narrative then "tests" the authenticity of this testament to the human spirit, as if, flooded by waves of unheroic memory, she realizes how alien her words are to the actuality she is about to recall.

She tells of a Jewish philologist, a professor from Vienna, whom she meets in the Lodz ghetto. He sits down next to her and says, "Let's talk about classical Rome." He then begins discussing the culture of ancient Rome with her, "in the middle of this bedlam and this hell," as she puts it. She remembers that he was perfectly dressed, in a beautiful suit and coat, and they carried on a learned conversation as if they were sitting in a coffee house or waiting for a train. If the drama ended here, we could celebrate it as an example of man's admirable refusal during the ordeal we call the Holocaust to let external circumstances affect the serenity of his internal life or the integrated identity that depended on it. But there is a second act. About two months later, Heda K. encounters the classical philologist again, in front of a building in Lodz, lying on a cot, dead. On his chest, she says, is a book opened to a gorgeous picture of the Venus de Milo—a tribute to the splendor and majesty of the human form. Both book and body are crawling with lice. "And that's how he ended,"[26] Heda K. solemnly announces, leaving to our imaginations any footnote on the fate of the distinguished heritage they represent.

It is as if an enduring form has been drained of its content; the shell persists, because even Nazism could not permanently destroy the influence on modern culture of the classical tradition. But the doom of its exemplar, the classical philologist, who begins imperturbably confident that his identity is intimately allied to his inner commitment and ends as terrain for lice, his cherished heritage spread out uselessly on his corpse—this doom operates as a kind of beacon to guide us through the desolate ironies that drain spiritual meaning from the parable. Classical wisdom pales in the presence of this abject end. As audience, we are unaware of any intermediate acts linking the initial vision with the closing one, and this in turn gives us a glimpse into the interior reality, so different from what traditional culture has taught us to expect, that occupies the unheroic memory of the former victim.

As heroic memory honors the connection between agency and fate, unheroic memory records its absence. The structure of many testimonies involves a shift from the one to the other. Midway through his narrative, Jacob F. insists that he survived because his (dead) mother and father appeared to him in dreams at crucial moments of his ordeal, guiding his actions and sustaining his hope—and, incidentally, cementing the union between generations, in spite of his parents' abrupt and baffling disappearance from his life. He refuses to accept physical explanations for his good fortune. He even remembers awaking one night to find himself speaking out loud. In fact, he adds in confirmation, "Two people in the room heard me talking and they asked me later on to whom I was talking. . . . I didn't want to tell them. I was afraid they would laugh at me." Whether reasons surface now to explain feelings of abandonment experienced then we cannot know; a complicating factor, as we shall see, because he was an adult at the time, is the memory of his *own* wife and two children, all of whom were separated from him and killed.

He plays two roles. As a son, he finds solace in the certainty of a flow from his parents to himself, expanding into the lagoon of a larger spiritual reality: "I believe my mother and father took care of me, and God protected me." But just before this tranquilizing statement, without preparation or warning, he suddenly recalls his murdered children and asks: "Innocent two children got killed by Hitler. For what? They were not politicians. They went to school, that's all." And he begins to weep at the barren landscape unfolding before him: "What's my life worth? Nothing. I will die, whom am I leaving? No one. My name—no more." He thus introduces (without pursuing) the obvious though difficult question of how one reconciles the hope springing from the bond he has created in memory between himself and his parents with the despair stalking his sense of discontinuity between himself and his children. Jacob F. offers us both points of view, but who can fail to conjecture about the unexpressed meanings lurking beneath his perhaps not so placid assertion: "I believe my mother and father took care of me"? What consolation lies in the reassurance that circumstances and not he were to blame for the contradiction?

Jacob F., an elderly man, admits during his interview that on his next birthday he will be eighty-one. "I never believed I would live that long," he confesses, suggesting, not for the first time in these testimonies, that a witness feels he has outlived his own death.[27]

His resurrection of his parents and his grief for his children both represent a dramatic instance of the dead overtaking the living, in a way that simultaneously confirms and erodes the ultimate value of survival. Whether or not we see this as a tension between coping via desperate illusion and confronting authentic loss, the *psychological* need betrayed by their coexistence divides reality and sends it careening into separate orbits, destabilizing the self and thereby diminishing its ability to make sense of its moral role vis-à-vis the past.

As witnesses to Jacob F.'s testimony, we are obliged by the structure of his narrative to admit that the promise of survival does not bear with it a guarantee of renewal. At every turn a remnant of the past lurks to disrupt the logic of the tale, to surprise the imagination, and to question the meaning of endurance. Unlike Proust's search for lost time, which culminates in the coherence of art, Jacob F.'s story cannot avoid the corridors of disintegration that no center of consciousness can transform from a labyrinth into an aesthetically reassuring design. Our reluctance to assent to the accessibility of his (and the other witnesses') experience may have as much to do with the familiarity of what we would have to surrender as with the estranging pain from what we would have to face, much as Jacob F. wavers between happily retrieving the family unit and sorrowfully conceding its ruin. As our consciousness is drawn into his (and their) discourse, the events that comprise their theme assume a triple reality: they *happened*, they were *remembered*, and they were *heard*. My own conviction is that our ability to gain access to these monologues of personal fortune and misfortune depends on what we are prepared to forsake in order to listen to them.

This in turn depends very much on what the primary witnesses (because our "new" identities as secondary witnesses are forged in the course of the interviews) are forced to abandon in the process of remembering at which we are present. The details of Pola J.'s odyssey sum up the challenge. Born in 1927, she grew up in a

small village in Poland. In July 1942, when Pola J. was fifteen, her
mother was seized in a roundup—and never seen again. Shortly
afterward, Pola J. was taken with a large group of Jews to a pit
outside of town. "We were asked to take off our garments," she
says. "At which point I made a dash and I ran away." "Into the
forest?" asks an interviewer, and she gasps painfully, "Yes." Escaping from the mass execution, she returns home at night to her
father and brother, who had already been notified of her death.
There she learns that her grandmother had been shot and killed
while running away. Reliving the terror, she seems shaken most
of all by her discovery now of what then must have seemed vague:
the gradual elimination of her family, who were *unable to do anything final to sustain her or themselves*. Together with an aunt, the
remaining family members dig a bunker in the woods, where they
hide until a peasant betrays their location to the Germans. They
change their hiding place to a farmer's barn infested with ven-
omous snakes and later move into a pigsty.

One day the Germans surround the area; her father and brother
panic, run out, are caught, and are shot. She and her aunt remain,
undetected, though eventually the farmer makes them leave. The
Germans spot them and shoot the aunt, while Pola J. once again
runs into the woods, where she unexpectedly meets some cousins. Together, they conceal themselves under hay in a barn,
where they remain until the Russians liberate the area. The only
uncertainty in her memory is the fate of her mother, for she has
been able to verify the deaths of the others. What "happened" is
their murder, which after all is not so different from the doom of
hundreds of thousands of others. What she "remembers" is the
stripping away, one by one, of the units of security in her life, the
most important source of her identity. What we "hear" is the
misshapen future that emerges from her narration, implicit in its
fragmentary form and the details she chooses to emphasize. Returning to her village determined to learn her mother's lot, she
recalls: "It became more and more apparent that my mother will

not come back. I never found my mother . . . and that was it." In her mind, this is the end of her personal odyssey, though she adds almost as an afterthought the by now deafening coda that after the liberation her first husband, also a camp survivor, was killed by a business associate who stole his money.

Her penultimate words are: "My friends, my relatives, I mean, they all perished . . . they all got killed, they all got killed!" Staying alive bears a legacy, to which she attaches no homily or moral injunctions, only an attempt to forestall the advent of what I call the diminished self, which is made inevitable by her simultaneously simple and complex concession: "I never found my mother . . . and that was it." Her subsequent words, the last ones in her testimony, constitute an appeal to the future: "If it [her testimony] goes into any archive, if an appendix could be made, at least of the people who have perished, the people I remember—I will send you . . . a list perhaps to use as an appendix."[28] At this moment the subtext surfaces and dominates—one might even say culminates—her narrative, the dead victims asserting their priority over the living ones. The "people who have perished" emerge as the real subject of the testimonies, while the circumstances of their death define the unheroic memory that tries to reclaim them, as it does the surviving self diminished by their absence and by its own powerlessness to alter their doom.

This memory, and the loss it records, has meaning only insofar as it engages the consciousness of us as audience. Otherwise, it remains mere archival anecdote. The appendix it entreats, however, must be moved from its position as textual supplement to the throbbing heart of the narrative of modernity. Resolute in its centrality to a search for the values that men and women hope to live by after the Holocaust, its corrosive reality continues to generate narcotic images of disappeared individuals, families, communities, and cultural traditions. Those remaining behind, the witnesses in these testimonies, although for the most part content with their compartmentalized *present* lives, on a deeper level acknowledge a flaw in that satisfaction. In spite of efforts to escape it, this corrosive reality retains a contemporary as well as a contemporaneous thrust. The fate of the "others" clings tenaciously to the present, harassing efforts to reestablish a normal identity for those who have survived the disaster.

Part of the unreconciled understanding resulting from this investigation, what I earlier labeled a threatening and perhaps a treacherous one, is this: the Holocaust does little to confirm theories of moral reality but much to question the reality of moral theories. We can of course dismiss this historical moment as a terrible but temporary aberration, during which human nature veered off course for a time but then rediscovered its true compass and restored direction to its moral voyage. But we do this only by ignoring the hundreds of voices of former victims, the details of whose memories frustrate such a placid view. Their shrunken moral universe, full of ambiguities concerning the basis for personal conduct, mocks conceptual efforts, from Plato to the present, to determine the relationship between duty and the good life, what it is right to do and what it is good to be.

I take this language from Charles Taylor's recent study, *Sources of the Self: The Making of the Modern Identity. My* subject appears to be precisely the opposite: "Sources of the Diminished Self: The Unmaking of the Modern Identity." Philosophical discourse on the nature of moral being is essentially an inquiry into the transfigurative impulse. It helps to define my own topic, which aspires to some practical reflections on what in the context of transfiguration appears to be a *disfigurative* impulse, although this description provides a convenient contrast more than an accurate designation. Taylor's work illustrates as well as any I know (though quite unintentionally) what happened to the self and its identity during the Holocaust, even though he attributes no explicit importance to the event in aiding him to develop his theories.

For Taylor, modern identity suggests "the ensemble of (largely unarticulated) understandings of what it is to be a human agent: the sense of inwardness, freedom, individuality, and being embedded in nature which are at home in the modern West." The videotaped oral testimonies we have studied develop an image of modern identity rooted not in theory but in experience, an image that articulates with more or less vividness what it meant (and means) in our time to exist *without* a sense of human agency. They reveal the consequences of a gradual attrition of the qualities of inwardness, freedom, and individuality, an estrangement from nature until one is alienated from the very self that Taylor equates with identity. When identity is forged by circumstances rather than by values, as was the case in countless situations presented in these testimonies, when "the good life" and "the right thing to do" lost their *relevancy* because particular situations did not allow the luxury of their expression (or even knowledge of what they were)—then Taylor's axiom that "the modern understanding of the self developed out of earlier pictures of human identity"[29] forces us to ask whether the "unreconciled understanding" we are in search of may not lead us down a different path entirely.

No one can quarrel with Taylor's conclusion that "understanding modernity aright is an exercise in retrieval" (xi), but the results will depend largely on what is retrieved. Unheroic memory is also an exercise in retrieval, as are all versions of memory in this study; but it raises for us the issue of whether the idea of the good life before Auschwitz, and the premises on which it was built, were of any use to the victim of the Holocaust universe. Few would have disputed Taylor's contention that certain goods are independent of our desires and inclinations, which in fact require the prior existence of those goods for their expression. "The goods which command our awe," Taylor argues, "must also function in some sense as standards for us." Family devotion and unity, parental care, filial affection, sibling loyalty—all certainly would have been included among these goods. But when the "goods which command our awe" suddenly collapsed on the ramp at Auschwitz, leaving nothing in their place, then identity groped for alternative moorings—and somewhere in our philosophical investigations we must find room for the diminished self that resulted, the one whose voice echoes sadly but frankly from the recollections of unheroic memory.

If identity or knowing who you are is "to be oriented in moral space," as Taylor says, "a space in which questions arise about what is good or bad, what is worth doing and what not, what has meaning and importance for you and what is trivial and second-ary" (28), then there is no doubt that arrivals in the concentration-ary universe needed fresh and unorthodox definitions of self in order to function even minimally. As for *survivors* of that universe—confronted with the insularity, not to say innocence of Taylor's definition, given their recent ordeal—how are we to re-turn them to the boundaries of moral development implicit in that formulation? Taylor's language is designed for a society in which the inviolable assumption of choice is the keystone of moral spec-ulation. His spatial metaphor assumes that the existence of frame-works always allows one to find deep in the psyche a gyroscope that insures moral balance. But as we have seen, circumstances in ghettos and camps were deliberately and systematically designed by the Nazis to destroy the functioning of that gyroscope. One of the many grievous burdens of these testimonies is the dizzying success of their efforts.

By a kind of default Taylor's formulations, never designed to shed light on the moral situation of the former Holocaust victim, help us to enter the realm of unreconciled understanding, where events remain permanently unredeemed and unredeemable. The thesis he defends in his book—"that doing without frameworks is utterly impossible for us"—is not so much contradicted as simply discarded by most witnesses, who experienced as "possible" cer-tain events that even they could not have anticipated in their wildest imaginings. Taylor intends no contingency for his thesis: "Living within such strongly qualified horizons is constitutive of human agency." But unheroic memory wrests versions of human agency from its past that are undreamt of in Taylor's philosophy. Unwittingly, he provides his own definition of the diminished self, though his tone, of course, reflects no approval: "Stepping outside these limits [that is, the horizons that constitute human agency] would be tantamount to stepping outside what we would recognize as integral, that is, undamaged human personhood" (27). When external events nonetheless compel one to enter a disintegrative milieu, as happened to the former victim, human personhood *must* be damaged, so that return to the pristine moral space Taylor describes proves impossible. The fault, however, may lie with the vocabulary of moral theory rather than with the individual who exists precariously in spite of it.

What are we to learn from this interlude in history, during which moral intuitions so often were useless because physical and psychological constraints like hunger, illness, fear, despair, and confusion created an unprecedented nonethical environment immune to the promptings of those intuitions? One of the unavoidable conclusions of unreconciled understanding is that we can inhabit more than one moral space at the same time—witnesses in these testimonies certainly do—and feel oriented and disoriented simultaneously. Another is that "damaged personhood" is one of the inevitable prices we pay for having lived in the time of the Holocaust, *provided* we acknowledge our active role as audience to the content of these testimonies. Indeed, it would be more than ingenuous to contend that the sources of such personhood in the twentieth century must be confined to this particular atrocity alone. History inflicts wounds on individual moral identity that are untraceable to personal choice or qualitative frameworks—though the scars they leave are real enough, reminding us that theoretical hopes for an integral life must face the constant challenge to that unity by self-shattering events like the Holocaust experience.

When we try to measure the vulnerable lives of former victims against the protected discourse of Taylor's text, we see how easily *terminology* may become a substitute for concrete human experience. Indeed, belief in the equivalence of terminology to behavior may have been partly responsible for that vulnerability. Taylor's insistence that the self "cannot do without some orientation to the good" (33) is for us, in the context of these testimonies, a revelation of how quickly such principles of identity can dissolve into illusion when they are stripped of their privileged security in the climate of "mere" discussion. The "exposed" language of Ely M., a Dutch Jewish girl who between the ages of ten and thirteen hid in various Christian homes, separated from her family, jars against Taylor's reassuring words: "You hear so often," she says, "that people start a new life and so on and how wonderful everything is. I personally . . . my feeling is that the after-effects are very hard for a child. When you come out of the war you don't want to be with your mother because you're estranged from your mother—for me it was [that way]." When one's moral space is invaded and disrupted as hers was—"You miss some part of your life somewhere," she says, "and people don't understand that"—one wonders how Taylor's formula is to apply to her life, during and following the events she describes.[30]

If the self cannot do without some orientation to the good, can it do without some orientation to the evil that Ely M. and other witnesses endured? Taylor maintains that the "full definition of someone's identity . . . usually involves not only his stand on moral and spiritual matters but also some reference to a defining community" (36). But the defining community of our witnesses is a dead community, or more strictly, an exterminated one; instead of marveling at the strength of the human spirit, particularly their own, they mourn its fragility when the isolated self has no support from the surrounding milieu to validate it.

Taylor virtually crosses the frontier separating theoretical discourse from oral testimony when he ventures "another basic condition of making sense of ourselves, that we grasp our lives in a *narrative.*" But if witness narratives make any sense, it is that the two planes of existence described in them do not intersect, that the coherence one expects from the life narratives Taylor speaks of cannot emerge from the simultaneous life-and-death narratives that we have been studying. The crucial difference appears in the ironic disparity between Taylor's neutral usage in the following maxim and the sinister charge his words carry to our overburdened ears: "In order to have a sense of who we are, we have to have a notion of how we have become, and of where we are going" (47). Could tainted memory ever have conjured such a tranquil formulation? Václav Havel's warning thunders here with a mind-stunning echo: "The meaning of every word also reflects the person who utters it, the situation in which it is uttered, and the reason for its utterance. The selfsame word can, at one moment, radiate great hopes, at another, it can emit lethal rays."[31]

Former victims speak of where they are going, but not in order to unify it with where they have come from. It would be more honest and accurate, when confronting their testimony, if we were to pluralize identity and address the question of multiple identities, not of course in a pathological sense but as a historical result of the value-dispersion that characterized their experience. Such an approach would naturally meet resistance from Taylor's quest for unity as the ideal of moral identity; the notion of a diminished self, with all that implies, stands in sharp contrast to his vision: "We want our lives to have meaning, or weight, or substance, or to grow towards some fulness, or however the concern is formulated that we have been discussing. . . . But this means our *whole* lives. If necessary, we want the future to 'redeem' the past, to make it part of a life story which has sense or purpose, to take it up in a meaningful unity" (50–51). All the key terms are there, including *redeem*, with whose misuse we began our investigation of Holocaust oral testimonies. Those are concerned with individual lives, unimpeded by the formal concerns that govern the creation of a *written* text. Taylor's text is no exception, forcing

us to face the difficult issue of how closely it mirrors some of the
most complex moral realities of our era.

To illustrate his position, Taylor turns to literature rather than to
life, as if the formal achievements of fiction—indeed, of only a
particular fiction—were enough to resolve the contradictions to
meaningful unity implicit in the uncertain flow of human effort:

> A famous, perhaps for us moderns a paradigm, example of
> what this can mean is recounted by Proust in his *A la recherche
> du temps perdu*. In the scene in the Guermantes's library, the
> narrator recovers the full meaning of his past and thus re-
> stores the time which was "lost" in the two senses I men-
> tioned above. The formerly irretrievable past is recovered in
> its unity with the life yet to live, and all the "wasted" time
> now has a meaning, as the time of preparation for the work of
> the writer who will give shape to this unity. (51)

Art may in fact achieve what life cannot, but this does not give it
the authority to confer on itself the role of model for moral unity in
the human sphere. Paradigms abound, ranging from the library to
the deathcamp, but whether "wasted" time has a meaning depends, I suppose, on which pattern we choose. Or which one
chooses us. Some writers, to be sure, have already shaped the
chaos of the Holocaust experience into a retrieved past, but their
insights prod the imagination to consider its relationship to the
future with greater restraint than Taylor or Taylor's version of
Proust allows. The raw material of oral Holocaust narratives, in
content and manner of presentation, resists the organizing impulse of moral theory and art. Does this keep these narratives
closer to their source in the pain of persecution? A kind of un-
shielded truth emerges from them, through which we salvage an
anatomy of melancholy for the modern spirit—part of our anguish and our fate. For the former victims, the Holocaust is a
communal wound that cannot heal. This is the ailing subtext of
their testimonies, wailing beneath the convalescent murmur of

their surface lives. We have little trouble listening to that surface murmur. When the subtext of their story echoes for us too as a communal wound, then we will have begun to hear their legacy of unheroic memory and grasp the meaning for our time of a diminished self.

■   ■   ■

From the testimony of Philip K. (T-1300):

I often say to people who pretend or seem to be marveling at the fact that I seem to be so normal, so unperturbed and so capable of functioning—they seem to think the Holocaust passed over and it's done with: It's my skin. This is not a coat. You can't take it off. And it's there, and it will be there until I die. . . .

If we were not an eternal people before, we are an eternal people after the Holocaust, in both its very positive and very negative sense. We have not only survived, but we have revived ourselves. In a very real way, we have won. We were victorious. But in a very real way, we have lost. We'll never recover what was lost. We can't even assess what was lost. Who knows what beauty and grandeur six million could have contributed to the world? Who can measure it up? What standard do you use? How do you count it? How do you estimate it . . . ?

We lost. The world lost, whether they know it or admit it. It doesn't make any difference. And yet we won, we're going on. . . .

I think there are as many ways of surviving survival as there have been to survive.

NOTES

PREFACE

1 Fortunoff Video Archive for Holocaust Testimonies, Yale University (hereafter FVA), tape T-94. Testimony of Max and Lorna B.
2 Ibid., tape T-1185. Testimony of Magda F.

CHAPTER 1. DEEP MEMORY

1 *Boston Globe*, Sept. 2, 1989, p. 18.
2 The first three volumes are *None of Us Will Return*, trans. John Githens (New York: Grove Press, 1968), originally published as *Aucun de nous ne reviendra* (Paris: Editions Gauthier, 1965), and the still-untranslated *Une connaissance inutile* (Paris: Editions de minuit, 1970) and *Mesure de nos jours* (Paris: Editions de minuit, 1971).
3 Charlotte Delbo, *La mémoire et les jours* (Paris: Berg International, 1985), p. 11. My translation. Subsequent citations will be included in the text. Rosette Lamont has recently translated this volume as *Days and Memory* (Marlboro, Vt.: Marlboro, 1990).

208 ■ Notes to Pages 11–28

4   FVA, tape T-36. Testimony of Celia K.
5   Zygmunt Bauman, *Modernity and the Holocaust* (Ithaca: Cornell University Press, 1989), p. 206.
6   FVA, tape T-108. Testimony of Anna G.
7   Tape T-882. Testimony of Sidney L.
8   Tape T-780. Testimony of Barbara T.
9   Barbara Fischman Traub, *The Matrushka Doll* (New York: Richard Marek, 1979), pp. 27–28.
10 Ibid., p. 28.
11 Although I believe there is often a *qualitative* difference between oral and written representations of that atrocity, I think the highest distinction must still be reserved for the latter, because no oral testimonies so far equal the *art* of writers like Primo Levi, Aharon Appelfeld, Charlotte Delbo, and Ida Fink—to name only a few. I would prefer to stress the dissimilarities between the two types of testimony, and the intrinsic value of the neglected oral form, rather than the superiority or inferiority of one to the other.
12 For a similar effect with an artfully contrived (and controlled) narrative voice in fiction, see Jorge Semprun's *The Long Voyage* and *What a Beautiful Sunday!*
13 Tape T-49. Testimony of Stanley M.
14 Tape T-295. Testimony of Baruch G.
15 Tape T-107. Testimony of Edith P.
16 Tape T-18. Testimony of Hannah F.
17 See Lawrence L. Langer, *Versions of Survival: The Holocaust and the Human Spirit* (Albany: State University of New York Press, 1982), p. 72.
18 Tape T-511. Testimony of Moses S. I have refrained from mentioning at this point the most painful episode in Moses S.'s narrative, which involves cannibalism. I shall return to it in chapter 3. Both the interviewers and Moses. S.'s wife are clearly unnerved by his mention of the subject and rush through it as quickly as possible, without comment. As far as I know, no one has yet dealt with this theme, though it has appeared at least a dozen times in the testimonies I have watched. I suspect that an equal number of witnesses, if not more, have failed to discuss it, for various reasons, most of them perhaps

obvious. But I do not see how we can ignore it, if we are to understand the disruptive effects of hunger in the extreme camp situation.

19 See Tape T-51. Testimony of Peter G.

20 Tape T-216. Testimony of Father John S.

21 Tape T-9. Testimony of William R.

22 Albert Camus, *The Myth of Sisyphus*, trans. Justin O'Brien (New York: Vintage, 1955), p. 91.

23 Tape T-99. Testimony of Hedda K.

24 Tape T-49. Testimony of Stanley M.

CHAPTER 2. ANGUISHED MEMORY

1 Maurice Blanchot, *The Writing of the Disaster (L'écriture du désastre)*, trans. Ann Smock (Lincoln: University of Nebraska Press, 1986), pp. 38, 8, 29. Subsequent citations will be included in the text.

2 Friedrich Nietzsche, *On the Advantage and Disadvantage of History for Life*, trans. Peter Preuss (New York: Hackett, 1980), p. 10.

3 Lawrence L. Langer, *Versions of Survival: The Holocaust and the Human Spirit* (Albany: SUNY Press, 1982), p. xii.

4 Charlotte Delbo, *None of Us Will Return*, trans. John Githens (New York: Grove, 1968), p. 72.

5 Ibid., p. 128.

6 Elie Wiesel, *Night*, trans. Stella Rodway (New York: Bantam, 1982), p. 42.

7 Viktor Frankl, *Man's Search for Meaning*, rev. ed. (New York: Pocket Books, 1984), pp. 87, 103.

8 Primo Levi, *Survival in Auschwitz: The Nazi Assault on Humanity*, trans. Stuart Woolf (New York: Collier Books, 1961), pp. 103, 105. Subsequent citations are included in the text.

9 FVA, tape T-35. Testimony of Zoltan G.

10 Tape T-3. Testimony of Sally H.

11 Picrinoires, so-called from the picrine (or picric acid) that they worked with in the ammunition factory at Skarzysko, led to a chemical poisoning that stained the flesh yellow and sometimes proved fatal.

12 Tape T-206. Testimony of Bessie and Jacob K.

13 Yosef Hayim Yerushalmi, *Zakhor: Jewish History and Jewish Memory* (Seattle: University of Washington Press, 1982), p. 94. Subsequent citations will be included in the text.

14 Tape T-206. Testimony of Bessie and Jacob K.

15 Tape T-1270. Testimony of Isabella L.

16 Tape T-107. Testimony of Edith P.

17 Carlos Fuentes, "Velázquez, Plato's Cave, and Bette Davis," *New York Times*, Arts and Leisure Section, Mar. 15, 1987.

18 Filip Müller, *Eyewitness Auschwitz: Three Years in the Gas Chambers*, trans. and ed. Susanne Flatauer (New York: Stein and Day, 1979), p. 24. The German title is *Sonderbehandlung* or "Special Treatment," the Nazi euphemism for death in the gas chambers. Complicating our response to Müller's written text is the note on the title page that Helmut Freitag was his literary collaborator, and Susanne Flatauer his translator *and* editor. In the German edition, we are told that Freitag was responsible for the "Deutsche Bearbeitung," which means the German "revision" or "adaptation" or "elaboration" of the presumably original Slovak text. The book is a valuable account of Müller's experience; but how do we separate his language (and hence ideas) from Freitag's? Beyond dispute in oral testimony is that every word spoken falls directly from the lips of the witness. Not as much can be said for written survivor testimony that is openly or silently edited. Whether this seriously limits the value of some written memoirs is a question that still needs to be investigated.

19 An ironic sequel to this statement is that Müller, as I have been told, *stammers* and that Lanzmann himself patiently edited out the speech impediments with a technological dexterity that must have been nothing short of Herculean.

20 Tape T-65. Testimony of Irene W.

21 Tape T-736. Testimony of Chaim E.

22 Tape T-18. Testimony of Hanna F.

23 In a follow-up videotaped interview with Hanna F., I asked her precisely this question. She explained that a transport *from* Auschwitz to a factory site in Germany was being prepared and that she joined the line of women being considered for this transport. Because of her extremely debilitated condition, she was pulled from the line and sent back to her barracks. Instead, she joined another line—a very

risky venture—and was warned a second time to return to barracks. But she stayed close to the cattle-car, and at the last minute, with the help of a friend who *had* been chosen, she somehow managed to clamber aboard without being seen. "It was the stupidest thing I ever did," she recalled more than forty years later. Detection would have meant instant execution. Thus, from her point of view, stupidity, at least for the time being, saved her life. Yet her original interviewers chose to see this as an example of pluck and guts.

24 Tape T-210. Testimony of Alex H.
25 Blanchot, *The Writing of the Disaster*, pp. 29, 33, 30, 38.
26 Tape T-1095. Testimony of Luna K.
27 Blanchot, *The Writing of the Disaster*, p. 51.
28 Tape T-1185. Testimony of Magda F.

CHAPTER 3. HUMILIATED MEMORY

1 Friedrich Nietzsche, *On the Advantage and Disadvantage of History for Life,* trans. Peter Preuss (New York: Hackett, 1980), pp. 14–17. Subsequent citations will be included in the text.

2 Nietzsche adds a third form of inquiry into the past, what he calls antiquarian history, which simply venerates the old while rejecting the new. There is little chance that this category will ever serve our study of the Holocaust—at least, not in the immediate future.

3 FVA, tape T-210. Testimony of Alex H.
4 Tape T-224. Testimony of Martin L.
5 Jean Améry, *At the Mind's Limits: Contemplations by a Survivor on Auschwitz and Its Realities,* trans. Sidney Rosenfeld and Stella P. Rosenfeld (New York: Schocken, 1986), p. 93.
6 Tape T-836. Testimony of Pierre T.
7 Améry, *At the Mind's Limits,* p. 29.
8 Tape T-37. Testimony of Leo P.
9 Améry, *At the Mind's Limits,* pp. 90–91. Subsequent citations will be included in the text.
10 Améry's struggle is especially poignant because his mother was Catholic and his father Jewish. The essay from which this citation is taken is called "On the Necessity and Impossibility of Being a Jew."
11 Tape T-938. Testimony of George S.

12 Tape T-628. Testimony of Leon H.

13 Here and elsewhere, I use *integrated* as a contrasting rather than a descriptive term. The idea of an integrated self is probably mostly mythical to begin with, though under normal circumstances—the opposite of the Holocaust universe—the armor preserving its external appearance seems more secure. The "integrated" self of the former victim, as do most of us, adapts to society's conventions by reembracing goals like marriage, family, and career. Oral testimonies reveal the existence of multiple selves that function in more or less satisfactory versions of equilibrium. Some may see this merely as an expression of the general human condition, though I believe that the exceptional nature of the former victims' experience is a crucial differentiating factor.

14 Tape T-628. Testimony of Leon H.

15 Tape T-192. Testimony of Viktor C.

16 Tape T-65. Testimony of Irene W.

17 Tape T-76. Testimony of Bronia K.

18 Tape T-1136. Testimony of Helena B.

19 Tape T-107. Testimony of Edith P.

20 See "Inferior Words," in Ilse Aichinger, *Selected Poetry and Prose*, ed. and trans. Allen H. Chappel (Durango, Colo.: Logbridge-Rhodes, 1983), p. 66.

21 Tape T-107. Testimony of Edith P.

22 See "Narrativity in the Representation of Reality" in Hayden White, *The Content of the Form: Narrative Discourse and Historical Representation* (Baltimore: Johns Hopkins University Press, 1987), pp. 10, 11. Subsequent citations will be included in the text.

23 Tape T-152. Testimony of Menachem S.

24 Tape T-134. Testimony of Malka D.

25 Tape T-1185. Testimony of Magda F.

26 There were of course many instances of family support, particularly between sisters who managed to stay together throughout the camp ordeal, but in these testimonies they are the exception rather than the rule. They cannot be considered representative of a way of behaving that insured survival. In addition, some witnesses report that the system of mutual support bred ironic results when the other family

member died or disappeared just before (or, in a few cases, just *after*) liberation, leaving a legacy of frustrated expectation that confirms the random and whimsical *cruelty* implicit in the Holocaust experience.

27 Tape T-134. Testimony of Malka D.

28 This is far from a singular example. At least a dozen other witnesses in interviews that I have seen (and one that I conducted) describe participating in or observing a similar experience. At least as many more mention scenes "too terrible to describe" and refuse to do so. One can only speculate on what lies behind their silence. Eberhard Kolb, in *Bergen-Belsen: From "Detention Camp" to Concentration Camp, 1943–1945* (trans. Gregory Claeys and Christine Lattek [Göttingen: Vandenhoeck and Ruprecht, 2d ed., 1988]), reports that one of the camp prisoner doctors, a Dr. Leo, "gave evidence of having seen [in the weeks before the camp's liberation] about 200 to 300 cases of cannibalism" (46).

29 Tape T-511. Testimony of Moses S.

30 Hayden White, *The Content of the Form*, p. 21.

CHAPTER 4.   TAINTED MEMORY

1 Blanchot, *The Writing of the Disaster*, p. 1.

2 FVA, tape T-82. Testimony of Joan B.

3 Tape T-299. Testimony of Myra L.

4 Heda Kovály and Erazim Kohák, *The Victors and the Vanquished* (New York: Horizon Press, 1973), p. 1.

5 Blanchot, *The Writing of the Disaster*, p. 2.

6 Heda Margolius Kovály, *Under a Cruel Star: A Life in Prague, 1941–1968*, trans. Franci Epstein and Helen Epstein with the author (Cambridge, Mass.: Plunkett Lake Press, 1986), p. 5. This edition, unlike the previous version, includes only the material by Mrs. Kovály.

7 Tape T-1123. Testimony of Arne L.

8 Tape T-107. Testimony of Edith P.

9 Tape T-48. Testimony of Paul D.

10 Blanchot, *The Writing of the Disaster*, p. 65. Subsequent citations will be included in the text.

11 The translation "unexperienced experience" is my own. The printed

translation reads: "Impossible necessary death: why do these words—and the experience to which they refer (the inexperience)—escape comprehension?"

12 Tape T-113. Testimony of Nathan A.

13 Tape T-934. Testimony of Julia S.

14 Tape T-11. Testimony of Schifra Z.

15 Tape T-18. Testimony of Hanna F.

16 Tape T-2. Testimony of Leon W.

17 Tape T-285. Testimony of Hanna H.

18 Tape T-192. Testimony of Viktor K.

19 Tape T-55. Testimony of Sigmund W.

20 Tape T-210. Testimony of Alex H.

21 Tape T-158. Testimony of Leo G.

22 Richard J. Evans, *In Hitler's Shadow: West German Historians and the Attempt to Escape from the Nazi Past* (New York: Pantheon, 1989), p. 120.

23 Tape T-250. Testimony of Vera B.

24 Tape T-927. Testimony of Irving F.

25 Tape T-205. Testimony of Mr. and Mrs. Leon S.

26 Tape 257. Testimony of Mira B.

27 Tape T-65. Testimony of Irene W.

28 Tape T-845. Testimony of Eva K.

29 Blanchot, *The Writing of the Disaster*, p. 42.

30 Ibid., p. 3. Blanchot also speaks of knowledge "via disaster" (*par désastre*), fusing consciousness even more keenly with the event. Apparently trying to convey Blanchot's unorthodox sense of verbal and mental intimacy, his translator renders *par désastre* as "knowledge disastrously," suggesting in English what is less obvious in the original French—literally, a new grammar of thought.

31 Tape T-729. Testimony of Leo L.

CHAPTER 5.   UNHEROIC MEMORY

1 Martin Gilbert, *The Holocaust: A History of the Jews of Europe during the Second World War* (New York: Holt, Rinehart and Winston, 1985), p. 828.

2   Ibid., p. 570.

3   Joseph Kermish, "Emmanuel Ringelblum's Notes Hitherto Un-published," in *Yad Vashem Studies*, vol. 7 (Jerusalem, 1968), pp. 179, 180.

4   Gilbert, *The Holocaust*, pp. 827–28.

5   Ibid., p. 827.

6   FVA, tape T-804. Testimony of Sol R.

7   Václav Havel, "Words on Words," *New York Review of Books*, Jan. 18, 1990, p. 6.

8   Joseph Brodsky, "The Condition We Call Exile," *New York Review of Books*, Jan. 21, 1988, p. 20.

9   Primo Levi, *The Drowned and the Saved* (New York: Summit, 1988), pp. 70–71.

10 Tape T-26. Testimony of Michael R.

11 Tape T-838. Testimony of Peter C.

12 Tape T-845. Testimony of Eva K.

13 See Miriam Novitch, ed., *Sobibor, Martyrdom and Revolt* (New York: Holocaust Library, 1980).

14 Tape T-756. Testimony of Chaim E.

15 Tape T-1095. Testimony of Luna K.

16 Tape T-61. Testimony of Joseph K.

17 Tape T-94. Testimony of Max and Lorna B.

18 Dissatisfied with his interview because he had insufficient time to tell his entire story, Max B. volunteered to be interviewed again more than eight years later (I was one of the interviewers). He told the same story of encouraging the sabotage of the relays, but his response this time to the hanging of the Ukrainians shifts its focus from the past to the present, confirming the idea of multiple voices that we have been exploring. In the first interview, we heard the voice of the self-ish self; now we hear the voice of the integrated self, judging its own earlier behavior: "They hanged them, and that's it. In the meantime, you know, my conscience was . . . I sent . . . this was my doing. I sent so many people, 15 people to death. It was very sad. Shaking like a leaf. At least I . . . calmed down because I was alive. But I was very sad for them." Tape T-1125. Second testimony of Max B.

19 Tape T-94. Testimony of Max and Lorna B.

20 Tape T-738. Testimony of Abraham P.
21 Jorge Semprun, *What a Beautiful Sunday!*, trans. Alan Sheridan (New York: Harcourt Brace Jovanovich, 1982), pp. 61, 105.
22 Ibid., pp. 106–07, 130.
23 Tape T-2. Testimony of Leon W.
24 Tape T-166. Testimony of Martin R.
25 Tape T-938. Testimony of George S.
26 Tape T-99. Testimony of Heda K.
27 Tape T-120. Testimony of Jacob F.
28 Tape T-640. Testimony of Pola J.
29 Charles Taylor, *Sources of the Self: The Making of the Modern Identity* (Cambridge, Mass.: Harvard University Press, 1989), pp. ix, x. Subsequent citations will be included in the text.
30 Tape T-1170. Testimony of Ely M.
31 Havel, "Words on Words," p. 6.